Sugar's Life in the Hood

'SUGAR'S LIFE IN THE HOOD

The Story of a Former Welfare Mother

Sugar Turner & Tracy Bachrach Ehlers

UNIVERSITY OF TEXAS PRESS ◆ AUSTIN

Library of Congress Cataloging-in-Publication Data
Turner, date–
    Sugar's life in the hood : the story of a former welfare mother / Sugar Turner
and Tracy Bachrach Ehlers.—1st ed.
            p.   cm.
ISBN 0-292-72102-1 (alk. paper)
ISBN 0-292-70195-0
    1. Turner, Sugar, 1945–   . 2. African American women—Interviews.
3. Ex-welfare recipients—United States—Interviews. 4. Poor single mothers—United States—Interviews. 5. African American Women—Social conditions—Case studies. 6. Inner cities—United States—Case studies. 7. Female
friendship—United States—Case studies. 8. Ehlers, Tracy Bachrach. 9.
Women anthropologists—United States—Biography. 10. White women—United States—Biography. I. Ehlers, Tracy Bachrach. II. Title.
E185.97.T98 A3 2002
305.48'896073—dc21   2001043475

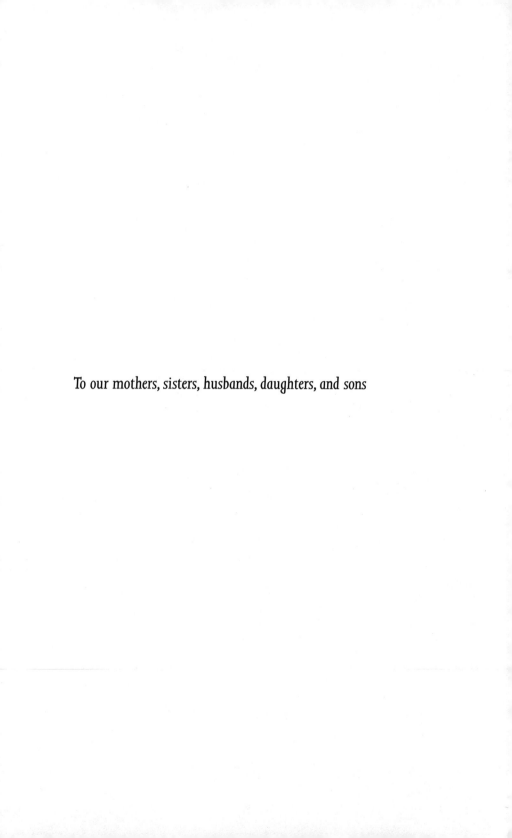

To our mothers, sisters, husbands, daughters, and sons

CONTENTS

FOREWORD Molly Ivins

Tracy Ehlers describes this book as what anthropologists call a *testimonio*, a voice, a story "told by nontraditional, previously silent voices, be they those of women, the poor or ethnic minorities. It allows those distanced from power to speak for themselves, to be witnesses to history and to culture, to re-create their pasts." I think this *testimonio* is more than that.

Among other things, it is the story of a most unlikely friendship between a black ho, hustler, and welfare mother, and a white feminist college professor of slightly daunting intelligence. Girlfriends in black culture are even more important than they are to white women, and Lord knows most white women can't get through without them. Scholars have only recently started studying the phenomenon, and as far as I know, this is the first report on a black/white, hustler/professional friendship.

Anyone who has known Tracy Ehlers during the years she has worked on this book knows that Sugar Turner is not a subject to her, Sugar is her friend. That's what makes this book work. A reporter or a traditional anthropologist would simply have written down what Sugar has to say, as Oscar Lewis did in *LaVida*. Ehlers is right there screaming at her, as any girlfriend would, "Are you crazy? The guy's a junkie! My God, let's eat."

And what a friend. Sugar's life may be a mess in some ways, but she has what Chris Hitchens once referred to as "that peculiarly British set of virtues—grit, spunk and pluck." She is also kind, devout, wonderfully funny and articulate, and a gifted verbal artist performing the equivalent of jazz riffs on the subjects of lousy men, the welfare system, and other plagues of our time. And finally, Sugar has a special gallantry, an almost heartbreaking courage of the "pick yourself up, dust yourself off, and start all over again" variety.

I have long been both annoyed and frustrated by the way Americans learn about "the poor." During my years at the New York Times we ran innumerable articles about poverty and "the poor" featuring the words of economists, sociologists, welfare experts, census takers, statisticians, religious leaders, drug counselors, and health care experts. The only people we never heard from were "the poor." I spent a couple of months wandering Red Hook, Green Point, and Brownsville, which are New York ghetto neighborhoods, just talking to people. My colleagues used to ask me, "Aren't you afraid to go there?" No. I was armed with a notebook, a pencil, and a simple request, "Tell me your story." Everyone wants to tell his story: what we all need, as Tracy discovered with Sugar, is someone to listen.

In journalism, we are taught to get information from those with credentials, with expertise, with titles. We always want to quote the chief of police, not just some cop; the CEO, not Dilbert. In politics, the president or the governor is always considered a more reliable source than a secretary. That's why it's called Establishment journalism. The result is a peculiarly distorted view of reality.

With a few noble exceptions, like the education writer Jonathan Kozol, most people who write about "the poor" never let us hear from them. The combination of anthropology and friendship Ehlers brings to this book makes it a completely different experience. Nor can it be read as though Sugar were an exotic specimen: "Ah, an actual poor person, how interesting." As Ehlers wryly notes, Sugar is a natural conservative Republican: in fact, she'd probably get along just fine with both Rush Limbaugh and Pat Robertson. It is Sugar, the individual, not Sugar, a black hustler, who lives in these pages.

And just in time. The degree of economic segregation in this country gets worse all the time: the famous "income gap" that separates the rich from the poor keeps growing and growing. And one consequence is the people at the bottom become increasingly invisible to the people at the top, and even to the middle class are an undifferentiated mass, a Them of color, crime, and fear. As we sort ourselves into suburbs by income level, the odds against our getting to know one another become ever greater. My black girlfriends are educated, middle-class women, both gender and class making it the easiest kind of interracial friendship to form. From them I have learned that special intonation and meaning of "Girlfriend!" I grew up in East Texas before the civil rights movement, and I can find just as many white people today who actually say, "Of course I know poor people: I talk to my household help all the time" as I could back then.

Ehlers's great contribution is to have written a book that breaks through color, class, and gender to give all of us a friend who has had to ho, hustle, and welfare mom it through part of her life. I'm proud to have her as a friend via this book.

MOLLY IVINS
AUSTIN, TEXAS

SUGAR'S PREFACE

Once there was a young woman named Sugar, who met a young woman named Tracy. The actual chronological "youth" of these two broads may be questionable, but within each was an innocence and a vigor that could only be termed "young." Now the two have aged and grown, and I hope I might shed some light on this process.

Sugar was a woman from a dubious background who, like many whores and saints before her, possessed a heart of gold. Also within her was a burning ember of a desire to know "Who am I and why am I?" and "When did I become who I am, and what will I be?" and "What does who I am have to do with what I will be?" Inherent in all these convoluted questions of the Id and the Ego were the questions of "Who were the people I came from?" and "Who helped make me who I am?" It was like being in a round room with many, many doors that would not open . . . and then one day, one of the doors cracked open, and peering in from behind it was Tracy. Sugar saw an opportunity to peek into the answers to some of her questions when she met Tracy. She found a person who would listen, and Sugar wanted to talk, to question, to shout "I want to know who I am!"

The reasons for writing this book have changed in many ways. I, Sugar, really can't speak for Tracy, but I am sure she feels the same. My goal at first was to begin the first step in a journey that would end in a movie of my life. This movie would bust open the closet doors of all my family's deep, dark secrets and give me and the world answers. It would expose all my kinfolk for the selfish charlatans they were, having hoarded the past from me and my siblings. I was so angry at them for not telling us the truth about ourselves, and I was jealous of people who had family histories that they knew and could recite, whether good or bad. At least they had a history, and I had none. My history was no more than whispered slips of non-stories and half-truths that got more fragile and elusive with time.

Also, I wanted answers for my siblings who did not have words for their questions. I wanted to speak for one and ask: "Why have I not had a life? Did someone take that from me or was it just my fate? Why was I chosen to be abused? Was I the likely candidate or did I do something wrong? Why the lies about all those years? Why did someone prey on me and hurt me?" And I wanted to shout for another: "Was I a child of shame? Why am I addicted and addicted and addicted? Why did people open my body to secrets that only adults should know and sometimes not even them?"

You know, Elton John once said that "sorry" seems to be the hardest word, but I think the hardest word is "why." But through the process of writing this book, I found out that my family is human and that I can't look to them to give me my answers. 'Cause family may never tell. No one will ever come forward and say, yes, it was me who messed with you. I learned that forgiveness is for the forgiver, and I have become rich in that knowledge. I learned that hurting people hurt people, and that's just the way it is. I learned that mistakes don't go away. They stay to make you strong and to remind you not to make them again. I learned that I am worthy of love and capable of some really funky choices, but they are my choices.

So the book, my perspective, myself, and even my reasons have changed. My real desire, besides making a lot of money to fulfill my dream of helping others, is to tell people that God can change anyone. I want prostitutes to know that God can bring you out of prostitution. I want drug addicts to know that the Lord will be your rock. I want young mothers to know that they are doing a great thing by raising their kids. I want young girls to know that they are princesses, even if they never hear it from anyone but me. I want young men to know that they are destined for greatness. I want parents to know that it's okay to let your kids know that you are human. I want ghetto folks to know that there is a whole world out there beyond the "hood." I want single people to never give up on love. I want white people to know that it's okay to try and know a black person. And I want black people to know that it's okay if a white person has questions about us. How else will we bridge the gap?

ME AND TRACY

One of my rotten men once said, "All you are is a specimen to her." At that time I didn't want to believe it. I like to think that everyone likes me, is as genuine and honest as me, and wants to see me do well. However, that is not the case, and in many ways, he was right, the bastard. My sister said that Tracy was exploiting me, and I acknowledged that she might be, but she couldn't have screwed me any worse than any of the countless fools I had chosen in my life. Just another screw, but it would be a good one because of what came out of it.

What a pleasant surprise that I got to study Tracy almost as much as she studied me, that our original relationship splintered into a number of others, not like broken glass in the street but more like broken colors in a kaleidoscope. Kind of the same thing but not—both broken glass, but one is useless, swept away, and the other is pretty, amusing, soothing, something you treasure and keep. We now have the multiplicity of being ethnographer and subject, girlfriend and girlfriend, colleagues and partners, kinfolks and loved ones. Who could ask for more from a chance meeting of a bigmouth girl and a nosy professor?

SUGAR'S SHOUTS

(Or, as Tracy likes to call them, Sugar's Acknowledgments)

First and foremost, I need to thank my Lord and Savior, Jesus Christ, to whom I owe my life and everything else.

Next, I need to thank my dear Mommy, who gave me life twice: once when she gave birth to me and, second, when she introduced me to Jesus.

Thanks to my dear children, who have given me so many reasons to live, to be, to strive, to go on.

To my sisters, for just being sisters, something no one can understand unless they have a sister. We are sisters by birth, but lovers and friends by choice. Thank you.

To my dear husband, for teaching me the joy of marriage and for showing me how to be and stay married. I love you.

To my sweet sister-friend Tracy: You helped me while my wings were drying. You embraced me when people were questioning. You encouraged me when I was doubting. You felt pain when I was crying. You worried when I was tight-rope walking (you gotta stop that). You laughed when I was laughing. Thanks so much. And to her dear husband, Michael: Thanks for supporting your wife. You remind me of still water, and you know they say it runs deep.

To my best friends who saw me through drugs, men, and bad-hair days: You came into my life and allowed me to share yours. So many times you were all I had. I love you.

To everyone who ever gave me a chance, opened a door, taught me a lesson, or showed me a vision: If perhaps I see farther than someone else, it is truly because I stand on the shoulders of those who came before me.

To all those who offered encouragement in the form of negativity, thanks for helping to lay a rocky path. I have learned to make my stumbling blocks into my stepping stones.

To young people everywhere, but especially young black people: Believe in something bigger than yourself and believe in yourself. Don't ever stop trying. Something's gotta work for you. It just *has* to. Don't give up. Even if you take a fall, don't give up. Even if you do the nastiest thing in the world, don't give up. Even if someone or everyone tells you you are doomed, don't give up. Try different things, new things, take something you've tried before and try it again differently. JUST DON'T GIVE UP!!

TRACY'S ACKNOWLEDGMENTS

In the twenty years that I've been a cultural anthropologist, nothing I have done has occasioned the response of *Sugar's Life in the Hood*. Since this book began, phone calls from friends and family usually begin with "So how's the book?" Everyone, it seems, is eager for Sugar's story to be told. Many people have supported me in this effort, and I'd like to thank some of them here.

The book emerged from an afternoon's conversation with the writer and historian Ricky Solinger, whose familiarity with welfare policy and the rigors of writing biography established the basis for telling Sugar's story. My sister Melissa Bachrach immediately shared my passion. She read my early efforts at what I thought were chapters and could not be dissuaded from her vision of *Sugar's Life in the Hood* as a best-seller and a movie. She directed me to Bill Contardi at the William Morris Agency, who acted more as an editor than an agent. Twice in the development of the book Bill read chapters and offered valuable guidance. I am indebted to him for introducing me to John Thornton of the Spieler Agency, who provided many thoughtful comments over a two-year relationship.

My family has been immensely supportive, especially my dear cousin Mark Larner, who has acted as lawyer and guide throughout the development and writing processes. Among my colleagues and friends, I have to single out Paul Shankman, who reads all my work the first time around. After reading a draft of *Sugar's Life in the Hood*, Paul just shook his head and laughed at my "telling all," a style both of us had scoffed at for years. I will always be indebted to Donna Goldstein, Paul's colleague and my friend. While deeply mired in the intricacies of completing her own book, Donna heard my cries for editorial support and promptly introduced me to Rick Camp.

Rick was in his early thirties, had a tattoo and a punk haircut, and worked at a gardening center. I was skeptical, but Donna insisted. Rick, she swore, was brilliant, and he had an ear for social science and popular writing. Of course, Donna was right. Rick Camp became my editor-angel during the spring and summer of 2000, the crunch time when Sugar and I swore the book just *had* to be finished. Rick took me in hand, and together we transformed unconnected chapters into a real story. Without his dedication to Sugar's voice, and his uncanny sense of drama and dialogue, this book certainly would not have developed as it did.

Others who have offered kindness or the chance to spread the word about *Sugar's Life in the Hood* include Margaret Maupin of the Tattered Cover Bookstore, who, early on, convinced me there were no other books like this in print; and Gregg Kvistad, my dean, who invited Sugar and me to read from the book as part of the Humanities Lecture Series. Jack Van Sandt and Rick Rinehart of Roberts Rinehart Publishers were invaluable in teaching me the language of book publishing. My sister Roberta Brady and my good friends Alan Stark, Jane Butcher, Michael Stoff, Stuart Schoffman, and John (Sonny) Tirman have given me endless good counsel, most of it very funny, for which I am so grateful.

I like to tell the story that Theresa May of the University of Texas Press agreed to publish *Sugar's Life in the Hood* over a lunch of chicken-fried steak with three vegetables at Austin's famous eatery Threadgill's. This is somewhat apocryphal, of course, and it turned out that publishing the book was no simple matter. Likely, Theresa was just cajoling me along as we were in the rather serious throes of readying another book of mine for publication. Nonetheless, Theresa's enthusiasm buoyed me immensely and injected tremendous energy into the project. Throughout the publication process, as I have fretted about almost everything, she has managed to distract me with deliciously amusing stories about her life in the theater.

I want to express the great and wonderful debt I owe to my husband of thirty years, Michael C. Ehlers, who first loved this idea. Through ten rewrites and countless frustrations, he continued to believe Sugar's story had to be told. I doubt that many men enjoy coming home at night to a spouse at the computer who is still in her pajamas. He listened, he made suggestions, he copyedited. Michael endured it all, and he has been immensely patient and understanding.

Lastly, my deeply felt gratitude must go to Ms. "Sugar Turner" for allowing me into her life. Together we peeled back the layers of her history until the inside story of her hustling came clearly into view. In the process, we both changed, and I have to thank her for what she put me through during these six years. I don't have another friend like her, and she will always be precious to me.

Sugar's Life in the Hood

TRACY'S INTRODUCTION

One Saturday morning in September, Sugar came to my house in Las Callas for a final day of taping. After five years, we had come to the end of our interview sessions chronicling the story of her life.

Before she arrived, I sat musing about the first time she had come to my house. It was December 1994. We had just begun our work and had decided to get the ball rolling with a marathon interview session at my house over the weekend. She called herself Shugie then, the stage name she had kept from her days as a whore and a model. She was thirty-five, had three children of her own, and was guardian for her cousin's two boys. Over the past seventeen years, she had worked some and had been on welfare. She was a reformed crack addict. There was a constant stream of men through her life; the latest one's name was Reggie.

The trip to Las Callas, which had seemed like a simple plan to me, proved to be an expedition for Sugar. She had never been much of anywhere. She was excited about coming to a white university town an hour from Springfield that was well outside her comfort zone of her hood in Springfield. Looking back on it, the trip proved to be a very big step indeed: an adventure was beginning.

She didn't have a car then, so she was taking the bus. I picked her up at the bus station when she missed my stop and had to ride all the way to the end of the line. In the car, she related the forty-five-minute trip, mile by mile. I was surprised at her wide-eyed, almost childlike enthusiasm. She had talked to this person, that person, seen some cows. It was all so different! Going to Las Callas cemented for Sugar the reality of what we were undertaking. It was scary and, at the same time, liberating.

She was hungry, so before we got down to work, we headed for the refrigerator. Ever faithful to the legions of good Jewish mothers in my family, I had stocked up on goodies in preparation for our two-day session: all kinds of fruit, cheeses, breads and bagels, turkey, carrots to munch on, and so forth. She opened the door, peered inside at all the food, and announced, "There's nothing to eat in here!"

This was not so much a slap in the face as it was a pronouncement of the cultural gulf we were trying to bridge. We looked at each other, both recognized the significance of the moment, and started laughing uproariously. Then we headed for the 7-Eleven and bought enough junk food to satisfy Sugar's appetite for sugar, salt, and carbohydrates.

From that day on we knew we had a problem when it came to food. She doesn't like the healthy food that I eat, and I don't eat the junk food she keeps in her house. We joke about this, but food is one of the most tangible and telling representations of culture. I live in a town with five natural-food supermarkets. I have the money to buy organic produce, while Sugar's shopping has always been guided by what her food stamps would buy, so she specializes in the convenience foods that I don't ever have in my house.

Given this conflict, it's ironic that at almost every taping session we were eating. Sharing food was a medium for conversation. And just because I don't have junk food in my kitchen doesn't mean I eschew eating most of a jar of jelly beans at Sugar's.

We ate out a lot, and the restaurants we went to pulled us into each other's worlds. We sat for hours in coffeehouses I knew. I introduced her to lattes and to scones. And she took me to Popeye's, to Kentucky Fried, and to a local rib place where she ran into a lot of her old gangster friends. For her birthday one year, I took her to a French restaurant where she asked the waiter if it would be okay if she ate her dessert first. This young man was so entranced with her, he forgot his own name.

I am embarrassed to say that sometimes I felt like Prof. Henry Higgins to Sugar's Eliza Doolittle. Yes, the elitist and patronizing self-congratulatory sense of "lifting" a woman up out of the gutter occasionally floated through my mind, especially when I took her somewhere she had never been . . . like the time we went to the Mongolia Exhibit at the Springfield Art Museum.

ST   I haven't been to the art museum since second grade. All the kids were laughin' and tittering at the—what do I want to say?—Rubenesque figure of this nude, this naked woman.

TBE   You have not been back to the art museum since you were in second grade?

ST   It's just that I rarely have time. It's always in my consciousness to go. I even put it on my calendar to take my kids, but Saturday's my workday, when I do hair. And that's the free day around town for museums and stuff. It just clashes. Or Saturday's the day when you've worked late Friday and you're just lazin' around. It's never a priority. So it was cool to be there today. It made my stomach feel funny. It feels strange. It's similar to what I feel in the library. It's a feeling of spirits bein' around you. Where other people have touched and done and made.

TBE   History.

ST   Yeah, that: history.

But such thoughts of Pygmalion were fleeting. First of all, she didn't want to be part of my world. Certainly, she took what she could, drinking in what she determined to be meaningful and useful to her. But whatever we experienced together she integrated back into her life in the hood. She sincerely likes who she is and doesn't aspire to a life among the middle class, either black or white. Once, when we were fantasizing about having lots of money, I asked her if she would ever buy a big house in a fancy Springfield neighborhood.

ST   No, I love my hood. I wanna stay in my hood. It's flavorful. I feel safe there. I know it like the back of my hand. My boon coons are there. They love me. I wouldn't want to live with white people. They may not love me. They don't know me. And they're afraid of me. So I would want a bigger house right here that I could renovate and make it look like a house in a fancy neighborhood. And you can bet I'd put up a serious security system!

Secondly, Sugar was no passive informant. She actively read, edited, and corrected transcripts and chapters. During that first year, Sugar accused me of "niggerizing" her voice. And although I defensively pointed out that I had it all on tape, when I went back to investigate, I found she was right. I couldn't completely understand what she was saying. All over the first transcripts I had written "clarify," or "ask Sugar." But worse, I had transcribed some words or phrases "down," making them more idiomatic or introducing more grammatical mistakes. I was unconsciously inserting stereotyped black speech. It wasn't until the second year that I had enough familiarity with her use of English and ebonics to no longer need her help translating. And by then, she had pointed out my "hearing" problem enough that I had stopped "niggerizing" her.

In addition, although my entry into her life created some adjustments, I was not the agent of change in Sugar's life. Sugar was. When I bought a new computer, I did give her the old one. But she didn't need any encouragement from me to become computer literate. She signed up for courses, asked every techie in the hood for advice, and just played around on the keyboard. In a remarkably brief period of time, she had transformed her back room into an efficient home office and immediately transferred to disk the documents and papers that had been in piles around the house.

Although traveling by herself to Las Callas had been a new adventure, Sugar is actually an oddly confident, even idiosyncratic, cultural explorer. She loves the challenge of the world outside the hood, but on her own terms. Her life, and what she expects from herself, is circumscribed by her worldview. She has been both hemmed in by those cultural parameters and able to, as Sugar says, "fly away" farther than her family or friends. But she also knows her life has to be firmly planted in the urban scene.

At the same time, she has always been an agile trekker through the wider Springfield scene. When she was a welfare mother, she regularly took herself out of the normal routine of the hood just to see what the bigger world looked like. She volunteered at the Springfield Marathon, handing water to the runners. She served on a cultural resources board that gave grants to art institutions. So, I think it is fair to say that Sugar has taken good advantage of what our partnership offers. Minimally, this means an occasional used computer. More important, however, just as I have had a front-seat tour of one woman's life in the hood, she has been privy to the less exciting but still challenging reality of the life of a middle-class academic.

To me, it has honestly never seemed an odd pairing. Of course, when we were taping in restaurants or at my university office, people couldn't really figure out what we were doing together, the red-haired black woman and the white fifty-something anthropologist. My friends were curious too, and they were just as befuddled by her as if she had been a huipil-wearing, Cakchiquel-speaking Mayan woman who had built a fire in the corner of my kitchen for making tortillas.

But to us, our collaboration is the logical extension of who we are. I had always been a curious, some might even say "nosy," sort of social scientist. Being in the field in highland Guatemalan villages and towns had been immensely satisfying to me partly because women allowed me to ask them absolutely anything about their lives. No one had ever been as interested in them as I was, so they seriously wanted to talk to me, simply to be heard. And, as a result, despite the strangeness of having a privileged professional American woman spending months among them without her husband, the locals befriended me, cared for me, and made me a part of their families.

So, for me, working with an African American woman who wanted me to write the story of her life seemed a natural research project. She wanted to tell me everything. She wanted me to listen and write it all down. I wanted to know all about her. It seemed pretty straightforward. What I didn't expect is that in documenting her life, I would learn so much about myself. The process of working with Sugar blurred the lines between subject and friend, and caused me to examine some uncomfortable realities, both about myself and about the world I come from. For years I had been researching women in poverty thousands of miles from home. Working with Sugar made me wonder what had prevented me from doing fieldwork among African American women. After all, despite seeming alien and a bit exotic, Sugar's world, unlike the world of the highland Maya, is my world, only a forty-five-minute drive away.

Sugar and I knew that in spite of our geographical proximity, we were from different planets, so we were constantly amazed at what we discovered about each other's habits and lives. But we gave each other the space we needed, although, for my part, sometimes the learning curve was pretty steep.

There was the time I brought my dog, Alma, with me to Sugar's house. Alma is the model golden retriever: playful, mellow, and loving. She hangs out at my office at the university, comes to class, runs around with students. People are always stopping me to admire and pet her. So when Alma and I walked into Sugar's house and her kids screamed in terror, I was surprised.

But the anthropologist in me spotted this as a cultural trait, something you learn growing up. I had been scared of dogs as a child growing up in urban Newark, New Jersey, where few people had big pets. But in Wisconsin, dogs are as common as hockey sticks and bratwurst. There are 25,000 dogs in Las Callas, about one per family. Most of them are well trained, or at least under the control of their owners. Thus many children have dogs and learn how to be comfortable with them.

In contrast, when I went to Guatemala for my dissertation research, I learned that dogs aren't pets. They are flea-ridden security systems who spend their lives on short chains, sounding the alarm if strangers approach. Most people there cannot afford to feed a dog, so many dogs become street scavengers competing with other animals for scraps of food. Little affection is directed toward these creatures. In fact, children learn to kick them or throw stones at them when they bark.

So when Sugar's children and their visiting friends ran upstairs in fear, I explained it as a cultural difference. I hadn't seen more than one or two dogs in the neighborhood, so being frightened of this big animal was, I thought, understandable. However, later, when Sugar's son hit Alma hard with a wooden toy and his mother laughed and thought it "cool," I stopped being complacently intellectual about dogs, children, and culture. I was in the field again, trying to identify with the folk and finding it difficult.

If Sugar was uncomfortable in any of the settings I chose, she never showed it. On the other hand, I always felt like an anxious interloper touring the cultural reality of the hood in an air-conditioned bus. This paranoia has been a troublesome handicap, one I couldn't seem to get around. But no matter how much fun we had at times, this odd partnership made us each feel awkward. We knew we were slowly overcoming our sense of being personal strangers; the cultural strangers, though, were harder to change. We were entering foreign worlds that we little understood: she, the white academic middle-class culture, and I, the reality of a poor black urban hustler. The partnership and the process evolved slowly. At first, we kept our distance. Our lives rarely intersected but for taping sessions.

I had never heard of Sugar's neighborhood, nor had I even driven through it. Once I became a regular visitor, I saw few white people on the streets. In fact, people who met me couldn't figure out what I was doing there. Often I imagined the neighbors thought I was Sugar's caseworker or the county home health care provider. Given the trajectory of my life, I didn't belong in Sugar's world.

Similarly, Sugar knew almost nothing about me or where I lived. She had never been to Las Callas and considered it the far-flung outskirts of Springfield, a place filled with boring white people. Although she had at one time considered going to college, she didn't know what an anthropologist did. But that was quickly rectified. On my first visit to her microenterprise class at the Coretta King Center for Women, I gave a slide show on my Guatemalan research. She was startled by her own ignorance of these Mayan women, but she quickly saw the connection and immediately began referring to them as her "sisters."

I had been dropping by Sugar's for five years, confidently chipping away at our agenda, when it became clear that our cultural gulf hadn't been entirely bridged. The work had made us good friends. That was true. But in spite of this bond, I still felt like a question mark. My self-imposed outsider status became clear to me around Sugar's fortieth birthday.

As her fortieth birthday approached, Sugar planned a huge extravaganza to which everyone she knew, including her third-grade classmates, would be invited by a billboard announcing the party. It was clearly an important milestone to her. Of course, she couldn't afford such a fete, so, eventually, the party ended up being an informal gathering at her favorite bar. I took her out to lunch on her birthday and gave her a gift, but I didn't go to the party. I had my list of excuses that I didn't share with her. I thought about the time when I had met Sugar's friends at her house. They were distant and wary with me, as if I weren't in the room. I saw this as a message. To my mind, the party would be the same kind of thing; I wouldn't fit in. I wasn't cool enough to hang with her set, I guess. I saw myself as this old boring white woman who didn't have the flashy clothes or cool dance steps that everyone else at the party would have. I wasn't snubbing her, I thought. I'm saving her from the embarrassment of having asked me.

Several days after the party, she showed me the photographs. There were all these people having fun mugging for the camera, and a lot of them were white teachers from the school where Sugar now works. They obviously didn't see themselves as unwanted party crashers; they were having a good time celebrating a colleague's birthday! I felt like a fool. It wasn't that I would have opted to hang out with these white people had I gone. But seeing their pictures, I knew that my being a cultural isolate in the hood was not just a problem associated with social scientific methods. I still had racial tensions to resolve. Ironically, my cultural comfort level was clearly more problematic than Sugar's. And, by giving into an unconscious need to distance myself, I had hurt a friend on her fortieth birthday.

For our last Las Callas taping session Sugar drove up in her little "hoopdy," the junker car that now got her around more efficiently. She again got lost, even though by now she had been to Las Callas many times. Sugar has no sense of direction and therefore drives by instinct. This isn't an exaggeration. She can't tell right from left. When our work started, and I was giving her rides home, she had to direct me. When I asked, "Which way at the corner?" there would be long pauses while she got her brain to say right or left. She ended up giving right and left names that came to mind quickly: Righty Tighty and Lefty Lucy. This problem has been partially addressed by her finally being able to afford a car and having to make fast directional decisions.

Once we got settled in my office, and I had turned on the heat so she wouldn't complain about it being "winter in here," we spent the afternoon reminiscing about our time together writing the story of her life. We clarified some material, but basically we laughed together and remembered. And she taught me her "I am a queen" mantra, something both of us now use on ourselves when we're feeling bad, or with students when they need some reinforcement. We went out for Japanese noodles, snacked on tortillas, cheese, and homegrown tomatoes, and drank some wine.

Just before she left, we were looking at a little shrine I had put together for a dear friend who had just died. I idly asked her if she had ever thought about her funeral. She was startled. No, she had never gone there, thank you. But it was a compelling idea. She started planning, and she had very quickly come up with specific ideas for the music, her clothes, an open coffin, which funeral home. She decided she wanted three people to eulogize her: one of her sisters, her dearest friend, and, much to my surprise, me.

I was touched and, at first, demurred. But the more I thought about it, the more I appreciated the logic and the sentiment of her choice. This was no empty gesture on Sugar's part. She understood by this point that I knew her better than many of her family or friends did. The process of writing her life story had allowed me to ask intimate and probing questions that propriety denies us even in our most important relationships. She had shared it all with me. And I had listened. In the course of our work, we had come to love each other. So, even though I knew I would feel awkward and white and uncool at the Pitkin Funeral Home in the hood, yes, I would speak about her when she was gone.

TRACY'S BACKGROUND

I consider myself an anthropologist of the Margaret Mead variety. Like Mead, an early anthropological pioneer, I study living peoples and cultures. And as Mead did, I try to connect the conditions of their lives to broader world problems. For more than twenty years, my research has focused on highland Guatemala and the women living in two communities there. Mostly, I've written about the strategies poor women must utilize in order to feed their children while unresponsive and often abusive men hover over their lives.

Three days a week I leave the sanctuary Las Callas provides to go to my office in Springfield. In spite of its stodgy reputation, Springfield is a real city. As have most U.S. cities over the last few decades, Springfield has experienced a rapid growth in the numbers of its citizens in poverty. According to the 1990 U.S. census, Springfield's poverty rate jumped to 17.1 percent from 13.7 percent a decade before. Outwardly, Springfield's poor neighborhoods do not resemble the bleak ghettos of cities like New York or Chicago. Nonetheless, Springfield's central city has one of the highest poverty rates in this part of the country. This is partially explained by the fact that during the 1980s the shift of jobs trickling away from the urban center and into the suburbs became a stampede. Springfield lost more than 15,000 manufacturing jobs, which contributed to an escalating poverty rate, especially among minorities with fewer skills and less education. Although the city's African American population remained stable during the 1980s, the number of poor blacks increased by 15 percent. Consistent with the national average, nearly 30 percent of African Americans in Springfield are now considered poor, compared with 9 percent of whites.

In 1994, inspired by the ethnic diversity around me, I decided to temporarily redirect my research interests from Guatemala to Springfield. I had written about women's small business efforts among the

Maya, and I wanted to do some cross-cultural comparisons among minority women in the United States. I began a research stint at the Coretta King Center for Women, examining and evaluating their female microenterprise training programs. The newest and most exciting of these, A Step Ahead, was designed to move women off the welfare rolls and into small businesses. That's where I met Sugar. She was enrolled in A Step Ahead, which she had determined was the most logical route from welfare dependency to entrepreneurial legitimacy.

I saw right away that Sugar was smart and that she was talkative. She had a lot to say about being a black welfare mother. Clearly, she and the system had been at loggerheads for years. Consequently, she was not ashamed of being a scammer and, in fact, touted her home beauty salon as the best in Springfield. She was eager and entrepreneurial. The modeling business she wanted to start was ready to go, she said, and she wanted to be a businesswoman now!

She was opinionated. She was funny. Her beauty and outrageously false red Afro only added to her charisma. We got to know each other a little. I started giving her rides home. I was mesmerized by her stories, her language, her enthusiasm. I knew immediately that she was an ethnographer's dream informant; that if I ever got her in front of a tape recorder, she would be dynamite. So when she asked me to write the story of her life, I immediately agreed.

Once we began, it was clear the book was not a welfare book. After each of us had read a few books about women on welfare, we figured there were sufficient experts who had covered the topic better than we could. Furthermore, we both found welfare much too narrow a focus to contain Sugar's story. Too often, welfare mothers are assumed to personify the daily grind of poverty and little else. That wasn't what either of us had in mind.

Sugar is far too multifaceted to be pigeonholed as a welfare queen. Beneath her flamboyant hustler skin is an extremely moral, thoughtful, righteous woman who runs her life almost along scriptural lines. She's made a lot of poor choices or downright mistakes in her life, but somehow she sees each one of them as a lesson. She almost died on crack, but she viewed this as God's thunderbolt, a not-too-subtle warning about the need to clean up her act. She was a whore for a couple of years, which she saw as an entrepreneurial start-up more than as a dangerous occupation. Men come and go in her life, and they've pretty much all been losers. The lessons they embodied are painful and complex, but she goes on after each of these affairs because of her certainty that God's got something better planned for her one day.

My reasons for working with her were not limited to the issue of welfare. I also wanted to attend to certain public policy issues. Then there was a scholarly goal that grew out of those. Finally, I had a personal agenda for spending time with Sugar in the hood.

Let me explain: I'm a 1960s progressive who grew up to be a "save the world" anthropologist and a feminist. As an anthropologist, I have been lucky enough to be able to combine my political perspective with a theoretical orientation, cultural materialism, which I feel nicely complements it. This approach downplays explanations based entirely on what people think or believe. Instead, cultural materialists search for explanations that emerge from the conditions in which people live. This idea becomes clear if you think about Karl Marx's contention that it is not people's mode of thinking that influences their social conditions, but the other way around.

As a cultural materialist, I've written that women's desperate economic vulnerability in highland Guatemala explains why they tolerate irresponsible husbands, even if the husband's economic contribution is small. The Mayan women I have studied do not believe they will ever have good husbands. They expect men to betray them in any number of ways, the worst one being that they will not be good providers. As such, they prepare themselves for that eventuality by developing their own small businesses. But these tiny cottage industries never yield enough to feed the family. So women accept beatings and infidelity because, materially, they need male income, however meager. And, in the long run, women want the children that a man can provide, for children turn out to be reliable workers from an early age. For all those reasons, survival depends on keeping a man around. The gravity of this situation is reflected in the Guatemalan saying: "How is a man like an avocado? A good one is hard to find."

What people think and the values they hold come into this model as a means to motivate and reinforce adaptive behavior. For example, Guatemalan socialization emphasizes subordination and passivity as appropriate for women. From an early age, women are taught to blame themselves for male shortcomings. If your husband is straying, it must be because you haven't been treating him right. If he deserts the family, relatives will say you failed in your duty to accommodate your husband's every wish. Perhaps he grew tired of your shrewish demands for more money and time at home. Girls are taught that women are strong while men are like children. Thus, women must endure men's irresponsibility and abuse, not only for the support the men provide but because the women believe that suffering at the hands of men is their destiny.

Similarly, when I see poverty in America, I immediately begin my analysis with the circumstances in which the poor are living. I examine institutional reasons for poverty that have proven to be almost impervious to change—lack of educational and economic opportunities or social inequities like racism and the concentration of wealth. In my university classes, I have tried to explain the feminization of poverty by examining the conditions that foster and support it, particularly the marginalization of poor blacks, both men and women.

I am particularly skeptical about those policymakers who blame single mothers for the disadvantaged and unfortunate lives their children are leading. Although cultural pathologies and dysfunctional mother-centered homes are consistent features of life among the so-called urban underclass, from where I sit, female-headed households are not the causes of poverty, but merely a symptom.

Outside the classroom, I have been more than a little impatient with the public policy rhetoric on welfare. But for years I had grumbled from the sidelines about White House or congressional missteps, feeling that because I had no research experience in urban America, I couldn't participate in the debate at the scholarly level as I would have liked.

When I met Sugar, however, I saw my entry point. I could have a firsthand look at the life of one single mother and, at the same time, learn whether the strategies black women used in their relations with men were anything like what I had seen in Guatemala. I believed that the conditions of poverty were likely the common variable in marital instability; that African American men mistreated economically marginalized women, who in turn accepted this abuse in hopes of whatever money they could eke out of their men. I suspected that because black women had a stronger sense of community and a better-developed state-level support system than did the more isolated Mayan women, they could more easily reject impossible men who were merely siphoning resources from the family. But how much did this happen?

What I learned from Sugar was that a mate was a very valuable commodity. Although men gave women little economic support, and they denied them long-term emotional satisfaction, what they did offer was romance, however fleeting, and, more important, the children that legitimated women by making them into mothers in the black community. I guessed that, like a good avocado in Guatemala, black men were scarce resources who were treasured far beyond their real worth. Little did I realize how right I was.

When Sugar and I began, I was just plain curious about this zany red-haired black woman. In my work in Central America, I have learned that women rarely have the chance to speak about themselves. Attentive listeners are hard to come by. So when I settled in for a long conversation in the home of a Mayan woman, and then came back repeatedly over the next year, I got an earful. The same proved to be true with Sugar.

She started out as a source, an informant. But as she talked to me, little by little the traditional social-scientific distance from the subject disappeared. It became evident that I was not writing a book *about* her so much as I was writing one *with* her. I think it was the familiarity Sugar encouraged that initially broke down the professional and personal barriers, not so much the unexpurgated nature of the material, but her eagerness to talk about it, to answer my questions, to fill out her life for me. Together we were reliving her childhood, the years on welfare, kicking crack—all of it.

Indeed, the intimate tenor of our conversations was a far cry from the kind of interviews either of us might have conducted with strangers, whichever side of the microphone we were on. We later found that our "girlfriend" status sometimes caused Sugar to reveal more about herself than she had originally intended. Later reflection on the content of the transcripts could be painful and at times embarrassing.

Over the years, we also worked through Sugar's latest realities: what was going on with the men she loved, the courses she was taking, or the jobs she wanted. This added a dynamic and decidedly different dimension to our sessions. The past is the past, but getting today's news on tape has palpable drama attached to it because the story develops while you watch. I once wrote that you don't need to have a television in highland Guatemala because every woman's life is a soap opera. The same goes for Sugar's little house in the hood.

People like to talk to me, to tell me things about their lives. It's partly why I'm a good ethnographer. I'd like to say that the basis of this confiding is trust, but sometimes it happens in the first interview. It may be that no one has ever offered them the opportunity to talk about their lives. Or perhaps it's that I am honestly interested in what they are saying, and it shows on my face. Just the other day, Sugar found something in the Bible about "the good listener" that reminded her of me. Perhaps people sense that. In any case, for five years I've been listening to Sugar. Apart from the substance of her story, her telling and my being a witness to that telling have brought us together as friends. We share a dedication to this process and to the level of honest oral narrative it elicits. But Sugar insists that the next time we do this, she'll be asking the questions and I'll be telling my story.

GIVING SUGAR A VOICE

For the past decade, Sugar has been renting a big ranch house in a black neighborhood in Springfield. To get there from my home in Las Callas, it takes only forty-five minutes. The trip has become fairly routine. I get off the highway, drive five minutes past the foul-smelling factories, the cheap burger place, and the check-cashing store. When I turn onto Sugar's street, I've entered a sprawling residential area of single-family homes on small, neat lots. By now, I've locked my car doors, feeling ashamed of myself, even though I know she locks her doors too.

The Marvin neighborhood is poor, and it shows in the old, run-down houses and the boarded-up stores. But it isn't one of Springfield's worst. Seventy percent black, its poverty rate is about 38 percent, which represents an 11 percent rise from the decade before, but is still better than other (largely Latino) Springfield areas where two-thirds of the residents live below the poverty line. While 71 percent of the Marvin district is made up of single-parent families, fewer than 20 percent of households receive public assistance. In poorer areas, this percentage is as high as 48. Still, the indicators aren't optimistic for the future. Last year, for example, more than half the Marvin births were to single mothers with less than a high school education. Clearly, these young, uneducated mothers will have a very difficult time supporting their children on low-paying jobs and increasingly inaccessible public assistance.

Sugar loves the Marvin hood. She adores her house and has even dreamed of buying it one day. The place is old and in disrepair, but to Sugar's way of thinking, it's practically posh. The house is decidedly bigger than anywhere she has lived before. The older kids have the run of the basement, with four bedrooms, a bath, and two phones, one for the boys and one for the girls. Sugar's bedroom and bath are off to one side, where she has carved out some quiet and some privacy amid the teenage bustle that blows through the rest of the house. In the kitchen, the appliances are old, but everything works. Her favorite room is the pristine living room with its red couch, black-and-white carpet, and big, engaging aquarium. One room has been set up for her hairdressing business. When there are no appointments, the teenage boys tend to gravitate there, dozing on the old couch and watching TV.

For me, there are two things that stand out about Sugar's house. First, it is always hot. She likes to "make winter go away," so the thermometer is usually set at 80 degrees. That makes it cozy for her, but uncomfortably overheated for me. Second, Sugar's home is cluttered. This woman has more stuff than she knows what to do with, and there are piles of it everywhere: clothes in the bedroom, toiletries in the bath, masses of papers on her kitchen table, magazines and bills piled up everywhere. Every surface of her tiny office nook is stacked with books and papers. It's not mounds of filthy laundry, but a "neat" kind of clutter, much like my own office.

My use of the word "clutter" in describing Sugar's home has become a standing joke between us. Obsessively organized, she objects to my choice of the word. When she was on welfare, I wrote in my notes that her defensiveness about her housekeeping was occasioned by her fervent need to avoid being stereotyped as a welfare queen, one who's too lazy to get up from the soap operas and talk shows to clean her own house.

Since getting to know her better, I understand that the ever-present piles can be explained by the fact that she has to be a worker, a student, a mother, and a businesswoman all at the same time. She's saving hundreds of clippings for future projects, sorting the clothes to give away to charity, and amassing books and activities for the students at her school. And she knows where everything is in that warren of papers. Once I had to drop off a transcript that she didn't want the children to see. She was away from home, but she was able to give me careful telephone directions to her hiding place, identifying each pile as it went by in her mind.

Over the last five years, Sugar and I have been able to clear a flat surface in Sugar's busy house to record her memories and her thoughts. This was usually accomplished when the four teenagers were at school and the youngest was at the baby-sitter's. Basically, our sessions were long oddball chats: the white anthropologist and the black welfare mother eat leftover Halloween candy bars and talk about Sugar's life. I select a topic. She talks. I ask questions. She talks some more. We laugh together at her obscenely candid description of old boyfriends or tricks and what they wanted from her. Or we get "deep" when she remembers the bittersweet fleeting delights of her youth, as when she received an award in junior high school, or the painful moments when she describes her mother rarely being there.

Sugar loves to be the raconteur, and I, of course, encourage her by my continued presence and persistent interest. After all, this is what I do for a living. But what is ethnography if not indulging one's curiosity about what's behind a door different from one's own?

I am interested in Sugar. In fact, I didn't realize when we began this work how "exotic" her lifestyle would prove to be. And I'm not referring to the hard-core side of her story. Sugar's world is so different from mine that the smallest details intrigue me: what television programs she likes, where she shops, or how she makes coffee. After twenty years as an anthropologist, I find the same desire to understand the day-to-day in Springfield as I do among traditional Maya in Guatemala.

However, the anthropologist I am in the 1990s is different from the fieldworker I was when I started out in the late 1970s. My entry into Sugar Turner's life is not as an ethnographic participant-observer, but as the sympathetic chronicler of an oral history. I care about her and am concerned about the world her children will inherit. There is no pretense of value-free science here. The irony is that as I guide her through the narrative of her life, she guides me into a world I have long misunderstood but always wanted to know.

One of the issues social scientists deal with is the veracity of the material they are collecting. In ethnographic research, there are versions of truth that anthropologists never discover because informants lie to us. Either there are holes in their memory or they only know part of the story. Everyone loses chunks of their own lives, and we have to turn to others present at the time for verification or details. In the writing of this book, every so often I found that Sugar had only presented one version of a story and that there was evidence of others. I don't think she ever intentionally lied to me. She was ignoring or forgetting parts of her own life, nuances and details embellished or omitted in her narrative recounting.

For example, the breakup of her marriage to Ernie T. was told to me as a straightforward list of conflicts, fights, tears, and tantrums resulting in her finally kicking him out. How did you feel about ending your marriage? I asked. *Good riddance! Never should have been married to him anyway.* That's how I wrote it down. A year or two later, Sugar gave me a notebook of letters and diary entries from that period. I found several emotional letters despairing of never being with Ernie T. again. She dreamed about him and missed him terribly. For this reason, Ernie T.'s role was fleshed out a bit, reminding me of how elusive the truth about someone's life really is. But the chronicling of Sugar's life was not a process of digging through archives or contacting relatives in an attempt to capture that truth. The book is neither biography nor autobiography. I consider it a testimonio.

The process of telling and listening has become known as oral history, testimonial literature, or, because of its roots in the social movements of Latin America, testimonio. Recording a testimonio is a very different literary process than the writing of popular autobiography. Testimonio gives voice to nontraditional, previously silenced voices, be they those of women, the poor, or ethnic minorities. It allows those distanced from power to speak for themselves, to be witnesses to history and culture, to re-create their pasts. As such, testimonios break from the "high culture" of the memoir by featuring the lives of the ordinary and the disempowered rather than those of historical figures, political leaders, and media stars.

Additionally, a testimonio is distinct because the process of writing one is facilitated by another person, usually a social scientist, who, unlike many of the storytellers, is literate and an experienced writer. The listener (or interlocutor) has multiple roles in the process. She organizes and guides the interviews, records and transcribes the narrative, and then edits the text, making a life story into a book. When the book is in shape, she promotes it and sells it to a publisher.

Few testimonios are widely read, since they tend to appeal mostly to academics and their students as yet another source of information about a subject area. However, one testimonio, I, Rigoberta Menchú: An Indian Woman in Guatemala, has been immensely popular. The book is the life story of an ordinary Mayan woman whose suffering and resistance to oppression came to symbolize the indigenous condition in Guatemala. The book propelled Rigoberta into the international spotlight. Soon after its publication, she was awarded the Nobel Peace Prize for her work. To me, this sequence of events demonstrated the potential inherent in giving voice to the poor and the powerless through *testimonios*. Readers, my students among them, were surprised and devastated by the intimate details she offered about her life in a traditional community and its eventual destruction at the hands of the Guatemalan military.

Recently, questions have arisen about the veracity of the story and whether Rigoberta embellished her situation by drawing upon the experiences of other, even more unfortunate, Maya in order to make a political point. My sense of this controversy is that a *testimonio* gives voice to a life history previously hidden or ignored, and if more than one life is uncovered, so much the better.

In many ways, envisioning Sugar's story as a *testimonio* helped me focus my agenda. Why was I was working with Sugar to tell her story through her words? I was doing so in order to insert an insider's view into what had become a biased, uninformed picture of life in the hood. A few weeks at Sugar's demonstrated how my own image of the urban ghetto had been skewed by misinformation. Policymakers and analysts produce a constant stream of data, but the stereotype of the ghetto family remains firmly fixed in the minds of most Americans. Perhaps, I thought, one woman's oral history, honestly told, would be an opening to a better understanding of what it means to be a poor black woman in America. Would focusing on Sugar's gaze and voice create compassion and interest where there had previously been scorn and half-truths? I hoped it would. Is this improving on history? If so, then I have done my job as editor or interpreter. I feel no guilt about using my authority to bring the story to the attention of the public.

Of course, we hope her tale of one woman's life in the hood will resonate far beyond Sugar herself; there is meaning to be found here for each reader. At the same time, we cannot deny the inherently off-putting nature of much of what she has done in her life. For many readers, white or black, the world Sugar inhabits will seem an alien place, and her approach to navigating that world unfathomable at times.

Even to me, who came to know Sugar so well, many of the choices she has made, especially about men, remain a mystery. It's not only that the line of losers is so long, but why does she repeatedly make wedding arrangements after knowing a man for only a few weeks? And I continue to be aghast at her persistent failure to practice safe sex, even though she has lectured her own children about condoms and AIDS.

Another thing that has always baffled me is Sugar's fundamentalism. From the first day we met, her sign-off line has been "May God be with you." She is a fervent Bible reader and analyst, and not a day goes by that she doesn't sit down to read and seek guidance from the good book. Where I would confront a problem by analyzing it, she says she's going to "ask the Lord." And she waits for the Lord to speak to her before she goes ahead with anything important.

This works for her, but I am quite sure she would refute such a pragmatic analysis of her faith. Sugar's spirituality is based on a profound commitment to God and to the moral order associated with the best in any religion. I respect her very personal connection with God and the marvelous sense of charity toward everyone that goes with it. Nonetheless, her fervent adherence to this approach continues to elude me.

A few months ago, she announced that she had decided I needed salvation. I laughed and said I thought it was a futile plan. I was stuck in my Jewish ways. Why, I asked, had saving me suddenly occurred to her? "Well," she said very matter-of-factly, "I've decided I don't want to be in heaven without you."

SUGAR, THE CONSERVATIVE REPUBLICAN

When Sugar and I first talked about politics, I was confronted with one of my own stereotypes. I thought that if you lived in the hood, you would be conversant with the politics of poverty. Furthermore, I assumed that most residents of the hood would be liberal Democrats, since those candidates most clearly spoke to the issues of the poor and disenfranchised. Not Sugar. Sugar sees the world like a conservative Republican. She's not savvy in the ways of the two-party system, and when I called her a conservative, she asked me to explain what it meant. Clearly, it is her personal philosophy that bespeaks a conservative bent. While I'm concerned about the triple whammy of her being poor, black, and female, to Sugar, those characteristics don't matter much in how you see the world. After all, "people are people."

If Sugar has been treated differently because she's black, she doesn't take it personally. Some of her friends explain their difficult situations by pointing to what she calls "the white man this . . . and white people that" syndrome; Sugar doesn't buy it. She was proud of a high school speech her daughter gave in which she said, "We can't blame our problems on the white people. We're the ones destroyin' ourselves." This is not a popular view among many African Americans, or people on the left, but it's a classic example of Sugar's iconoclasm.

When the story broke about Denny's restaurant mistreating black customers, Sugar's response was, "Well, you can't force Denny's to treat you good. It's their place! If they don't want to serve you, get your ass out and go someplace else!" When I pressed her with an example of a country club or college refusing to admit women or minorities, she said,

It's not cool and it's not fair, but it's theirs. Now if you're a public thing, the machinery is already in place to make you change that. But the real deal is that they own it. When black people own colleges, we won't have to keep grovelin' and beggin', 'Please let us in your college.' Get you a college! Get somethin'! Own somethin'! Don't always be on the end of wanting to be a part of somebody else's thing.

Similarly, Sugar's not a feminist and, for a while, she wasn't even sure what the word meant. The black men who dominate and mistreat black women are welcomed one after the other into their female-headed welfare homes in spite of their reprehensible personal habits and consistently empty pockets. I argue that, given the abusive irresponsibility of so many poor black men, maybe solo parenting is the way to go. Thus, to my way of thinking, the absence of male income is the most problematic issue for the family. Sugar says it's men, period.

TBE   If someone asked me, how can we cure poverty in America's inner cities, I have one word: *jobs*. I believe decent jobs would change inner city culture.

ST   What you really mean is decent pay.

TBE   Yes, jobs that weren't dead-end jobs, jobs that had decent pay. And if there were decent jobs, it makes for an ever widening circle of the demand for decent education to train people for those jobs, etc. How do you feel about that?

ST   By now these men are so rotten that if you was to give them a good job, they're so into themselves that it wouldn't make a big change. Say this man got a raise, he would start doin' things for himself. A little might trickle down to the family, but most of it would stay in his pocket. He'd buy shoes, he'd fix his car, he'd get a better car, he'd flash money, he'd buy clothes, jewelry, but probably not books. There's a saying, if you want to hide something from a black man, put it in a book.

In the end, Sugar believes every individual is responsible for his or her own situation. Although she is knowledgeable about the broader socioeconomic factors impacting her life, she believes the most important factor is how the individual manipulates the situation he or she is given. This is one part of Sugar's hustler identity. Since no one else is going to get her out of a bad situation or solve a problem, she must do it. That attitude leads her, to some extent, to be scornful of those neighbors and friends who are not proactive. To Sugar, non-hustlers are passively accepting what is doled out to them, not striving to produce more. Thus, they have only themselves to blame for their downtrodden state. Don't get me wrong, Sugar is a kind and understanding woman, sympathetic to the pressures of *everyone's* poverty, but her solutions are still disarming to me.

I am a listener, but I also dole out advice. I am solution-oriented, and I know it's judgmental of me, but I have little patience for passivity in the face of personal challenges, even difficult ones. Though I understand that people just can't snap out of trying situations, I expect them to get past the whining stage in an appropriate amount of time and move toward taking action. I was therefore fascinated that although from time to time Sugar bitterly complained about and shed copious tears over the pressures of poverty, single motherhood, and the abusive boyfriends who stole her food stamps, she wasn't wallowing in these misfortunes. She had taken control of her life and repositioned herself toward a future in which she was legitimate and clean. I love that about her. Moreover, she wasn't ashamed of her past. It was Sugar who had initiated the documenting of the sordid and messy trail behind her. She did it for herself and she did it for what she sees as her ministry: to share what she is learning as a survivor.

Sugar's attitude about herself is so positive that she calls herself a "Pollyanna." Sometimes it's laughable how sunny the world looks to her. For example, she argues that closing down the welfare system could be a good thing in that everybody on welfare would have a chance to see what they're really made of! She accepts problems as challenges from which there is a lesson to be learned. I don't exactly roll my eyes when Sugar says things like that, but she knows me as a serious skeptic.

THE HISTORY OF OUR PARTNERSHIP

Beginning in 1995, Sugar and I worked together for a year or so, during which time we established a comfortable routine. Focusing on a particular issue or time period in her life, we would tape-record for two or three days in a row, until we had covered the topic to our satisfaction. Then I would transcribe the tapes and give the written transcriptions back to Sugar for her to correct or amend. Little by little a life emerged. I thought we were being productive, and we were. We had the tapes, and the transcripts were evolving. Then, Sugar broke up with her second husband, Mr. Lester. At that point, a whole new chapter in our relationship opened up.

Until the breakup, when I had asked Sugar how she was doing, her response had always been something like, "Oooooh! My man and I are soooo happy!" I accepted this, but was somewhat suspicious of the overexuberance in her voice. For two years, I was careful to say nothing as she painted a rosy picture of her marriage. Once free of Mr. Lester, however, Sugar finally allowed herself to be completely honest with me. She no longer needed to create the pretense of marital bliss out of loyalty to her new husband. Moreover, she wanted to complain about what she had endured! As a result, we were able to talk about the fact that she hadn't ever confided in me or to the tape recorder about the trials of living with a junkie. This marvelous turnaround in our friendship, and in our work, began one afternoon at a Mexican restaurant where we were having margaritas while we talked.

TBE   I *told* you Mr. Lester was a junkie when you first met him!

ST   You did not!

TBE   I most certainly did! Hello? I have this on tape!

ST   Bullshit!

TBE   Remember where you asked me, "What does it mean if a man is nodding during a conversation?" And I said to you, "It means he's a fucking heroin addict."

ST   No, you're *not* getting credit for that!

TBE   Oh, God Almighty! I can't believe you don't remember this! I told
        you from the first week I met the guy that his eyes were pinned!

ST   You did not! Oh, I'm shouting . . .

TBE   In a public place. Just a little spat, people. Nothing to worry about.
        [*Whispering now*] Talk about denial. I even know the first time you
        fucked the guy!

ST   Do you?

TBE   Yes, I do! In his apartment, unless you did it earlier on some bus
        that I don't know about. The way you even described the guy's
        apartment . . . it was definitely the apartment of a junkie! We said it
        then! You just don't remember.

ST   It was a fucking drug den. I remember. I just don't remember *you*
        telling *me*. I told *you*!

TBE   Okay, right, I *never* said it. She just knew it herself without any help
        from me!

ST   Not only that, but that fat track sittin' on his arm that he told me
        was an old track.

TBE   At that party, he was stoned out of his mind!

ST   Okay, I'm in denial. You think?

TBE   I swear I should be charging you for these sessions.

After that lunch, everything changed. The barriers between us collapsed. No holding back now, either on tape or in our relationship. I confessed that I had felt ridiculously embarrassed in front of her sister. She confronted me about holding back, being social scientific and distant sometimes. I jumped all over her for not using condoms when she was sleeping with a needle user. She chastised me for worrying too much and for being impatient. I finally told her I felt bad when she didn't invite me to her wedding. And even though I'm not sure I believe in it, I asked her to pray for a friend who had lymphoma. I came to rely on her for advice when I knew no one else could help me. We began to talk on the phone about everything, but I didn't tape those conversations, or even take notes.

The day we did the final taping we reminisced about our time together, crying a little:

ST   You were the first person that listened to me, the first person that was
        interested. You listened and you drove me to my home in the hood.
        You didn't drop me at the bus stop. You went that extra mile for me.

TBE   I wonder whether it was just, "Well, this is a person who needs a ride, I'll take her home," or the anthropologist eager to go anywhere. It doesn't matter. The world is a fascinating place to be.

ST   Can you separate those? I don't think you can. I think it was all of the above. Here's a wonderful specimen. And she's pretty nice.

TBE   I wonder when we got past the specimen to where we were partners.

ST   I remember Reggie used to say, "You're just an experiment to her." And I'd be like, "No, that's my friend." And he'd be, "Dream on, bitch."

Sugar's life in the hood has seeped into the deep structures of my mind. There is no book or library of books that could have made me see her world the way I have come to see it, firsthand, personal, committed. It may sound frivolous, but now I get Chris Rock. I have a much greater appreciation for his references to how black men and women interact as well as for the ethnic perspective underlying his humor. And I totally see where Terry McMillan's Stella was coming from, while she was trying to get her groove back. I loved spending time with Stella's voice (it was a book on tape) because it was so much like Sugar's voice. It had the music and the jargon, the words dancing from her lips as she told her tale. I could see Stella's head move about and her hands do their part as she played with this language so different from my own. It was magical, just like Sugar.

TBE   I'm jury-rigging this tape because we don't have any more tape.

ST   What does "jury-rigging" mean? Where'd you get that term from?

TBE   You know, improvising: taking something from here, something from there, sticking it together.

ST   Is that a real word?

TBE   Yeah.

ST   We call it "nigger-rigging."

TBE   Well, we *don't*!

ST   I thought *we* made it up.

I need to say at this point that *Sugar's Life in the Hood* makes no claims to being a stereotype-free ethnography of the ghetto. We are both strong-minded, opinionated women, and we have influenced the direction of the book in countless ways, not all of them positive or unbiased. But neither of us tried to create the quintessential account of the black experience. Nor are we affirming that Sugar's experience speaks for anyone else but Sugar. This is her story, and I believe that it is as true as we could make it. But it should not be generalized to all women or all poor blacks. Its value lies in its being a kind of *testimonio*, in its getting out the word. As such, it will dispel some ghetto myths and reinforce others.

This book is the story of one woman's life. More broadly, it is a story about the friendship that developed between one black woman and one white woman. Just as this is not an attempt to generalize Sugar's life to a larger reality, neither of us represents all the women of our respective races. But Sugar's being black and Tracy's being white are obviously part of the story.

It is not a goal of this book to represent the authors' interaction as some kind of archetype of racial conflict resolution. The goals of the book are smaller and more personal. They are to give voice to this one remarkable woman who may not ever have had the opportunity to speak in this way, and to chronicle the friendship and respect of two women across a cultural gulf that is still crowded with stereotypes and bigotry, a mental landscape rife with the potential for misunderstanding and suspicion. We do not claim to have solved the questions of race, even between us. But we have found a mutual respect. And we have formed a friendship that will continue long after this book is forgotten.

When we began this book, Sugar and I were strangers. It's true that we laughed a lot, and shared intimate recollections of her life, but what we did together was work, little more. It's true that Sugar exulted in being in the limelight I shined on her, and, like a new patient on a psychiatrist's couch, was pleased to be getting her side of things on the record. As for me, I hoped that the retelling would shed some light on Sugar's dramas, uncovering for her, and for the reader, the meanings embedded in the paradoxes that were everywhere in her tales.

Of course, we both wanted to get rich from Sugar's life story. Many times we fantasized about the money we were going to make when the book became a best-seller or a movie. We choreographed her first appearance on *Oprah*, down to what she would wear and how she would do her hair. Should we both appear, or just Sugar? Would we arrive in a limo? And, of course, we spent all our millions in our shared fantasies, even to the thrill of surprising our mothers and sisters with big checks or cars.

Our worlds never should have intersected, but they did. Over the years devoted to this project, collegiality turned into friendship. Now, like close friends everywhere, we send each other notes remembering special days, hug and kiss each other's family members, leave loving phone messages, and buy special gifts that express our bond. We can disagree, confront each other, complain and cry in each other's arms. Most of all, I respect Sugar, and she respects me, each for being our own person. At the same time, though I am confidant of the strength of our friendship, only time will tell if we can continue to bridge the cultural chasm between us.

Sugar isn't an ordinary woman. If she were, I would not have devoted five years to collecting her story. The truth is, I find many ethnographic life stories useful but tedious to read. They provide access to those routines and details that open up hidden worlds, but often this is more than the reader wants to know about the recollections and meaning of otherwise mundane lives.

In my Guatemalan fieldwork, I have recorded many life stories of ordinary women, but for the entirely different purpose of enhancing my analysis with case materials. For example, I selected a few romantic moments from the life of an eighty-five-year-old great-grandmother to illustrate the point that extramarital affairs were nothing new in this traditional Mayan town. Another woman's memory of her life before electricity is used to chronicle the advent of this technology and how it enhanced textile productivity previously done by candlelight. Each of these women is certainly a special individual, but at the same time, their narratives represent a broader, more general existence. They speak to a culture in which female potential is decidedly limited and therefore somewhat predictable. That is not to say that the sameness of their lives removes them from being valuable subjects of anthropological inquiry. It may be useful and informative to add these Mayan lives to the spectrum of voices, but I don't think they necessarily make good stories.

However, when I met Sugar, I immediately knew that her life was the stuff of great narrative. She didn't represent any kind of cultural model to me. Hers was, like those of the Mayan women, just one life story among millions. But what made it amazing and compelling was how clearly Sugar fulfilled the ghetto media image of "welfare queen on crack" and simultaneously contradicted those same long-held stereotypes with her moral resolve and steadfast self-improvement program. She is a conundrum, a real-life puzzle that insists we rethink whatever well-ordered system we are using to describe or explain life in the hood.

In short, her story is offered as neither the "truth" nor anything more than one person's essential reality. But Sugar allows us a moment to gaze upon the world behind the distorted façade of racial tensions, poverty, and crime. It is this glimpse through the parted curtains we hope this book offers.

When we started out, there was so much sex appeal in Sugar and her vivid grip on life that I thought this was what Sugar was all about. She was still investing in her gangster persona. It was a fantastic, pornographic, wild, dangerous life she was retelling, and, as far as I could tell, although she had retired from prostitution and had sworn off crack, she still liked being a "hustler," with all the guile and flash that came with the name. I was convinced people would want to read about the reality of a kind of life they had only heard about or imagined. It was the life most white people associated with the word "welfare": dysfunctional families, abusive men, drug addiction, and crime. And Sugar would tell all.

But as it turned out, Sugar's tale wasn't the lurid, back-alley show I had imagined. For instance, her love life was pretty active and very steamy, but she wouldn't dwell on that. I wanted to make a whole chapter out of the "list of men" I found in her Bible, a list she prayed over on a regular basis. Although we did produce several tapes about the men on the "list," in the end, she cut most of them out of the text. What she wanted readers to know was that the men she had slept with, johns or not, had been pretty decent to her. The men who had caused her pain or beaten her were the two or three men in her life that she had loved, lived with, or married.

True, she called herself a hustler, but early on I didn't really know what hustling was. What I learned was that, to Sugar, being a hustler was more than a seamy brush with crack or prostitution. It was an approach to life in the hood, a philosophy and self-image designed to meet—head-on—the demands of the conditions in which she lived. And calling herself a "hustler" made her feel good because it showed she wasn't a "slug." Slugs are what she calls people who are so comfortable with their life of poverty that they simply go along, cashing their welfare checks and doing nothing more to help themselves. That isn't Sugar.

Hustler that she is, Sugar's story convincingly demonstrates that in the end, welfare or jobs didn't matter all that much in terms of the quality of her children's lives. It was a trade-off. Like most single mothers, Sugar begins her workday long before the office opens. It involves waiting for two buses to get to the day-care centers and schools before taking two more buses to work, and then not having the energy to help with homework or cook dinner at the end of the day. Welfare allowed her to stay at home, and when she added in money from home businesses, Sugar found that her family's standard of living hadn't changed from when she had a job. Welfare or job, her kids had the same toys and the same clothes, and she was still worrying about the same bothersome debts.

Sugar's story shows how she carefully juggled those options to extract the best possible outcome for the family. Most important, through style and dedicated strategizing, she managed to dissuade her offspring of the notion that they were poor. Her children recognized that they were urban, black, Christian, and, like everybody around them, hurting for money, but Sugar never let welfare or poverty be the guiding principle of their existence. The result is that neither sons nor daughters feel trapped in a racially tense inner city. They love their neighborhood, feel comfortable there, and because of that, are determined to one day be able to give something back to their hood.

Ultimately, Sugar's story cannot help but have relevance beyond her family and herself. It connects to the centuries of poverty and discrimination that have indeed created a culture of poverty, a community stamped by deep-seated hopelessness, fragile family ties, and emotionally distant males, similar to poor societies everywhere. The men she loved had been demeaned to the point of being ignored as potentially viable citizens, fathers, or workers. In their despair, they had come to hate themselves and to despise and abuse this woman who loved them.

Right now I'm an anthropologist just back from the field. We've finished our work, and I feel much like I did when, in 1977, I came home from a year in highland Guatemala, where I had been doing my first ethnographic research. Living among the Maya had affected me in ways I couldn't begin to understand just then. During the first week home, I remember turning on the TV and there were Lucy and Desi arguing as usual. I was only half listening. Suddenly, I realized that for the first time, I understood what Desi was saying—not just "Lucy, you've got some 'splainin' to do," but all of Desi's angry Spanish sputterings. I didn't even have to think about what he was saying. It was just very clear to me. Like the Spanish in the deep structure of my mind, Sugar's life has penetrated some invisible mental barrier. Somewhere inside myself, I'm beginning to get it, to physically and emotionally understand. When I told this story to Sugar, she said, "You're going to be an honorary sistah!"

For the chapters ahead, I offer this version of a reader's road map. We organized *Sugar's Life in the Hood* to tell Sugar's story the way she told it to me. Because we did not envision the book strictly as an autobiography, it isn't organized in the standard chronological order. Instead, the chapters are focused on topics that resonate throughout Sugar's life, like welfare, being an African American mother, or Sugar's faith. Thus, discussion of Sugar's childhood doesn't come into play until Chapter 4, while the very first chapter deals with men, a theme that reappears again and again throughout the book.

Readers may notice that from time to time Sugar's voice changes. For example, in one place she dots her language with a lot of ebonics, or she may be concocting sentences with a grammar all their own. Elsewhere there is none of that street color in her voice. This reflects the fact that Sugar's life was evolving and as it did, her language changed as well.

One final note: In an attempt to protect Sugar's identity, we have located our story in a fictitious place. Sugar Turner is a pseudonym. We have changed certain characteristics of Sugar's work, family, and habits. None of these changes seriously compromise the tale. All they do is allow Sugar to privately pursue the good life she now enjoys.

1 THE LIST OF MEN

FIELDNOTES: *Sugar's Kitchen—As usual, we're snacking. I'm eating cold leftover sausages that are sitting in a skillet on the stove; Sugar's eating scones and coffee I picked up on my way over. Last week, while going through her Bible, we came across a list of the men she had slept with.*

ST   We're not going to talk about this on tape.

TBE   Yes, we are.

ST   Oh no, no, no.

TBE   Why not?

ST   NO!!!

TBE   You don't want to talk about it?

ST   Heck no!

TBE   Oh, it would be such a great device.

ST   A device for what?

TBE   We have a whole huge chapter on men . . .

ST   Why would we need more?

TBE   We don't need to go through the entire list. It would just give you something to jar your memory.

ST   Okay, let's. [*Laughs*] This is a list of all the men that I've slept with in my life. When I started out, I was a girl. I'm not going to tell you the exact number, but believe me, it's a lot!

TBE   Why are you keeping this list?

ST   I asked the Lord to show me these men because I wanted to pray for them, ask forgiveness, and just hope that I didn't ruin their life in some nasty little way. I was part of their unhealthiness. Some of 'em were married. Some of 'em were preachers. Some of 'em were one-night stands. Some of 'em were tricks. Often I wonder what part did I play in their lives? Yeah, I'm retired from ho'ing. But I still love men! Hence the list! But it was never just looking for sex. I was searching for Mr. Goodbar. I was looking for a good guy, a mate, a companion. I'm still looking for my prince.

TBE   Okay, I'll buy that you've been searching for Mr. Right. But I have to ask you this. From this list, it looks like you're just switching from one loser to another. You're too good for these losers!

ST   Ain't I just!?

TBE   You need to get some help!

ST   Don't I know it! That's why I'm takin' a break. That's why I quit all my boyfriends. I'm gonna do my clothes, I'm gonna do my nails, I'm gonna read my Bible, I'm gonna read books, I'm gonna do things. I'm planning on being dateless, manless, loveless, totally sexless. I'm taking the rest of the year off. I ain't screwin' nothing. I'm back on my celibacy kick, believe me.

TBE   All right, speaking of losers, let's hear about Mr. Lester.

ST   No, I don't want to talk about Mr. Lester right now. I miss him.

TBE   You are so male dependent! He is a real certified junkie! He's a smackhead!

ST   I like him!

TBE   They're worse than tweekers!

ST   I bet! It doesn't mean I don't like him!

TBE   Have you ever thought about raising your sights a little?

ST   To what?

TBE   Nonjunkies! People who don't get high for a living! You ever heard of 'em? I know, it's a new concept! What I don't understand is why you need to go to bed with some godforsaken junkie to feel special? It's not like you're desperate for male attention. Look at this list. I mean, there are men lining up down the block.

ST   You're mad. [*Both laughing*] Tony called me and wanted me to go to a concert with him, but Tony's a booty call!

TBE   What's that?

ST   A booty call. Tony just wants to have sex.

TBE   You need a whole new line of potential lovers. I mean, who is this woman who is choosing this kind of low-life scum?

ST   At the time that I'm choosing 'em, they ain't visibly low-life scum. Like I keep tellin' you, hey, I never chose a loser in my life. What I chose, like with Reggie, I thought I chose a Christian man who loved the Lord and loved me. Reggie was articulate and smart. That's what I chose. Mr. Lester, I thought he cared about me. That's why I chose to marry him. Nobody goes out there and sez, "Today, I'm gonna put on my nice dress and go find me a fucked-up man!" Nobody chooses losers.

FIELDNOTES: *Sugar was an ambitious college-bound teenager until she met Ernie T. Johnson, the man who became her first husband. Ernie T. seems to have cast an as-yet-unbroken mold for Sugar's men. He was seductive, cool, unreliable, violent, and broke. Without a backward glance at her derailed education, Sugar invested in hanging with Ernie T., eventually becoming pregnant, going on welfare, and being pushed into a marriage she did not want. But this rocky union had two very positive results: in the few years they were together, they produced two daughters, Dolly and Tina.*

ERNIE T.

I met my first husband, Ernie T. Johnson, walkin' down the street, comin' home from modelin' school. I remember it *real well* 'cause that was my last youthful autumn. I was full of hope. I had started attending community college, been there two weeks. And then I met this guy and that was it. The end. College, modeling school, everything. Good-bye!

I was eighteen and still a good girl. I just liked bad boys. He was just out of the penitentiary, for armed robbery or drugs *or somethin'*. I don't know. I never been a asker. Subsequently, I got the short end of the stick forever. Started out he asked me if I wanted a ride.

"No, thank you."

"Oh, baby, come on."

"No, thank you."

"Oh, baby, please."

"Oh, okay!"

So I get in the car, and he brings me home. And, of course, I fell in love 'cause I was locked out of the house and he climbed through the window to let me in. Wasn't that gallant?

The next day, I went over his house. We end up in bed. I get Dolly. I knew the exact moment that I got pregnant. I was supposed to be on the pill, but I obviously wasn't 'cause I got that baby. I don't even remember thinking of an abortion. We liked each other, and so we started seein' each other. So the first nine months of our "courtship," I was pregnant. Of course, I'm growin' every day, gettin' bigger and bigger. And he's this young man who would like to be responsible, but I don't think he ever had the wherewithal to do it.

I remember that September of not goin' to school. I felt so lonely, detached, thrown away, broke off. I missed the sounds of kids goin' to school. I didn't get to smell schoolbooks. I didn't get to smell erasers. And I had a child in me.

I stayed at my mom's house. When Dolly was about four months old, I moved out and got my first apartment. Cost me $125 a month. I had a job workin' for the state. So now I got my own place, a job, and my man can come and stay with me when he's in town, which he would do. A lot of the time he spent in St. Paul because he had, like, been banned from livin' in Wisconsin 'cause of somethin' havin' to do with his legal stuff. So he spent a lot of the time away from me, but I was cool with the deal.

However, soon after that, since I had a baby, my mom forced me to marry him. I didn't have to end up having a life with him. I just coulda screwed him, and got a baby, and left him alone. But now because of my mom, I suddenly gotta be in love, and we gotta be a couple. I didn't know nothin' about that. I didn't want that. I wanted to go to school.

But my mom was like, "Get married, get married, you gotta get married." She was harpin', "It's better to marry than to burn. The Bible says marriage is noble."

She never asked, "What do you guys have in common?" Not, "What do you like about this man? What can he do for you? What will he do for this child?" Never cared nothin' that matters to a real marriage. But her whole thing was that she was this staunch figure in the church and she wanted her daughters to be married. She wanted to maintain this upstanding image. So, me and Ernie T. got married when Dolly was about eleven months old. And her little sister, Tina, wasn't far from being on the way.

Tell ya how funky my wedding was. I was wearing an ugly old dress that didn't even belong to me. It was my sister's and looked like an old chenille bedspread. I look about forty years old in the pictures. I'm really only nineteen years old, my hair's nappy, and they're marrying me off to this guy—in a borrowed dress with my little Avon ring that cost me all of seven dollars. The boy couldn't even buy me a ring! I couldn't afford a dress! We had no business bein' married.

It was only two years and a month that we were married. Most of the time we fought. We had our first fight two weeks after the wedding. Knock down, drag 'em out! We boxed! I don't know who hit who. We were playin' in the kitchen or somethin' and somehow I ended up throwing a cup of water on him, playfully, but it ended up in a fight. We spent our marriage kinda going back and forth like that. It was stressful. He was very jealous, very protective. Later on, I found out one of the reasons he was so protective of me was that my mom had pulled him to the side and said, "Keep Sugar outta the streets!" Can you believe that? My mom wanted to run everybody's life.

I was a kid! I wanted to go party! He figured the way to keep me out the streets was to go upside my head! That wasn't goin' to work. He would pick fights with me, knowin' that I would fight. He would get up in my face, he would talk nasty, he would berate me. We'd be fightin', and I'd say, "I hate you!" And he would slap my mouth. I'd say, "I hate you" *again*, and he would slap my mouth. Every time he slapped me, my lips went up: "I hate you." I wasn't gonna let him know that I feared him in no way. I didn't care what he did. He'd break tables. He'd tear up stuff that I loved.

One time I remember I had to go to work, and he threw my purse on the roof, with everything that I needed to get to work! So now I gotta climb up on the roof. Plus he was drinkin'. He'd drink and go rant and rave. He'd tear up the house. I never really knew what was goin' on with him.

One night I just decided I couldn't handle it anymore, and I told him I wanted out. I ended up movin' into a little low-income apartment. He moved me there, and then he began to come over. That was defeating the purpose of me gettin' away from him.

Another time we were fightin' over there. He threw a lot of my stuff over this third-floor balcony. I'm lookin' at my stuff layin' there in the street, and I just ran. I had to get out of there. I remember cowering on somebody's porch in my nightgown.

And it just kept on like that. Finally, I told him one of us was gonna hurt the other if he didn't please leave. I was feeling myself on the verge of what I know now to be insanity. I was sitting in a corner, pleading with him to go. I was blubberin', I was cryin', I was incoherent. We were fighting so much, I couldn't handle it no more. Once Dolly came over to me and she was wipin' my tears. It dawned on me then that my three-year-old child should not be wiping my tears, telling me not to cry. I should be doing that for her. And that's when I knew I had to get out of this marriage.

I guess he finally saw that it wasn't workin' and he left. I'm not sure where he went. But we ended up bein' separated forever. But it sure wasn't easy.

In the beginning, he was stingin' about our breakup. He broke out my windows in my apartment. He slashed my tires. He did any number of stupid stuff. After six months I guess it dawned on him what a fool he was bein', and he stopped. But he didn't contribute a thing to me or his girls. And I wouldn't ask. That's one thing that black women believe: "You don't have to do nothin' for mine. I'll do for mine. Even if it means sellin' my ass, whatever. You ain't got to do nothin' that you don't want to do."

It wasn't like he didn't have any money. For the most part, he had a job. He was a hard worker. When he wasn't workin', he was lookin'. He was a gardener. I remember him workin' in a factory. The last job that I know he had was being a plumber's assistant. So he worked.

Of course, me bein' on welfare, it was okay for him. A lot of men think if you're gettin' a welfare check, you don't need nothin' else. And so they don't contribute. "You gettin' that check, ain't you?" Matter of fact, I would even protect him. When I went on welfare, they would try to make me ask him for child support and stuff, and I would tell them I didn't know where he was, just to keep 'em off his track.

I was gonna divorce him. But when I first started looking into divorce, I was working, so legal aid wouldn't help me, and it cost too much. It wasn't worth it to me. I thought, "I'm single. I know I'm single. I don't need no white judge to tell me that I'm single!" After that, it kinda slipped through the back of our minds.

Ernie T.'s been fairly present in later years. The girls, Dolly and Tina, they'd call and say, "Well, Dad, I need some shoes when you get paid." And he'd go take 'em to get shoes. He'll take 'em to get a coat. They call him a lot. They see him often. He borrows money from me on a regular basis.

FIELDNOTES: *As Sugar mentioned, Ernie T. continues to be a part of her life. This is largely due to their connection through their daughters, both of whom are devoted to their father and his family. Like many other inner-city black men, Ernie T. has established a permanent residence with his mother, who lives only a few blocks from Sugar.*

Throughout this story, there are many references to both the blessings and the problems associated with Sugar's mother-in-law, the judgmental "Grandma." Grandma has played a vital role as caregiver to her granddaughters and support system to Sugar, something a single mother must have to successfully raise her children. We anthropologists call this pattern "matrifocality," a kind of family organization designed around mutually supportive women and their children.

Whether the peripheral status of men in this system is a cause or a consequence of matrifocality continues to be hotly debated, but one fascinating by-product that I have seen is the utter disdain that Sugar has for men as providers. If she needs help, she can ask her female relatives or friends. Most of the time, however, she can manage on her own, thank you very much.

LETTERS TO ERNIE T.

FIELDNOTES: I had known Sugar for a year or so before I read these letters to Ernie T. In our interviews, she hadn't related the depth of her feelings for him, preferring to emphasize the negative, conflicted nature of their relationship.

1983
Dear Ernie T.,

How are you doing? Fine, I do hope. This is just a little note to tell you a few things that you probably don't want to hear anyway, but it is worth a try.

I just want to tell you that your girls love and miss you very much. I think it is so sad that you don't care enough to answer their letters, or send them a picture or a card for their birthday, or get them something for Christmas, or just send a note to let them know that you do love and care for them. They are not some woman that you can quit or divorce. No, they are your girls, no matter what happened or happens between me and you. I hope you have matured enough to stop holding a grudge on them because of what you and I did.

You always tried to accuse me of trying to poison Dolly's mind against you. And I always tried to convince you that was not true. I told you many times that the ideas she had of you were what you instilled in her. I told you that I would never try to turn them against you, and I never will. All I say to them about you is good things. I will never let them disrespect you, because that is not the way I was taught.

I know that we will probably never be a complete family again unless God knows something we don't know. And I know that you can't be with your girls 100% of the time. But please, don't miss out on sharing at least a little part of their lives. They love you and have never stopped loving you. I hope you are man enough to set grudges aside that they had nothing to do with and let them know that their Dad loves them. Love, S.

Dear Ernie T.,

Well, here they are! The pictures of our daughters. As you can see, they are healthy and well taken care of. I hope you will enjoy the pictures very much, and if you get a chance, send my babies one of yourself so they will not feel that all is not forgotten about them. They talk about you frequently, and the other day when Tina got in trouble, she was hollering, "Daddy, Daddy."

So, how are you doing? I am just asking, but I surely don't expect you to answer. Of course, you never do. You must be a busy man.

I and your girls are fine. Dolly will be starting kindergarten on the 31st of this month. She is going to ride the school bus to and from your mom's house. I was worried about my baby riding the bus, but she assured me, "Mama, I won't get lost on the bus." I don't suppose you care to make any contribution to their school clothes? I know times are hard, so I don't expect anything. But, rest assured, they will be well and fashionably dressed. I will see to that.

How am I? Well, I am sure you probably don't want to know, but I will tell you anyway. I am fed up, fucked up, confused, happy, sad, lonely, mean, bitchy, nice, need some loving, want my man but know that can never be, want to make some money but I am too scared to go into a life of crime, want to settle down but still want to run free. In a way, I am not sure what I want, but I guess I will figure it out.

You just don't know what I would give for one happy night with you. I know it couldn't be forever, but one night is my wish.

I hate to think of you with someone else. I try to fool myself that you don't, won't, can't, shouldn't have someone to show affection to, but I know I am just fooling myself to keep from seeing the truth. These couple years have made me see many of the mistakes I made. But that, as they say, is water under the bridge.

Well, I am feeling quite sentimental now, and getting teary eyed. So, I will bring this letter to a close. I wish God had seen fit to bless us with a stronger devotion to each other and a better understanding of each other. Also, me with a little bit more patience and foresight. But He didn't.

Enjoy the pictures and keep your self safe. And as I always said, "Be careful." S.

THE DUSTY STORY

FIELDNOTES: *Dusty Howard might have been just another man on the list had he not fathered Sugar's young son, Terrell. The Dusty story is amusing, but the reality of Dusty is not. He wanted Sugar to love and support him, but he soon lost interest and moved on to someone with more resources for him to exploit. Unlike Ernie T., Dusty only reappears in Sugar's life to drop off an occasional Christmas present for his son.*

I tell you I'm a fag hag! When I met Dusty, I suspected he might be a little sweet. Because I was down in Antoine's, this club we go to. I was on a bar stool, sitting there with my girlfriend. Dusty walks by and he had on this velvety suit, almost a real deep maroon. And he had a purse. You know how men carry those portfolio thingies, but it was a good size. Dusty's real flamboyant. I turned around and sez, "Is that your bag or are you carryin' your lady's purse?" I laughed. It turned out to be his bag. The rest is history.

We exchanged phone numbers and we talked that same night. He talked about how with many closet faggots you really wouldn't know. So here's this man in a velvet suit carrying a purse and talking about faggots. Can you believe he became the father of my son!?

After we had talked back and forth on the phone for a month or so, I went over his house. What an ordeal! It was the most horrible experience of my life! I called a cab and I waited for that cab about four hours. So it wasn't till about one in the morning that I finally got out of the house. Why didn't I say after thirty minutes, "Hey, the cab's not comin'," and take my ass to bed? I really wanted to see this man. So I wait and I wait and finally I get in this cab with my little overnight bag.

I tell the man where I'm goin', someplace on Midland Place. I'd never been there before. But the cabdriver, little do I know, takes me to the next block over. So I go, "It's 1836," and he takes me to 1836, but it isn't an apartment building. It's one of those huge gothic houses. So I tell him, wait until I get in. So the cabdriver waits, and I go into this building, and I push on the door, and it's open. So I go in, and the cabdriver leaves. I look around, and it still doesn't look like an apartment building, but I'm thinking that it might be okay because, you know, they split those old houses up into apartments. And, of course, I'm also thinkin' the cabdriver's *gotta* know where he's going. So I go in there and I look around, and I'm on this enclosed porch. There's all this furniture covered up and bicycles. But there's also another door, so I go in.

I'm lookin' around for #301, but there's no three floors in here. I go up the stairs, and I see that there's some kids' shoes by the only other door. Okay, he didn't mention any kids. I'm thinking I'm in the wrong place, but in case I'm not, I leave my bag on a chair inside the foyer when I go back out, 'cause now I'm gonna walk the block to find where I really need to be. I go out and I pull these doors. Little do I know that when I pull the second door, it locks *behind me*. So now, I'm locked out! It's one o'clock in the morning and I'm walking up the street and down the street and up the street and down the street, but I can't figure out where the hell I am. I can't see any street signs. I was scared as hell: girl walkin' up the street by herself, guys on motorcycles passin' by. So I decide to go back to the house and wait until daylight. I go back. I get into the porch area, and I try the door to get my bag, but I can't get in. Now what do I do? I don't want to wake these people up. And I surely don't want to make a lot of noise so that I startle them and somebody comes to shoot me because they see this black girl out on their porch where she has no business. So there's a chair, and I pull a sheet off of one of the bicycles and I cover up in the chair 'cause I'm gonna wait there till morning.

But it's February, really cold. There's a window, and I hear a person breathing. So I tap a little, but they don't wake up. Now I'm freezin', and they have this porch enclosed in plastic, and it's scary as hell. Finally I can't stand it no more. I'm gonna knock. I start tapping on the glass, tapping on the glass. Still nothing. I start tapping harder. Finally, a guy comes—a white guy. He lifts up the curtain.

He's like, "What the hell you doin'?"

And I'm like, "Please, sir, let me explain, I'm lost and my bag is there on the chair, and I just need my bag."

He's like, "Yeah, right!"

And I'm goin', "No, please, I'm a Christian!"

He looks at me.

"Well, how do I know that's your bag?"

"Please, sir, that's my bag! I don't have my money. I don't have any ID, everything's in there."

And he's sayin', "Yeah, well, what's in it?"

And I go, "Well, there's a teal-colored lingerie and there's a wallet with $10."

And he pulls it out, but he still doesn't believe it's my bag after I describe everything that's in the bag.

So, finally, from upstairs comes "Tom, what's goin' on down there?" and Jane or whoever comes down the stairs.

And he goes, "Jane, is this your bag?" and she says no.

I'm just about hysterical. "It's my bag!" I try to explain that I just need my bag and directions to Midland Place. Finally, he opens the door, thrusts my bag at me, tells me Midland Place is around the corner, and he warns me that I better get out of there. I run around the corner, and by the time I get to Dusty's, I'm a mess.

This was my first time seein' this man since the night I met him. It's four in the morning. I'm blubbering, and he's wonderin' where I am. He was almost out in the hall looking for me. When he saw me, he hugged me. It was so nice after this ordeal. So because of all this, I'm suddenly in love now.

That's not when I got Terrell, but soon thereafter.

So after that first night, he's my man. I'm his woman. We go together. He stayed on Midland Place, and I don't know how much of that was only for me to see. He says he lived with his cousin in this little efficiency apartment, just one bed and a couch. Now two men are not gonna sleep in bed together, but he would say the cousin stayed over his girlfriend's house most of the time. But I think it was just a decoy. Like a place to bring me to make me think he lived there. I know that he had other women in Springfield. And I know he had a ton in Kansas City, and at least one in Vegas. I think he was livin' with a woman in Springfield, for real. Like a girlfriend. But the woman he really lived with, like a marriage situation, lived in Kansas City. I know because I called there. Dusty would sit on my phone and make all these long-distance phone calls. So I had this list of phone numbers.

One day I called all the numbers to see which ones women would answer, and this one a machine answered and said it was the St. John and Howard residence. And I go, "Ah ha! Got it." But I didn't say anything right away. I just took some notes. Then, one day I called, and he answered. That's how I found out where he lived. He tells me he lives with his mom in Kansas City, but ain't no thirty-nine-year-old man is living with his momma. Not a man like that.

Back then he said he had sixteen kids, almost all with different women. The most one woman had was four. A couple may have had three. The rest are maybe two, and then one, one, one. He was like a fuckin' honeybee! I think his first child may have been born when he was in the ninth or tenth grade. So he's been having kids ever since. Why? Because he doesn't believe in condoms, number one. And Kansas City, Missouri, from what I understand, ain't a helluva place to come from. At least not the ghetto or the area where he comes from. He grew up in the projects, very, very poor. So he's a big man on campus down there. That's supposed to be my claim to fame. I'm Dusty's baby's mama. Basically, I think that's his claim to fame: that so many women have his kids, That's one reason why me and him didn't really last. Because I didn't revere him like I was supposed to.

He had a job in a school. I don't know what, but he wasn't no janitor. He told me that when things would go on, a bad kid or something, they would go find Dusty. He knew this kid. He knew this kid's mother. He probably was this kid's father. From what I understand, he's a minor celebrity in Kansas City. So I can see how he has sixteen kids.

Now, why he came to Springfield is a mystery (you know I don't know anything about these men I deal with). I think he was running away from having to pay child support for these children he's fathering. He couldn't work there 'cause they were on to him, so he came here where he has a few relatives and friends. So he stayed here until they caught up with him, which they did. But then, conveniently, his high blood pressure got so high, he can't really do the kind of work that he had done, and he can't do enough work to pay off his child support. So he's sort of off the hook.

In the beginning, he spent a lot of time in Kansas City. He'd come and he'd go, doing whatever it was he did—taking care of business, making babies, whatever.

When he was here, we would see each other fairly regularly. We would go do a little shopping, mostly when he was buying himself something. I would go over to his place in the evenings when he would get off of work. We'd eat together, drink coffee, have sex. We'd watch basketball. Of course, you can't talk when he's watchin' basketball—"Hush! Shut up!"—so I'd sit there, and I'd read. We went out maybe a couple of times to this club called Jimmy's where his cousin is the disc jockey. A lot of people from Kansas City go there. So, once again, he's the big man.

At Jimmy's, I'd always have to sit there, be window dressing, can't dance. He wouldn't dance. Sure, he'd slow dance because slow dancing is suave and everybody sees you; there's not as many people on the floor, so you can gyrate with your woman and look like the big man. Whenever I'd be wanting to dance, he'd get some other guy to dance with me—some guy who was one of his friends from Kansas City that he knows real well. I get to dance maybe twice in a night. That and maybe one slow dance. Yeah! And the rest of the time I'd pretty much just sit there.

And guys were always comin' over and talkin' to me. And he would promptly come over and run them away, but in a suave way. Like one time I was talkin' to some motorcycle guy. This guy came over from across the room, and he says, "Lady, I just got to tell you, me and my club brothers over there, we have voted, and you are the most beautiful woman in here tonight. We just wanted to know would you come over and join us."

I say, "Well, thank you. But no, I can't join you."

Then Dusty comes over, puts his hands on my shoulders, kisses me on the forehead, gives me a rose. "Back off, man" is basically what that says. And it's all real obvious, so nobody else approaches me all night. So I sit there and look pretty.

Hell yes, I complained! But what ya gonna do? Jump up and dance with somebody and get ya ass beat on the dance floor? Your man said you couldn't dance. And not only that, there's like this code that men know. These other guys aren't gonna disrespect him. So you sit there like some hoochie all night.

I got pregnant in March, three months after I met him. It was okay. This is my man! I was pregnant before I found out he had sixteen kids. After we'd been screwin' for a while, it dawns on me to ask, "Well, how many children do you have?" And he sez sixteen. And I'm waitin' for the "ha, ha!" and it never came. I hadn't been on birth control for about four years. I'm thinkin', old broad, thirty-two years old, probably not gonna get pregnant. It wasn't a conscious thought. It was that in four years I hadn't gotten pregnant, so that wasn't a worry or a concern with me. I just wasn't thinkin' birth control.

I felt good during the pregnancy. I worked the whole time. I was trim. I was beautiful. I was glowing. Dusty was there a lot of the time. For a while after Terrell was born, he would just come over and we would kick it. The kids were in school.

He didn't deal with my other kids at all. That wasn't unusual. Men don't really interact with my kids. Maybe it's something I adopted to shield my kids. Black women always say, "Well, if he can't deal with my kids, if he can't love my kids, he can't deal with me." That makes sense to a certain degree, but every man that comes into your life is not gonna be your man forever. So you don't necessarily want to expose your kids to all these people. And also, I tell my kids, "You don't have to like 'em. All you need to do is respect 'em. Because they're not your friend, they're my friend." So every man I meet, I'm not gonna say, "You gotta like my kids. You gonna be their next daddy." I would see if we were gonna be something before I put 'em on my kids. So, no, he didn't have a relationship with my kids. He'd come in—"Hey, how ya doin'?"—and he'd go into Terrell's room and he'd play with his son, and that's about it.

FIELDNOTES: *This idyllic family scenario was blown to bits when Sugar discovered that Dusty was fooling around. His betrayal was particularly painful, as the other woman, Regina, was one of her beauty shop customers. Even though it all happened more than five years ago, she is still steaming.*

Regina. I don't do Regina's hair anymore because she fucked my man. End of story. She's a two-faced, dirty old tramp. But she's not really. I'm not really mad at Regina. I feel that I can't blame a woman for likin' what I like. If I think Dusty's handsome, and tall, and dark, and charismatic, why shouldn't another woman think that he's those things. And why should she not think 'em just because I do her hair? Anybody can fall prey to a man. Loyalty is a scarce commodity in the nineties. So I'm not really mad at Regina, but she can't come and get her hair done anymore. I'm not *that* liberal!

Regina works over at the employment agency where I go to find jobs and have for a thousand years. I sent Dusty over there, tryin' to look after him and help him find a job—I always want to mother these cads. So he went. You have to pay your two dollars, and Regina is the one who takes your two dollars. Regina is one who, at the drop of a hat, will brag about what she has; how much of it she has, how many apartments she has, how many cars she has, how big her house is. Of course, Dusty has radar for that type of woman, and he picked up on it. Basically, Dusty goes to the highest bidder, and Regina was the highest bidder. Dusty says, "I'm a poor woman's lover and a rich woman's dream."

So he was seein' Regina. I found out because he called me from her house one time, although I didn't know he was at her house. After we chitchatted for a while, he says, "I'm on my way over there. What's Terrell doin'?"

I'm thinkin', cool. We hadn't seen him for at least three weeks because he had been in Kansas City. The killing part is he comes into town, and he goes over this girl's house first. We had been together eighteen months, and he goes over there first. And now he's comin' to see us.

When he gets off the phone, a few minutes later, she calls back. She says, "Well, I have to tell you something. I have a guy I been seein' for a month, and he was just talkin' to you." She says that when she heard him say Terrell, that's when she picked up that he was talkin' to me and that she put the connection together that this is Terrell's father. She said she asked him who it was he was talking to, and he said that's my hairdresser. Like it's no big deal.

Not long after that, she came back to my little shop one more time for a touch-up on her hair. When she came back, she was so syrupy sweet that she had to have been having designs on my man. I guess I really shouldn't say "my man." He wasn't my man. Anybody that has sixteen kids is not my man.

She said she had been "seein'" him for a month. But he had been outta town for three weeks, so she's full of bullshit. He'd been up her house a few times, but as far as seeing her, bullshit. She comes in for her hair appointment, all under the guise of "I'm loyal to you, you're my hairdresser, that nigger can take a hike. He ain't all that, because you've been good to me, you're such a sweet girl, why would he do that, men are dogs." She hugs me, she plays with Terrell. But she never comes back. She never calls again. I never see her again.

During that last visit, she's saying, "Oh, guess what I bought!"

And I'm goin', "Okay, I'll guess. Is it bigger than a breadbox?"

"Noooo."

I'm guessin' and I finally give up. Turn's out it's this huge German bed.

And she says, "You know I'm just a welfare girl, so this was a real deal."

Said she saw this bed when she was over in Germany in the military. She met a guy in Springfield who had one just like it, and he wanted $6,000, but she talked him down to $3,000. It's got like a seven-foot headboard and it's seven feet long.

"So big I had to move all my dressers out into my other room, so I could get it in."

I didn't say it, but I was thinkin', "Sounds like you tryin' to get a big bed for a big nigger." Dusty's not no little bitty man. That's the story.

So I call her Regina, the Buffarilla. It's a word. It means a big, burly, stank, ugly, black, fat, stretch-marky, lisping, glasses-wearing, fat-faced, ugly black broad. A cross between a buffalo and a gorilla.

I told Dusty you can't fuck her and me too, so you better go with rich ole Buffarilla and see what you can get. 'Cause that's what he's about. He's a name-brand guy. He's very gold and diamonds. He tells you how much things cost, sez shit like, "I know I look kind of casual, but I got on over $700 worth of clothes right now." Myself, I could look that good and go spend $5.50 at the Goodwill. For him, it's what it costs. This is Georgio Butani, and this is Luis Vuitton, and this is Polo. But that's a sign of somebody who grew up with nothing. I've seen it. Black people know. He's wearin' it like this badge of honor. And I'm feeling compassion for him. Every time he'd pull this shit, I say to myself, "Damn, Dusty, you must have been really poor."

I felt hurt at the end, but I understand it. He was not looking for love. He had love at home in Kansas City. He was materialistic, and this woman had more than me. I'm not mad at her because she's a fucking Buffarilla. Why would I begrudge either of them what it is they desire? And for neither of them was it me.

But does he help me out? Hell no! He sends me fifty dollars for his son's Christmas. For Mother's Day, he gave me twenty dollars from my son. No, he doesn't help out at all. He calls once in a while.

Life is life. I still love Dusty. My girlfriend was askin' me the other day if I would get back with him. I'm not mad at him, so maybe I would get back with him. But soon as another higher bidder comes along, he'd jilt me again. But I liked some of the things that he made me feel. He would come and we would just kick it. And I liked that. There wasn't no sexual pressure. I'd be lucky to get it once every three weeks from that man. His high blood pressure is what I thought. But now I think it's because he had to service so many women. That's what I think the real deal was. So I still love Dusty. And I love Ernie T., although he's like a brother now. I love my men. I'm very generous and good and loving. And love is not something you can turn off and on because they do you wrong, no matter what.

REGGIE

TBE   So having a man, whoever he is, is important to you—so important that you'll be with a man like Reggie, who's a lying crackhead. I just don't get it. Why do you subordinate yourself to a man who you know is not as good as you are?

ST   They say the devil you know is better than the devil you don't know. So, okay, I can deal with Reggie and hope that Reggie gets better or I can take a chance on finding a worse devil than him. It's like a bird in the hand is worth two in the bush. I got this one. Let me work with this one. Otherwise I gotta go back out there!

TBE   Let me continue to hammer away at this feminism thing. You know you're a better human being than most of the men in your life.

ST   What does that mean?

TBE   What you told me. There are five things that make somebody a good person. You gotta be honest, fair, a provider, spiritual, and loving. You are all those things. Reggie is not.

ST   That's true.

TBE   None of the men in your life have any of those qualities. Or maybe they have one. So just on that scale, you're smarter, you're better educated, you have more of a sense of the world around you, et cetera. I'm sorry, am I putting words in your mouth?

ST   No, it's true. I am those things. I have more goals than them. I've asked Reggie several times, "What do you want to be when you grow up? What do you want to do?" He can't tell me. He don't dream. He's content, complacent. I know the world is so much larger than me. That I am nowhere near my apex. But the men that I have to choose from are in the world that I am in now. Even though I know there's more out there, it's not like I can choose a man from out there. Because I'm not there yet.

TBE   I can't wait till you have enough money to get your head shrunk. [*Laughs*]

ST   Aren't you shrinking it now?

FIELDNOTES: *I met Reggie in the beginning of their relationship, when Sugar was falling in love with "the man I'm gonna marry." I was parking my car at Lucille's, where Sugar was doing one of her fashion shows. I was a little nervous about being alone, white, and clearly out of place at a nightclub when I got a big welcoming smile from the skinny guy running the lot. He called me "Baby," and he showed me where to park. It was Reggie, and I was immediately charmed. The next week, I ran into him* at Sugar's, where I learned that he had gone to college at SUNY, Albany, where he had studied sociology. But he didn't graduate and went on to be a cabdriver for eight years in New York. We chatted about moving to Springfield, about life in New York, what Sugar's kids were up to. About six months later, I wrote the following fieldnote about this same man, who had seemed so delightful and intelligent:

> January 12, 1996
> Called Sugar at 9:50 A.M. She was crying hysterically. Reggie was there. She said he's been verbally abusing her, telling her she's worthless and will never amount to anything, that she thinks she's a star, that he wants a plain woman. She keeps saying she has to get rid of him. He's got to go. Meanwhile, he won't leave. The phone kept getting disconnected. The last time I heard her pleading that he had to leave: "Please, you gotta go!" I called back repeatedly. She called me. Each time he pulled the plug on the phone. She sounded more exasperated than scared. So I'm laying back, not running down. The next day I called to find out what had happened. She downplayed the whole thing; it was "nothing."

FIELDNOTES: From early in their relationship, being with Reggie proved to be seriously problematic. What she had fallen for was a serious crack addict (a "tweeker") committed to little more than satisfying his habit. He stole from Sugar, he couldn't keep a job, he was unbelievably irresponsible and a chronic liar. On top of his somewhat predictable deviant behavior, however, Reggie overlaid a careful veneer of religiosity that successfully confounded the issue of his addiction for both himself and Sugar. Was it the Lord's challenge to her to reform him? Should she be apologizing for expecting too much of him when, after all, the Lord has His purpose?

Sugar's slide from foolish innocent love for Reggie James to bitterness, anger, and despair is not intended to depict a victimized woman. Sugar is clearly the one making the choices about her future, whether good or bad.

More than anything, Reggie was a project for Sugar. She was convinced that her love could change him; that he would eventually realize that he was a king and could thereby pull himself up out of the gutter. She had used this counseling before as part of her motivational work with neighborhood teenagers. In this case, however, Reggie's bad habits were so deeply ingrained that her positive attitude had no influence on him at all.

"I REALLY WANTED TO MARRY THE BOY"

I knew I was going to marry Reggie from day one. I've said I was done with love, but I formulated that view when I was like twenty-one years old. It's just been such a struggle! How can you talk about bein' in love when your gas and light bill is due and it's $400? I've always said that poor people shouldn't screw. I almost can't imagine why Ethiopians, starving people, have babies, hungry babies. When did you find time to lay down and make a child when your other kids are starvin'? Your thing should be about getting food on the table, getting some maize, some grain, somethin! But now it's years since I said I was done with love. That's a long time to be a jaded old bitch that won't let herself love. I guess I just needed to seek love. Which is why I think I liked bein' with Reggie so much.

But from the start, Reggie was gettin' pissed off 'cause all my ex-men were coming out the woodwork. Reggie was like, "These other nigs had all this time to tell you you were special. They had all this time to ask you to marry 'em. They had all this time to raise up your kids. Now that I'm on the scene, everybody wants to be in your life. But how come you weren't special to them *before*?"

That's why I think I thought Reggie was so special. I felt that Reggie loved me *for me*. He wanted to be a part of my life. He seemed actually and genuinely interested in my kids. I started tellin' him some of my kids' issues. Anyone else would have bolted for the door, but he was still like, "I love you." I always told Reggie love is tangible, love makes you go beyond *saying* you'll do something and *walk* the walk.

Reggie had *no* money, but the countless guys before Reggie that *did* have any money to speak of weren't generous with the money. So I thought, what's the difference? I was tryin' to look past his financial status because I didn't want to miss out on somethin' good just because he was a poor man.

The truth is, I don't know really what love is. Growin' up, we never saw a successful marriage. I can't think of one. Ask my sister. I doubt she can think of one either. We don't have any examples. Images of mothers, grandmas, and aunties is what you have. A dad was another thing. I remember when we were in school and somebody had two parents; I mean, kids would almost gather round: "You got a dad! You live with your dad?" It would be like this shock thing. That was a strange being who had a dad. Nobody had dads. So we haven't seen an example of love. What we know as love is maybe the violence, the jealousy, the pryin'. So how the heck are you supposed to know what love is?

So, did I love Reggie? I've found that I did love him in spite of myself. What attracted me to Reggie was that he was a Christian man.

He loves the Lord, and he's very well versed on the Bible. The one thing I had not experienced was the love of a man who loved the Lord and loved me. I've known every other combination, so why not try this? It gets to the point in every other relationship where I would quit. With Reggie, you couldn't quit. If he ain't got no paycheck, he sez, "We're under attack. The devil knows that we have good things in store for us, so that's why nothin's goin' good right now." Where otherwise I would say, "Get the fuck outta here, you freeloadin' bum," with Reggie it's: "Let's pray about it. The Lord will bless us to do better." So you give it another chance. You stick it out a little longer, 'cause you don't want the devil to have a victory.

One day we were in the kitchen together and there was just a good feeling of bein' in the kitchen and my mate is across the table. And, no, there wasn't a whole lot of money, but it didn't matter. I think we were havin' coffee or somethin'. It was those little things I hadn't enjoyed before. Havin' coffee with your mate. Hangin' out in the crib, just chillin', like old married folks.

Another time we were walkin' and holdin' hands, and it dawned on me: thirty-five years old and I couldn't recall but maybe a couple of times as a teenager of just pure walkin', holdin' hands. Before I was with Reggie, if you weren't drivin', I wouldn't look at you! I would never look at a man on the bus. So here was a man who's walkin' 'cause he don't have a car, so I got to enjoy walkin' in the fall through leaves with this man who makes me feel good, not showboatin' in a big car.

One time with Dusty, he drives up in his big Lincoln. I'm a black woman strugglin'. Dusty claims that he's a Muslim, so you would think, this black man, first thing he's gonna do is try to help a woman strugglin' to raise up young black men. And I says, "Can you take me over to the store so I can get my boys some shoes?" And you know the first thing he wanted to do was spread newspaper on the floor of his car so that their feet would not get his car dirty! I was like, "Well, never mind!"

That's like my defense mechanism. The minute somebody rejects you, you throw up your Black Matriarch, your HNIC, "Head Nigger in Charge" attitude: "That's all right, nigger, I'm used to doin' it. I'll do it. I got it covered."

But I was findin', with Reggie, I just didn't want to have to be in charge all the time. Sometimes I just wanted to be soft. I wanted somebody to hold me. I love the romantic stuff. But Reggie didn't get it. Whenever I was sayin' I would like to go on a date, Reggie was always thinkin', "Well, I don't have any money, so I can't take her on a date." What Reggie didn't get was that I didn't need him to take me to some fancy place and feed me lobster! If he would have just said, "Let's go get an ice cream cone. Let's go walk downtown. Let's ride the bus to the lake. Because I love you." That date would have been better than any date. But he wouldn't even do that. Stupid! He didn't have a clue.

Despite this, by little bits and pieces, he was taking over areas in the house, getting all tangled up and becoming part of the family. There was a fight in me not to let it go on, but there was another part that was appreciative. Like one day he said he was gonna go upstairs and talk to the boys 'cause they gotta get their rooms clean. After all the struggle I have had with those boys and their nasty rooms! We can't get uncles, brothers, nobody, to help us raise these boy children. I've had men come into my life, wanna screw me, whatever, and never say, "So, boys, what kinda sports do you like?" I'm tellin' you! And here was Reggie, askin' about their homework, helpin' them with their projects. He sat down and played cards with them for hours.

And, not only that, but I was gettin' somethin' for me. I've had men that have been so-called "involved" with me who, if I come out less than beautiful, my hair standin' on end, these nigs is goin' through all the doors and windows, can't get outta here fast enough! I never get to be off! I never get to be ugly! I never get to be just me! But with Reggie it was different, like I got to come down off the pedestal for a while.

I really wanted to marry the boy! There's been times in my relationships when the minute there comes a speed bump, I'm like, "I can't do it." I don't waste no time even tryin' to figure it out or work it out. That's been my way. It's a throwback to the old days when if he ain't got no money, I get rid of him. That's the only value we black women have because throughout our lives we've been so hungry. We don't value emotion. We haven't valued trying to work it out. It's just, "You don't have no money? You gone!"

Reggie had no money when I met him. He was workin' on gettin' some, but for some reason there ain't never nothin' clickin' for that boy. I was prayin' that somethin' would change for him, 'cause then it was gonna be some change for me.

FIELDNOTES: *Soon after Sugar wrote the following diary entry, she read it aloud to me, crying the entire time. It conveys some of the contradictions and confusion inher-*

ent in the Reggie story. She had let herself fall in love with Reggie, investing in a romantic fantasy about couples, communication, and holding hands. That young-love idea was shot to hell when she discovered that Prince Charming was a crack addict. As we will learn later, Sugar had already gone through her own struggle with drugs. She had cleaned up her act and was no longer a tweeker. Consequently, to have been foolish enough to invite a tweeker into her house and her bed, when she should have known better, was a bitter pill.

Sugar's Diary

November 1995

I can't love a tweeker!

My man is using drugs! My love-blind eyes would not, could not see. And yet, I *did* see, and *asked* and pleaded for some sense to be made out of all the puzzles that he used to placate me. I am hurt because I have allowed confusion to come into my life. I have slept with it and fed it. I have bought confusion shoes and clothed it. I kissed it and professed my everlasting love for it. I cooked for it and caressed it. And now I sit here stunned.

I am disillusioned because I am torn by my Christian beliefs. Why would the Lord send this man at this time? Why am I always designated to be the caretaker of the world and never anyone to take care of me? At this time, I don't even have anyone I can tell. I can't tell my daughters, whom I have confided in since they were old enough to have understanding. How can I? If I am going to be with a smoker, I could be with their father, couldn't I? As hard as I stay on him about getting off drugs and improving his life, and here I am sleeping with the enemy. I am alone in this. I just feel it. I could just scream.

How was I so foolish, how did I, Ms. Hip and Knowledgeable of the nineties, get caught up in such a fucked-up trap? Was I so desperate for love that I would take anything? Was I smarting so much from Dusty's rejection that I ran as fast as I could to the first man who professed to love, even *like* me? Is my judgment so clouded that I could not take my time and make a right choice for my and my kids' life? Why are my choices always so fucked up? Am I just a beautiful package that no one but the handicapped want? Kinda like Christmas wrapping, good for nothing but to throw away? How can I go to my Mom, who I asked, "*Would* the Lord send me a dirty man?" And she said, emphatically, "*No.*" And I asked her what was uncleanliness a sign of, and she said it was a sign of something deeper. I knew she was right, but chose to ignore it. What a stupid bitch I was! But *could* the Lord have sent him into my life and, if so, why? Does the Lord only send good? Well, then, why do we say that He sends trials to make us strong? Is this not one of the worst trials in my life so far?

Why did I ignore all the blatant signs of a smoker? Signs I would not have tolerated in any other person? The burnt lip. The poor hygiene. The emaciated look. The poor excuses. The street walking late at night. The unexplained absence of money. The food stamps missing. The dark circles under the eyes. The excess sleeping. The pawning of the diamond ring. The lack of desire for sex. My daughter telling me she thought she smelled cocaine in the house one day. And the lies! Lies! Lies! Lies!!! What the fuck was I waiting for and what the hell am I waiting for now? What the fuck is wrong with me? Why can't I let go?

Is being a Christian another word for being a fool? Does it make me blind to everything? If I can't help this man, am I Christian enough to help another downtrodden soul? Why is the faith that has given me so much comfort and peace eluding me now? How do I reconcile this issue? And what's next? I know that I may love the man and the man may truly love me. But the cocaine don't love or give a fuck about me or him or my kids or anybody. Cocaine will fuck you up and leave you laying there, as it has done to countless of our people. What is the lesson in here for me, Lord? How can I overcome this? Do I wait until something else comes up missing? Do I wait until he threatens my life? Do I wait until everyone in my community knows I am engaged to marry a tweeker? Of course, the answer must be *no*. On the other hand, do I not help a person in need if I can? Can I help at all? How can I help? Do I kick him out at his weakest point? Do I fucking try to save the world? What is the lesson, Lord? I am pleading to you, Father, to give me a sign, a note, a thump on the head. Something to tell me what is wise and prudent and fair and right and Christlike to do. Please, Lord, I'm begging, and I'm feeling very lost and alone. Help, please.

FIELDNOTES: *The revelations about Reggie's addiction opened the gates to two years of conflict and tears. Sugar's life was so subsumed by Reggie's lies and his irresponsible behavior that we barely spoke of anything else. The transcripts show that I let her talk. She thought it therapeutic. We sat companionably taping while she relived every detail of every fight. I voiced my objections to his behavior, but at this* point in our friendship, I wouldn't let myself interfere to the point of saying, "Dump the bastard." I wanted to, but I didn't.

The following segments are excerpted from Sugar's diary written during the Reggie period.

I don't know what this man is doin' in my house! Reggie went and spent his paycheck on dope. And then after he tells me, he says, "I'm mad at you," *because I made him admit it to me.* Because none of his stories would wash and he kept on with lie after lie after lie after lie and he finally admitted to having been on drugs for ten years. He says the Lord healed him and he's been off for the last three. Which is fine. But I can't tolerate him bein' on it again. My heart goes out a long way, but I know that I can't conquer dope. I know that Reggie may love me, but dope will steal from me. Drugs don't give a damn. He's sayin' it's not a problem, and that's one of the problems. You don't have a healthy respect for it, you think it's not a problem. It *is* a problem.

He was on crack for ten years in New York. He tells me he was clean for three years, but he's been druggin' for the whole time I been with him. He has several ties with many good women such as myself, hardworkin', attractive women, but he's probably burned all his bridges. For some reason he's not even allowed to see his youngest daughter. There's nothing in New York for him. He's probably already stole from everybody he can think of there.

I feel that the only way that Reggie is gonna leave drugs alone is to do it through the Lord, like I did it. And he doesn't have that much faith, or don't want to that bad, or hasn't been broke down enough. I think Reggie wants to do right. So my thing is that it's not really that Reggie has to leave; cocaine has to leave. And since it's in Reggie, that's how it has to go. Some other things I would be willing to work with him on, but not crack. I feel angry and I feel sad. I told him it's sad to see you destroyed and knowin' that you're ruining yourself. It'd be different if he came home and somebody had beat him up. I'd have somebody else to be mad at.

I don't know what Reggie's doin', but like two weeks ago he promised me his check, and no check. Last month my food stamps came up missin'. Three hundred and some dollars. I'm sure he took 'em. They were in my jacket pocket and then they weren't. And that's the night that he went out walkin', left, and didn't come back till the next day. And, by the time he came back, he had pawned my diamond ring. I let him wear it. He didn't have it two days and he had pawned it. And then he says he pawned it for ten dollars. He goes to sleep, I look in his billfold, and he actually pawned it for $25. So none of this is washin'.

It wasn't until almost 2 o'clock that afternoon that I saw the food stamps were gone. I've made my shopping lists. I know my food stamps are there, because when I put something there, it's there. Then, they're gone. He doesn't know what happened to 'em. I'm not makin' no connection to the fact that at one o'clock in the morning, he went for a walk. Duh!

I began to backtrack. It's what I do. I didn't directly turn to him and say, "Okay, nigger, what the fuck happened to my food stamps?" He's cool, 'cause he knows I don't fret over this kinda stuff. You know me, I don't worry over spilt milk, lost money, lost jewels. Matter of fact, I pray for the person that finds 'em. So he knew enough about me. He's thinking, "I can take the food stamps. If she don't find 'em, in a minute, she's gonna go, 'Oh well, the Lord blessed *somebody*.' And I'll be cool." Eventually, everything pointed to him, but he's such a skilled liar. He helps me look all over the room. He lifts the mattress. He looks up. He looks down. He looks everywhere. Meanwhile, he had stolen the food out of my kids' mouths!

I've told people, "I don't fuck with cocaine, I don't fuck with people that fuck with cocaine." That's been my bottom line. Okay, I could be your friend, I could associate with you, I could party with you out in the street, you could buy a ticket to my fashion show, but as far as you bein' my man, *never*! Not even a man who toots. And now I got a smoker!

Not only that, I usually can spot a tweeker a mile off. How did this man get in my drawers and I didn't even know he was smok-ing? I can't love a tweeker! But now he's in my home. I already warned him. He got to go. I'm tryin' to ease him outta there. I'm tryin' to position myself. See, with somebody like that you don't wanna just go off and say, "Git out!" 'Cause maybe they're in some drug-crazed stupor, and go, "Bitch, okay, I'm gonna get back at you and come and shoot up your house!" I'm not gonna do anything drastic. I'm just like biding my time. I'm not gonna put his stuff out 'cause he's gonna be mad, and then I'm not gonna know if he's gonna turn into this crazed, love-sick stalker.

Reggie's an ass. The Lord moved as I knew He would and I trusted that He would. And it was interesting to see how He moved, especially the timing. Remember how I told you I was going to give Reggie enough rope to hang hisself? He's getting closer and closer to the end of that rope.

This must have been Tuesday. I told Reggie I was broke and I needed some money. And we have this joint account at the credit union. And so I sez, "Baby, well, I need some money." He's, "I'll git you some money *tomorrow*. I'll have it for you *tomorrow*." I sez, "Well, no, that's not how this works, okay? You ask *me* for money. I say, 'How much do you need?' I give it to you. I ask *you* for money when I'm broke. You say, 'How much do you need?' You give it to me." He sez, "Ah, Sugar, I'm in here tryin' to sleep!" He's always tryin' to put me on the defensive, like I'm doin' somethin' wrong. He sez, "Well, just don't mess with what's in the credit union. That's in the joint account. That's *for* somethin'." And I'm like sayin' to myself, "I'm goin' to the credit union and take care of my business. You about to make me mad. Fuck you! I don't have to ask you for money. I've *got* money!"

You see I'm tryin' to let him be the man and do his manly thing, give his woman ten dollars to go on her little rounds and everything? He says the money's in the credit union. It's pretty much do or die time: if the money's in there, then it's there. And if it's not in the credit union, you've told one lie too many, and I've had it.

FIELDNOTES: *For Sugar, looking over these diary entries brought up all the frustration, anger, and disappointment she went through with Reggie. Laughing and crying at the same time, she itemized Reggie's deceit and the games he played, all of which she had blindly accepted in her futile attempt to "save that man."*

I stretched myself to the limit with that nigger. The thing of "Well, let's wait and see if it works out" or "How will you ever know what's on the other side of this door if you don't get to the other side?" and all that. I mean, I waited for him to get a job. He got the job. But when he was doin' all his temp stuff and day-labor things, there was never no money. Somethin' always happened to it. There should have been some kind of injection into the household. Somethin'. Anything. But no. And if you can't do nothin' after livin' with me for all that time, then what? Come on Sugar, get a grip! So the credit union was kinda like the final straw. I felt that if he really had the money, we could keep on

going and we could try some more. But if there's no money, which I
suspected would be the case, it would be my out. In the back of my
mind, I was hopin' it wasn't there, 'cause you always want an out.
And marriage is like no out.

So I went to the credit union to get my last forty dollars.

I say, "Ronald, might I be able to access my joint account?"

And he says, "No, he's been here."

This asshole Reggie had been tellin' me not to get into the credit
union because *he's already been there*, maybe four days before, when he
left for work. He emptied out the account, but didn't have the damn
gumption to say, "Well, babe, you goin' up to the credit union, I
guess you're goin' to find out there's no money in there."

So I'm at the credit union and there was no money. I was totally
pissed, but I went on about my business. And I didn't say anything to
Reggie 'cause I said to the Lord, "You givin' me my out. I asked You
specifically to make him right or make him get out of my house."
Here was my out. So I'm cool. And at night he's still cuddlin' up to me
all in the bed and everything. Asshole.

I didn't want to tell him anything before Thanksgiving. I didn't
want him to say, "Oh, you wait until the holiday and then you break
my heart." Holidays are traditionally when people either go commit
suicide or get real depressed or stupid. I was just gonna hold my
peace until after the holiday, play the role.

So we went and we did Thanksgiving, just the happy couple. I'm
not mad at him, 'cause I knew that the Lord was moving. And everybody sayin', "Throw the bum out!" But I kept sayin' that I was waitin'
on the Lord, and they would kind of look at me like, "poor dear." But
I had asked the Lord to put ninety days on Reggie stayin' or goin'.
Ninety days is enough for you to either tear your ass or not tear your
ass. And from the time that me and him started goin' together to
Thanksgiving was exactly one hundred days. So I'm pleased. It was
like the Lord said, "Okay, ninety days is up, now watch me move!
Watch me come in here and start workin'!"

I wasn't expecting Jesus to come down and do it for me. I knew
that I would have to take some action. But what I had been doin' in
the previous time was startin' to get my ducks in a row, things that I
was puttin' together so that shit just started falling into place.

Finally, I couldn't hardly hold it any longer. He was tellin' me he's
goin' to go get some money. He's gonna go work at Ready Pool. He's
supposed to go get thirty dollars. He thought that was gonna placate

me. Duh! What I wanted to say was, "Why do you have to work at Ready Pool when there's already money in the credit union?" But I had already made up my mind. I was waitin' on the Lord to give me the words, and I didn't want to jump the gun.

That night we were supposed to go to a friend's fashion show. The doors were gonna open at seven. And I told him they probably wouldn't even go on stage till like 9:30. So he calls me and tells me he's stuck out wherever they have sent him on some job. But I don't believe he ever went to the Ready Pool in the first place.

He says, "I don't think I'm goin' to get out of here till six o'clock. And it will probably take me about four hours to get home. Ten o'clock."

I was thinkin', "What bus in Springfield do you know takes four hours?" He was so full of shit. He conveniently made it so he'd miss the fashion show.

Earlier, he was already sayin' I didn't want him to go with me anyway 'cause he don't have nothin' to wear. I had been harpin' on him, "Honey, please put your coat in the cleaners and get it cleaned. We may wanna do somethin' one time." But see, when you're on drugs, any little money you spend you always regret because it could get you high. Like when he bought his tennis shoes, and he's, "I didn't need these," 'cause now he's thinkin' what else he could have done with $20. So he didn't put his coat in to the cleaners and no way was he gonna go with me 'cause I was gonna wear this long black dress and full-length leather coat and all that.

So he called with this bullshit and finally he sez, "Well, what's wrong?"

"Oh, there's nothin' wrong."

"Yeah, well, I can hear something in your voice."

So I say, "Well, there's no money in the credit union."

He goes, "Hey, I knew that! I knew you was goin' to do that. That's why I took it out. And that shows that you disrespect me because you don't obey. I told you not to go into the credit union."

I go, "Fine." I say, "Fuck you, Reggie James! I've clocked out emotionally and I'm through. You're outta here."

So then later, he comes home about twelve o'clock. His heart was beatin' so fast, I could hear it! He done been off gettin' high somewhere. I tell him I need him to leave. I need him to go. I decided that what I would do was not put him on the defensive, but make it look like it was me: "Honey, you deserve better. You're such an upstanding man, and I'm just a wretched bitch." So he can feel good. I even wrote him a letter and made him a copy, so he could take it to his friends and say, "See, she was a wretched bitch. And I'm really an upstanding Christian man. See she sez it right here in the letter."

Go! You want your reputation intact? Go!

So I told him that he had to leave. He begged me and begged me not to break up with him. "Okay, we're not breaking up, just go!" So he leaves.

I didn't pack it up. I told him, "You can leave some of your stuff here. We still go together, but we don't live together. You can come over and chill, have a meal, or whatever. But you don't live here."

I thought I was easin' him out. Of course, two days later, he was back.

FIELDNOTES: *What appealed to me about Reggie was that he was smart and well educated. Not that I had much contact with him—over the years we had maybe two or three short conversations. Usually, I ran into him at Sugar's house, when either he was just leaving or Sugar was ushering me out the door so he wouldn't overhear our conversations. I had no experience with the inner-city culture of the addict. So I didn't know what a crackhead would be like to talk to. When we did have a chance to chat, I always walked away amazed at how articulate and worldly he was. So when he got a job as a counselor for delinquent boys, I was pleased. I foolishly thought this professional-level employment was proof that he was on the road to redemption.*

"YOU AIN'T GOT THE SENSE GOD GAVE SMOKE"

A couple of months later, Reggie's got this pretty good job as a counselor in a halfway house. What's he do but steal the van from work! He works at one house. He finishes two days there, he goes to the other house to relieve somebody else. They sent him from that house to relieve at the third house. He never showed at the third house. He took the van! Gone all night.

You know where he tells me he was? First he says he ran outta gas. I sez, "You're an asshole. Who do you think's gonna believe that? You're stupid."

He ran outta gas in a dope zone! He comes in here, eyes ringed, dark. He's all funky.

I go, "You been out doin' dope, asshole!"

"I didn't have no money to be doin' dope," he sez.

"Hey, I been there. You don't have to have no money to be doin' dope! For all I know you might've been out there suckin' dicks! I don't know what you will do, but all I know is this story is not what you say it is."

You know what he says he did to run outta gas?

"I went joy ridin'," he sez.

"You're forty-one fucking years old! So either you're stupid because you're doin' dope or you're stupid because you're an overgrown juvenile delinquent goin' joy ridin'. Who's gonna believe that?"

And he's tryin' to get me to give him some money to put gas in the van. I sez, "I'm not doin' shit. I told you I would be behind you if you wanna do right, but I'm not gonna uphold you in wrong. I'm not gonna continue to enable you. You do whatever the hell you gotta do!" I sez, "You're fuckin' crazy. You ain't got the sense God gave smoke. You're a fool." I told him to get out. I finally end up giving him a dollar. I tell him, "If you pack your shit and tell me I'll never see your ass again, I'll give you money. Otherwise, I don't have it."

So then he's sittin' there trying to figure out what can he tell the people about the van.

I sez, "You're probably reported as a stolen vehicle. If you have any sense, you would go to those people and explain yourself.

The last time he missed work, they called. They were cool. They sez, "Reggie, we're a group home. We got a whole series of group homes. If there's anything we got, it's counseling. If you need counseling, come to us."

I sez, "Reggie, if you got any sense, you'll go and tell those people you want some help. If you tell people you ran out of fucking gas and went on a joy ride, they won't accept that. They can understand you having a little breakdown. They cannot understand grown men of forty-one running out of gas and not calling."

He'll never be able to get another counseling job. How can he counsel these boys not to run when running is what he does? And the funny thing was I've heard him give these boys some good advice: "Man, it's your choice. Nobody's holdin' you. If you want to run, it's stupid. Don't do it. You're supposed to be in here tryin' to make things better for yourself." Blah, blah, blah, blah, blah.

FIELDNOTES: *When we recorded the first part of the next section, "A Lie a Week," we were lying across Sugar's bed, giggling like teenagers at a slumber party. Sugar had actually kept a list of Reggie's lies. And as she checked off each lie, our laughter grew. We howled, we cried, we gulped for air. It was all so stupid and so futile!*

"A LIE A WEEK"

The boy lied to me from the git-go! I had realized that he was tellin' me a lie a week coinciding with payday. When I first met him, he told me he owed money to a loan shark, so he would begin contributing to the household if I could just see him clear to pay the loan shark off. This was like a knee-breaking loan shark, so that lie bought him a lot of time.

Once, he said he couldn't give me any money 'cause he bought a plane ticket; since he's a man without a country, he likes to keep a way out. "I never know when you're gonna put me out or when you're gonna flip," he sez, "so I keep a plane ticket." This man who doesn't even have bus fare! I never, of course, saw the ticket.

Then there was one time when he bought $20 worth of lottery tickets and they were all losers!

Once when I bitched about him not havin' any money in October, he sez, "I can't even surprise you! On Christmas mornin' I wanted you to look out there and see a car. I'm saving for your car." Then he sez I'm such an old evil bitch, I done spoiled the surprise, and so now I don't get the car.

See, Reggie thought, if he does *tit*, he's gonna get *tat*. He didn't know that he was gonna get *rat-a-tat-tat-tat* comin' back on his ass. That's what he was expectin', that he's only gettin' as much as he puts out there. But I think as it goes around that 360 degrees, it gains momentum. So that's why I try as hard as I can to put good things in my circle. By the time they come around, they are better things. I'm not all good, and I'm not all perfect, but I just try to do right.

See, my shit's taken care of. My kids is off to school. Baby's gettin' dressed. I'm goin' to do somethin' positive for my life. You wanna tear your ass, you tear it. I'm not goin' there with you.

You know there are men out there who *can't* make a living. But I think men like Reggie *won't*. I think it's worse to "won't" than to "can't." He's able-bodied. He's smart. He's articulate. Sure, I'd like to lay in a fetal position and stay covered up in a blanket all day too, but I'm a mom and I can't. I gotta get my ass up and go. But Reggie, he won't. He wanna lay there and die. I don't have that choice.

Black men say that we black women *castrate* 'em, we don't let 'em be a man. So I'm sayin', "Okay, you wanna be the man, I'll let you be the man. Do what a man's supposed to do, Reggie. You take care of business. You don't necessarily provide, but you help. You bring food.

You contribute. You know what? It's all bull 'cause I been doin' it this whole time. I'm the Head Nigger in Charge, not Reggie James!"

So at this point he was seein' that he's losin' hold, and he turns into this mad, jealous fiend. If he had had his druthers, the mailman couldn't deliver mail 'cause else I'd be fuckin' him. We'd be walkin' down the street, and he'd be sayin' to guys in cars, "What are you lookin' at?" And I'd be, "Man, ain't nobody lookin' at your woman."

I'd come home, and he'd say, "Who tried to talk to you today? Who rapped to you today? I know when you wear those pants, I know your butt is looking too good, I know somebody tried to rap to you."

I'm goin, "Nobody."

"Yeah, right. You just not tellin' me, which means you're covering up somethin'."

Total insecurity. He's gotta wonder who tried to talk to me, who made me feel good today? Who smiled at me and told me I was pretty? Because you know his ass wasn't doin' it. So he was always worried.

FIELDNOTES: *Sugar loved the fact that Reggie was a Christian, the first man in her life who shared her faith. She talked about it all the time. How he was knowledgeable about the Bible, how he had his ministry, people with whom she regularly prayed. But in the end, his avowed devotion to God proved to be yet another scam and manipulation.*

"HE BEATS YOU UP WITH CHRISTIANITY"

Loving the Lord didn't necessarily make Reggie a good Christian or a good man. I told him, "You pimp in the name of Jesus. You've stolen in the name of Jesus." But he was able to turn his knowledge of the Bible around to use it for his own good.

Like one day he says, "Well, are you my Abigail?"

Abigail is a woman in the Bible who was brave, all these good things. So he likens me to Abigail, and I'm so flattered, I fall for it. But eventually, I got smart.

One day, I asked him, "What was Abigail's husband like?"

Abigail's husband was David. David was a provider. He was brave; he was a warrior; he was a king. *He wasn't no broke nig bastard!*

But Reggie just hems and haws. He doesn't want to touch on David.

The boy was sly. He preys on Christian women because he knows he can hit 'em over the head with that Bible. A non-Christian woman gonna say, "Nigger, get the hell out with your broke ass!" But a Christian woman's gonna go, "Okay, well, I'm supposed to turn the other cheek. I'm supposed to go the extra mile."

We read the Bible together, yeah, but it's totally different when you read the Bible with Reggie. He beats you up with Christianity! Like you gotta be torn down. You gotta be debased before the Lord will work with you. On days I felt pretty, Reggie told me I was vain. Days I'd be proud of an accomplishment, well, he'd be, "pride cometh before a fall." When I would have money coming in, he was all, "a rich man will have more trouble getting into heaven than a camel getting through the eye of a needle." Always somethin'.

I was tellin' him, "But the Lord promised me life more abundant and I plan to get the abundant life."

"Oh no," Reggie sez, "that's one of the reasons why I don't have anything. I don't care about anything, 'cept for the coming of Jesus."

And I'm sayin' to myself, "That's why at age forty-one, you don't have shit, you homeless nigger!"

Like he would say, "The Bible says you're obligated to forgive me. No matter if I kick you in your ass. Smoke up everything. You're obligated to forgive me and I don't have to make a damn change." See, for him, being a Christian meant he's not responsible for anything in his life. Either a spirit did it or a curse or the devil jumped up. So he just had no concept of owning up to nothing. And I don't know what in childhood makes that happen, but whatever it is, he didn't have a clue about being responsible for himself.

When Reggie first came in, I opened up my home to him and told him, "You're the spiritual head. You're more learned than I am." What I thought would be ideal would be a Christian man. But what did I get? Is this what the Lord requires of me? To help him do wrong? I don't think so. My Bible didn't say that. So all of a sudden I didn't have no concept, no picture, and I was almost right back at square one, not being able to identify what man is healthy and good for me in my life; what type of man do I want to influence my children?

FIELDNOTES: *Overwhelmingly, men are the batterers in cases of domestic violence. But women can also lose it. Sugar has gotten violent with the men in her life, but none of them have set her off like Reggie did. In the following segment, Sugar tells us how Reggie so infuriated her that she considered setting him on fire.*

"I JUST WANTED TO BEAT THE DEVIL OUT OF HIM"

I have this little affirmation over my desk that says, "I am who I always was." I was a good little girl. I still am. I put it up 'cause Reggie was tryin' to change me.

The violence—I can't pinpoint when it began, but I know a lot of it was probably during the first seven months. I began to jump on him 'cause nothin' made sense. So I'd be like, "You don't have no check!! What the hell do you mean you lost it!?" And then I'd go off 'cause it didn't make sense.

Oh, I know the first time: when he pawned my ring. That was right after he stole my food stamps. I slapped his face. I tried to slap his head off. And that was the first time the police got called in here, too. I called them to tell them he stole my ring, and they didn't do anything that time. Reggie just played it off: "Oh, officer, we're just having a little spat here. I pawned her ring, and I'm gonna get it back."

That was where it started. After that it just escalated. I just wanted to knock some sense into him. I just wanted to beat the devil out of him, knock the drugs out of him, make him responsible, make him tell the truth. I hate lies. And he'd be lyin' so much that my reflex was just to hit him. And I know he could've snapped my neck at any time. But I couldn't help myself.

We fought all the time. I called him names. I beat on him. I whupped his ass. I sent him to the hospital one night. This was a real ugly scene. This might have been the moment when we really fell out of love. We spit in each others' faces. Is that the grossest, dog-nasty, horriblest, basest thing you can ever do to another human being?!

Well, this particular night, he was in a snit. I don't know why. Who ever knew why he was in a snit? And it began by him bein' in the room playin' music, some Christian music. That's what he listened to. It was around ten somethin'. So now it's time for me to go to bed, and I'm sayin', "Honey, I'm gettin' ready to come in and go to bed."

And he's, "Well, I just want to listen to this one more song."

So I'm, "Well, honey, you know I can't sleep with music, but go ahead, I'll compromise. Listen to the one more song."

After the one song, he keeps rewinding to listen to it over and over and over. He's tryin' to start a fight. But how do you fight somebody who's listening to Christian music? That makes me the devil. What do you say? "Turn off that damned Christian music!?"

I kept unplugging the music. And he'd plug it back up. And I'm sayin', "Please, honey, I don't want to fight, I want to go to sleep." And he'd plug it up, and play his music. Anything to keep from doin' what I need him to do.

I told him, "You take my power."

I was powerless to do anything. I couldn't even faze him to turn the music off. So I had no control and that was really makin' me lose it. I kept jumpin' off the bed, hittin' him. He had vowed he'd never hit me again. I was all upside his head. I was slapping his face. I hit him wherever I could hit him. Finally I kicked him in his ass. Hard. I thought maybe I had paralyzed him. But it didn't do no good.

Finally, I snapped. I went and I got some lighter fluid and I creeped very slowly and I squirted him with it. I got a match. And I debated whether I should strike the match. Oh, he had taken me to the edge. I was crazy. My eyes were glazed over. After fightin' me, beratin' me, talkin' about me, he was sayin' that I wasn't worthy to go to church. Said the women in church should watch out 'cause I would fuck their husbands, and just horrible, horrible, horrible stuff. And I sez to my-self, I'm just gonna kill him. I'm just gonna set his ass on fire and kill him.

That was after I went to try to get my gun, this little inoperable piece of nothin'. I had never even shot it or put bullets in it. It was in a lock box and I was tryin' to get it, but he took that. After I couldn't get at the gun, that's when I decided I was just gonna set him on fire. But then I couldn't do it. I could see what would happen. I could see that one match bein' my whole future—my kids' future, my school, my ministry, my hair business, my customers, my everything, in one match. So I was sane enough not to. But I'd been close to that edge before. I had placed razors strategically in my room. There was one up top on the shelf. I had one on the mirror, one in a basket, one in my jewelry box. I had knives to be able to get at him if I needed to. Ugly. Ugly! I was gonna slice his ass up.

But he was doin' more damage to me. The stuff that he did to me! By the time he'd called me the last douche bag, bitch, whore, I didn't know any way to hurt him and make him leave me alone. There was the time when he told me, almost literally for four hours straight through, how pitiful, sorry, worthless I was. Never even took a breath! By the end of those four hours, I was gone. I called him a faggot. He tipped me over in a chair and was chokin' and twistin' me and every-thing else after I called him that!

Then there was all this Christian bullshit. He'd say, "Don't you see how Satan's attacking us? He's attacking our ministry. It's not really us. It's just Satan doin' this. And I love you and the only reason I can hurt you is because I love you so. Oh, honey, I'm so sorry . . . " Then in the next breath, I'd be some douche bag, bitch, whore, flat-back tramp, stank, crazy, schizophrenic again!

He was so good at making me feel so bad. I mean he'd make fake phone calls. He was so skilled. I mean this boy had been doin' this so long, any person would think he was holdin' a phone conversation. Like he would act like he was calling another woman, and he'd talk about me. What better way to get a woman crazy than to talk about her with another woman? He'd do it in the morning while I'm lyin' in the bed. It was a stupid ploy, but I still would get caught up in it. He'd go in the bathroom and close the door. Then he would talk loud enough so that it would go through the door, and I'd hear every word.

But one time I caught him. He was talkin' for thirty-five minutes and after he was done, we both realized the phone wasn't even plugged in!

FIELDNOTES: *Sugar once told me that Reggie wanted to hide himself in her life, like a hermit crab that wanted to crawl up in somebody else's shell. He took on the identity that came from being Sugar's fiancé, not just for other people, but for himself as well. When he lived with her, he wasn't a hungry, homeless junkie. He was a hardworking Christian. "Being an addict is just a small part of my identity," he tells himself. "It's my sickness, but I ain't a junkie. I really am gonna marry this girl." So he wanted her life. He needed her shell just to have a reason to wake up in the mornings.*

He was just such a confused, really demented type of man. He was really hurtin' bad. He was a very, very dependent type of person. And I guess he felt he was losing me, which he was, and felt he needed to do something, anything, to draw me back in. You know how it is with kids, it don't matter what kind of attention you're payin' to 'em, even if you're hittin' 'em, as long as you're payin' attention to 'em. Reggie hated for me to ignore him or go off and do things by myself. So he would draw me back in to the fight with him. And I guess he thought fightin' was better than nothing. He would always say, "I don't care what you say. I don't care how bad it gets. It's still better than bein' alone."

He claimed he never hit a woman before, that he had never been violent. Said that there was a spirit of violence in my house and that's what really came over us. Not that we were fighting, but that the spirit of violence had settled down upon us. What bullshit! His sister told me he had a tendency to be violent. I talked to her on the phone one time. She lives in Mississippi. She was callin' him for something and me and her just got to talking.

I remember I said, "I don't know where he is. I hope he never comes back!"

She had heard that before!

I was sayin' somethin' about myself, and she says, "Oh no, you don't have to tell me. I can tell you about you. You're attractive, you're articulate, you're smart, you're a hard worker."

She just ran it down.

"These are the types of women that he gets. You fit the stereotype."

She told me! And she said that he had a tendency toward violence. But at the time, this didn't set off alarms!! It was just another red flag I was ignoring because I am going to try to save the world! I was going to love this man out of anything bad you told me about him.

There was tons of battering, and then one time I had his ass put in jail. Supposedly, he was getting ready to go into drug rehab. So he goes out on this one final binge before he's gonna get cleaned up. But I had decided that after his drug binge he couldn't come back in the house. So when he comes rolling in about 2:30 the next afternoon, I told him, "Your stuff is out in the back."

I had had the windows bolted down for a time when I knew I would need to put Reggie out. But he had previously *removed* the bolts, and so he came through the window.

He was trying to restrain me, to keep me from getting to the phone. But you can get pretty physical trying to restrain a nut like me. I was tryin' to get up outta there. So what he did was cut the phone cord. But he cut it a split second after I punched in 911. And after that, the police was like five deep. They came and took him to jail. Sent him away for fifty-two days.

2 THE HUSTLE
WELFARE AND WORK

FIELDNOTES: I had known Sugar for a year before we started talking about poverty and welfare. Up to that point, we found ourselves deeply involved in recording the drama of her relationship with Reggie. When that sorry love affair ended, our concern with the mundane reality of poverty began.

One September morning, Sugar initiated me into the Springfield welfare bureaucracy with a guided tour of their offices, located in a dreary, half-vacant shopping mall. The offices are divided into the dilapidated, depressing Springfield Family Opportunity (SFO) center for job training and counseling and, next door to it, the only slightly spiffier welfare office itself. The few stores around the offices are designed for the quick and easy extraction of what little money the poor might have: rental furniture, liquor, confirmation dresses, gang paraphernalia, and burritos.

At first we laughed as Sugar did a running commentary on the institutional poverty scene, but the visit eventually made her very angry. By allowing herself the distance of being a tour guide, she was able to express her frustration and rage at being treated as a dependent child by the very system that despises and denounces the dependency of the poor.

By this time in our friendship, I was past my confusion about what she meant when she described herself as a "hustler." She didn't mean a hooker or a liar or a schemer. I now understood Sugar to be a "hustler" in the sense that she interacts with her world by melding honest values with intelligence, industriousness, and the readiness to take advantage of opportunities at every turn.

In terms of her financial status, hustling means using her wits to find the money she needs to support her kids and herself. As long as Sugar's got her brain in gear, she doesn't think of herself as poor; she's a hustler. Hustling isn't a scam. It's a style, an attitude. It shows you care about yourself, that you've got some pride, that you are somebody who takes care of business. Hustling comes from the kind of self-reliant initiative welfare critics are hard-pressed to find among the poor.

What follows is a very personal, and often judgmental, indictment of a welfare system that psychologically demeans and financially handicaps women, maintaining them in poverty, so that they cannot achieve self-reliance even if they wished to.

"THEY'RE TELLIN' YOU THAT YOU ARE NOTHIN'"

ST   Like I said, I avoid the welfare office. I haven't had to be down here in a long time. But when you're on any type of job training program, you gotta come down here to see your technician to talk about your progress or what you're doin' in the program or changes that you made. You come to this gross, dirty place where people are supposed to come and want to uplift themselves. How the hell would they? It's disgusting. It is trash, it's dark, it's dirty. The signs are nasty. There's no colors. It hasn't been swept. It hasn't been mopped. Even the railing, you don't want to touch it. You might catch some welfare germ. The stairs is gray. The walls look dirty. How much does it cost to get a coat of paint? There's no toys for the kids. What's wrong with some dinosaurs for these kids while they sit there with their moms? There's one trash can sittin' there in the middle of the foyer. They don't care if somebody bumps into it.

       How the hell are they gonna make a woman feel better about herself in a place like this? Look at this training room? It's gloomy at best. The carpet is filthy! It's dark. It's shitty. Gross. I hate it.

TBE   What's the message that this gives to the women who are coming there?

ST   They're tellin' you that you are *nothin'*. That's what it says to me. You are nothin'! How many pieces of tape does it take to make this poster about mammograms neat? Four little pieces. They have one little piece that's stuck up there like they don't *care* if I *get* a mammogram. Be a good example! If we supposed to do better, *show* us some better! How the hell am I gonna get inspired?

FIELDNOTES: On this day, there was little happening at the SFO. A few clerks shuffled papers in their offices, but Sugar and I wandered around with impunity. We walked into barren classrooms and looked around people's offices until we got bored with the sameness of it all.

The immediate targets of Sugar's resentment were the welfare workers and the power they wielded over her check and, thus, her family's survival. Our tour allowed Sugar to sit in judgment of the staff, whom she eagerly scanned (and denounced) for fashion flaws and sloppy habits. These, she attested, were signs that they were doing a poor job as community servants.

ST   They don't even care enough about themselves. The employees feel like shit comin' in there. Look in here. All those technicians are fat! Do you think they love their jobs?

TBE   What does fat have to do with anything?

ST   Ugh! When you're all fat like that, you're unhealthy, you're unhappy. This is where you get your inspiration, by looking at these women? And they don't give a damn about you, no matter that you're more presentable and cleaner than they are! I've seen technicians stand and hold conversations with their clients in the damn doorway. Like, what? I can't go in your office? You put my business out on the streets where other people can stare? You would think that the nature of this work should make you want to do more. It's human services. You're in the service of *humans*!

TBE   What *should* this room look like?

ST   If I ran this place, it would be brightly lit. It would be bright colors. I would probably have a radio playing very low, smooth jazz or somethin' during the time out. There would be lots of magazines. I'm just such a particular type of stickler for things to be neat. It would be organized. The damn carpets wouldn't be filthy. I might encourage the women to all bring pictures of their family, and I'd make like a family wall. You know, show off your kids, show off what you take pride in. Of course, brochures. No chairs stored in the class! Is this a fuckin' storage room, excuse me, or is it a classroom? We don't rate that much, so we have to sit where you store chairs too?

TBE   It would be cool if this room were done like a living room, with nice furniture to make you feel better, raise your expectations.

ST   Or even if it felt more like a classroom. Classrooms should have *information*. What do you see on the wall now? Ground rules. Stuff like, "Respect each other and speakers. No food during class. Follow class dress code. Be on time. Have fun." That is bullshit. That's the stuff you want to remind me of every day? Not "You're special. You

can do this." You tell me to dress and be on time and don't eat.
That's crappy.

TBE   So what does it feel like coming in here now?

ST   You know what this says to me? How little the state cares. 'Cause
there's no money in that office at all. The building looks like it's
been shut down, torn down, and abandoned! It's a wonder why
women don't get up and come here with gats and shoot up the
whole place! Let's get outta here.

FIELDNOTES: *Our next stop was the nearby welfare office itself. On the way,*
we passed the Springfield Public Schools Resource Center, an inviting, bright, well-
decorated office. Sugar was stopped in her tracks.

ST   Look at this place right next door! There's tapes, there's books. Plants
and mobiles. There's resources! Education! It's not open to the public,
but things are catalogued and lined up nice and neat so teachers
wanna come in. And it's right next to that depersonalized crap!

FIELDNOTES: *We sat down in the waiting area in the welfare office. Sugar applied*
her critical eye to a scene she had witnessed hundreds of times before, but without
such a willing audience.

ST   It's neater and cleaner than the last time I was here. But look at that
technician. She looks like hell. She looks like somebody whupped
her last night. And you want to serve *me* and help *me*? There's a
smiling technician that appears to be enjoying her job, but she's ill
dressed. It's too damn cold for them open-toed shoes, and they too
high for her. Look at that technician over there: raggedy old washed
out jeans, lookin' like poor white trash. And she's dispensin' food
stamps, or I think you can go in there and get diapers. They never
have diapers when you go. Unless you hit 'em at the first of the
month, you ain't gettin' nothin' from General Assistance. Oof! That
technician woman look like she's comin' off a drunk. Her health is
horrible. Look at her figure. She don't have no bra on. Her stomach
is stickin' out.

TBE   What an attitude you have, your highness! I love that even though
you're on welfare, you're not demeaned by it.

ST   I'm a hustler. I know hustlers. Not everybody's a hustler here,
specially not the help. She obviously not 'cause she's workin' behind
that counter lookin' like hell. That girl that walked past us ain't a

hustler 'cause she got on them cheap-assed clothes and thinks she's looking great. Look at *that* technician. He ain't a hustler, stuffed into them clothes like that, big old fat unhealthy thing. And he's regulatin' somebody's life!

From what I've seen in the welfare bureaucracy, there's people like me that are civil servants. And there's others like that fat, ugly one right there. She don't make no more money than I do. She could be a welfare person but she's on the other side of the desk. She looks horrible; she doesn't love herself. She is probably barely makin' enough to get by.

TBE   Is there anyone in here who looks good to you?

ST   That red-haired welfare worker over there—*she's* tryin' to do something different with herself. There's a healthy lady. Now she knows these people. She's laughin' and she's happy. She's a human services worker. It's her community that she cares about. And, that girl right there could be a hustler. She's comfortable. She has a nice purse. Her hair is combed. She has on nice glasses. She walked through here with confidence. She's doin' somethin' else than getting welfare.

TBE   So you're saying that besides the technicians, the people who are dependent on welfare are the sad sacks in here.

ST   When they're totally *dependent* on welfare, they're definitely sad. They don't have no choices. They *gotta* take the shit. There's the difference. Here's a man filling out some welfare papers. Maybe he's on disability. Now *he's* a hustler. A straight-up hustler. He has on nice clothes. He's tall, he's robust. He's in good health, seemingly, for a man his age. He got a nice cap, and it ain't cheap. I bet his shoes are good. Socks that match. His gold necklace. Hustler.

TBE   What's his life like outside this office?

ST   He gambles. He plays the dogs. He kicks it. He has a wife or some women. He has grown kids. That girl over there, she's pretty much a hustler too. But she very well could be a smoker too. And cleaned herself up to come in today, but she's hustlin' to get her drugs.

TBE   What makes you think she's a smoker?

ST   Because she's so thin and skinny. You can be thin, but so skinny gotta be from the pipe.

FIELDNOTES: *Sugar has the remarkable ability to switch from bitchy commentary to personal experience to adroit analysis. Our welfare visit allowed her to combine all of these skills.*

Waiting time is stank. There's lots of people. All those welfare people are sitting around. Kids with dirty faces. Because you're poor, your kid's face doesn't have to be dirty. Unruly kids running around. Because you're poor, your kids don't have to be wild. And what's even more depressing is the number of men who are in there now. It used to be only women and children in the welfare office. And now there's men, and they appear to be able-bodied men, a lot of 'em. And they are there sitting right beside you in the welfare office. There's no jobs. They may be drugged out. They may be alcoholed out. Whatever. They are disabled. So now they're relying on a check too.

If there were jobs in Springfield, this man would not be there today. That didn't happen overnight to get him there. It's a process to get a man till he's so downtrodden, till he's so disabled that he's in the welfare office. He doesn't have one bad time and go, "Well, I'm gonna go get on welfare." He still has the desire to want to provide for himself. And two, or three, or four bad times still don't kill that desire. But after you get kicked in the head more times than you can count, well . . .

When I used to come here, I set myself apart. It's like I would go to the food-stamp office at a certain hour 'cause I didn't want to stand up in the line with all those welfare people lookin' hungry. I wouldn't *dare* go to the food-stamp office lookin' hungry. I don't want to be that needy. I don't want to be that dependent. I don't want anybody to think that I'm not gonna eat if I don't get food stamps. I'll make a way. I'll figure something out. I would not stand at that window and cry. If my kids are waiting for me outside in the car, I can't come out of there cryin', goin', "They wouldn't give me my food stamps." I can't do that. I'm a hustler. And I gotta figure out whatever it is I gotta do to get some food goin' on.

Inside yourself you feel embarrassed, because if you go to that window and you turn away with nothing, everybody knows somethin's wrong. Course they've all experienced it too, so everybody has the fear that if they go to the window, something could be wrong. You never know. The computer could be down, there could be a glitch, something could have happened to your paperwork. Each time you go up to their window, you're at their mercy. You can't call and ask, "Am I on the computer?" You have to go down and see. So you always have to present your face, and there's always the chance that your face could get egg on it.

The workers at the Springfield Family Opportunity office are just sad. Anytime I went to see my technician, she'd never be dressed as good as me. Pills on her clothes. No jewelry. Nothing matching. I'd almost feel guilty. I'd turn my rings around. But of course, she probably drove, and I took the bus. And she probably has a life insurance policy for her kids, and I didn't have that. But on the surface, she never looked as happy as me. But look at her job! I feel sorry for her. She's dealing with welfare people every day. They're comin' in, dumpin' on you. So who's really poor? She's got all this baggage that's comin' in the door and it's her job. She's makin' $5 somethin', $6 somethin', $7 somethin' an hour to have people dump depression on her. I can't see that it would be worth it.

Day in and day out you got people with sob stories. I respect 'em, and that's one of the reasons why I never gave them a hard time. They're human. They have feelings. So I think my experience with technicians was never terribly unpleasant because I was never terribly unpleasant. It all has to do with how you treat people and how you feel about yourself.

Also I knew that that's their job. And I realized that it didn't have anything to do with me. It might be that her husband half-did her last night. Maybe she didn't come. But I just know I've never done nothin' to this woman, so it couldn't be me. So I never took any of that away with me.

You can have the butt-ugliest woman for a technician. Good Lord in the morning Jesus, her figure is horrible! She's totally unhealthy. Or you can have someone ugly as a mud fence but who you can tell loves themselves, cares about themself. She obviously doesn't.

FIELDNOTES: *The welfare field trip opened my eyes to the day-to-day reality of Sugar's being on welfare and, specifically, to how much strategizing and hustling she must do in order to make it through the month. Hustlers like Sugar are fairly common in Springfield. Identifying them in the welfare office, however, revealed an elitism that I hadn't recognized in her before. You can see how Sugar had her welfare class system all worked out. She let me know just which clients were "sorry welfare bitches" and which were "hustlers." The hustlers were the better-dressed, more self-contained, confident welfare clients whom she knew had something going on the side—an illicit source of income that lifted them from the insufferable and demeaning poverty afforded by a welfare check alone. In this view, nonhustlers were entitlement junkies doing little to make their children's lives more pleasant than cashing their monthly check.*

We sat in the welfare office for a few hours while Sugar provided a running commentary on every client, clerk, and administrator she saw. Even as we drove away, she was still madly sputtering about inflexible, uncompassionate clerks failing to treat clients as human beings who have individual lives and problems. As I listened to this funny but highly judgmental monologue largely directed at the sad state of the nonhustlers, I was startled by how fundamentally opposed we were politically. While I saw single mothers strategizing around historical and socioeconomic conditions beyond their control, she saw pitiful, inherently weak-willed women too comfortably accustomed to feeding at the public trough. Here we were looking at the welfare system from two different perspectives, but I knew that it went further than the obvious insider-outsider dichotomy.

Although Sugar personally identifies with other welfare recipients—"They are me. They are my sisters and brothers"—there is an element of self-hatred here as well. She adamantly denounces those women who verbally advertise the pitifulness of their poverty by complaining loudly on buses or who declaim the injustice of the system in front of the food-stamp office. She goes out of her way not to identify herself as a welfare mother, either in her own community or outside it. No new nails or nightclub binges on the first of the month for Sugar!

Regarding the dismal hopelessness of welfare, Sugar reminded me that no one can live on welfare alone; they can only exist. Most welfare mothers, she pointed out, have so few resources that they only make it through the month by hanging on to the thought that the first will eventually come, and with it their check. Those women who decide to work instead of eking out a welfare subsistence find they can't earn enough in the marginal minimum-wage jobs that are out there. But even with the depressing reality of these conditions in mind, Sugar characterized those who do little or nothing to enhance their checks as "weak, fat girlfriends layin' up with nothin' to do all day but watch the soaps."

> You don't want to be no welfare bitch—which is just an ignorant, loud-mouth, collect-a-check, don't-do-nothin', don't-comb-her-hair, don't-keep-her-kids, just-don't-care-who-knows-her-business type of broad. That's who she is. You can talk about welfare with other women, but you don't tell your business out loud in a parking lot! There's a certain protocol.
>
> No way would I do that. I'm a hustler, and I have faith that the Lord is going to make a way for me. And my faith is not in man. So if the office is closed, I'm cool. If I'm standing at that window and they're telling me my food stamps aren't there, and they really aren't there, then maybe there's a lesson in there for me. Maybe there's a reason

why my food stamps aren't there. My faith is in the Lord. I'm goin' to eat. I don't know what I'm gonna do, but I'm goin' to eat. I'm gonna pawn my rings. I'll go over to Grandma's. There's any number of people I can call. These aren't people I could say, give me a thousand dollars, but a meal, that I could ask for. There's no way I could look my kids in the face and say we not eatin'.

And I'd never bring my kids to the welfare office. Because kids don't need to see it. They don't need to grow up knowing that welfare is their daddy. Kids can grow up and not know they're on welfare if you try hard. But you can't deny it bringin' 'em into the office.

It's like if their daddy's in jail. You don't take them into the jail because then they get a whole sense of it, a feel, a smell. As long as it's just in their mind, they don't have nothin' to really attach it to. You bring 'em to the welfare office with those unhappy people waitin' around all day, then they know what welfare is. It makes a mentality that they don't need to have. It's a handicap. Because then they know that they're different than other kids.

Repealin' welfare means you gonna find more newborn kids in trash cans. You're gonna find more crime, more drugs, more violence. People are gonna be frustrated. It shouldn't be this way, but sometimes welfare is people's only hope. If you're struggling for the month, sometimes your only hope is that the first is coming. That might be the only thing that keeps you from killing these kids, beatin' 'em, throwing yourself over a bridge, droppin' 'em out this window. If you can just hold out till the first and you get your check. On the first, you feel better and they feel better, and you can hold out till the next first of the month. It lends some hope.

If the government takes away their checks, welfare mothers will be up the creek. It'll be a struggle. Every day they'll feel like shit. They wouldn't start robbin' banks or whatever, but their lives would be even more dilapidated. The only jobs they could get would be just like welfare, only worse. You can't tell somebody that they're gonna get some positive feelings sweeping sidewalks for forty hours, and they're supposed to feel some satisfaction about going to work to earn your food stamps and your check. They're gonna be a mean, disgruntled bunch of bitches. Ain't nobody gonna be able to stand 'em. They're not gonna have any purpose. At least if you're on welfare, you have the purpose of staying home, taking care of your kids, keeping the cleanest house on the block, being able to go to maybe some PTA meetings, and everything.

And now, the government's beatin' you up for doin' it, and for valuin' being a mother. If you take that away and you say, sweep sidewalks all day for this funky-ass check, there'd be a whole class of really mean people with nothin'. No dream, no nothin'.

FIELDNOTES: *One day I used the word "proactive" to give Sugar my feedback to her welfare story. She didn't know what it meant. After I defined it, she gave me her usual response to unfamiliar words when they came up: "Yeah, that." She recognized herself as a woman who doesn't wait for things to happen to her; she takes charge, she schemes, she grapples with reality instead of meekly accepting what comes her way.*

Sugar knows she is different from what she considers the typical woman in the hood who simply "goes along." Like Sugar, ordinary welfare mothers are "broke, broke, broke." And although some women have scams or businesses to supplement their checks, most do little that would help them emerge from what can become an insidious welfare dependency. Sugar recognizes this, and she has predicted the panic that would ensue when welfare reform results in mothers losing the checks they have placidly been cashing month after month. They have nothing else, she explained, and even before the government "gits a broom and sweeps bitches offa welfare," women will be twirling around helplessly, unable to envision a life different from the one they have been dealt.

I have seen this same kind of fatalism among women in highland Guatemala. Recently, I interviewed some market women whose businesses were being undermined by cheaper competitive goods from Mexico. I asked them what they were planning to do about making a living in the future. They shrugged and said, "Well, when we can't do this, we'll do something else." They weren't scrambling around looking for new products, customers, or investment opportunities. They accepted their struggles as God's will, something to be reckoned with day by day.

Although it may be too much of a generalization, I believe that there is an important connection here: Guatemalan women and welfare mothers lack the basic resources required to be either entrepreneurial or proactive. It is only the rare woman, like Sugar, who manages to drag herself out of the gender constraints her life imposes, be it a lack of capital, education, or family support.

To exacerbate their impoverished situations, in both these cases, women are culturally assigned to be mothers who are supposed to manage pretty much on their own. The men in their lives either can not or will not provide for them. Thus, as the providers of last resort, the women must juggle their meager resources in order to clothe and feed their kids.

Neither has enough money, not from welfare nor from meager market sales. Living on a difficult financial precipice means these women are very vulnerable. As a result, they must turn to the unreliable men in their lives for some level of support, no matter

how minimal. They are often obliged to accept the attentions of abusive or irresponsible men because they have no alternative. Old boyfriends who drop by once a year
with $50 for the baby are not greeted with disdain, but rather with open arms.

Once women on the edge are denied their welfare checks and are really scrambling,
they will be forced into accepting even more mistreatment from men. And, as Sugar
says, there will be more screaming on the streets and more babies in trash cans. I agree
with her that being pushed off welfare might be an opportunity—for some women.
But for most, job training, microbusiness loans, or minimum wage salaries are too
little, too late.

TBE   So, are you glad you spent seventeen years on welfare?
ST   Can I say that welfare has been very very good to me? Welfare's
       great. Because if you have the thought to, the want to, the will to,
       you can use welfare as the basis for getting what your family needs.
       I guess that's the way it was intended.

"GOIN' ON WELFARE IS WHAT YOU DO"

Well, you know, I've been on welfare on and off for a thousand years.
I went on welfare the first time when I was eighteen. It was 1977. I
was pregnant with Dolly. In those days, they gave a pregnant girl a
check, so I went. I was living with my mom and I had been working
when I got pregnant. I did work out the Christmas season. I had a job
selling clothes at a department store downtown. I've worked since I
was thirteen years old, when I did janitorial at the finance center.
When I was about fifteen, I worked at the airport, and then I went to
the telephone company when I was about seventeen. Then I went to
the state. I went from there to the Post Office. And I went from there
to Prudential. In between, there was a real estate office and various
temporary jobs.

I was about three or four months pregnant and I stopped working.
It was about when I was first showing and my clothes started to be
tight. And after that job I didn't get another job. Just stayed home
bein' pregnant. Hung out with Ernie T. I knew I didn't have to work
then. I didn't have a lot of needs. I lived at home. It's not like I was
startin' some college fund for this kid or anything. So why not enjoy
your pregnancy?

I wasn't getting any more than $120 a month before I had the baby.
After Dolly was born, it was maybe $220 or something like that. I

lived with my mom till Dolly was four months old. At that time, you didn't have to live independently to get a check, so it was the best of both worlds.

Goin' on welfare is what you do. It's like, there's money for you, go get it. You lay down with the man, you done got pregnant, you goin' to have a baby, you might as well get a check. It's almost like a bonus. I was building up my little hope chest and getting my stuff ready for my baby. And my mom didn't have the money to do that. I didn't have a lot of options. Maybe they were there, but I wasn't aware of 'em.

In my community, the images kids have of success are definitely lacking. There's not that many role models. What's typical is to become a mom. So success is either that you can make it in the hood, which you can with the child, or that you're Janet Jackson, which is so far out in the universe, you ain't never gonna be it. You don't see no in-between. You don't know women who went to college or had a certain level of success, whatever that is. You don't see Susan Taylor Smith, the editor of *Essence*. It's like, "Well, my mom's a cook over at the elementary school, and she had me when she was seventeen. She's made it." That's your model. You don't see that there's higher than the cook. That is success to you. And, in terms of gettin' a check, if I saw my mom slavin' at some poor cafeteria job with no more success than somebody's mom who was on welfare, it wouldn't exactly entice me to go on welfare, but it wouldn't discourage me either. Welfare or crummy job, the picture of success looks the same.

Mostly everybody my age had kids when they were young. Everybody did it. I don't know of any of them that wasn't on welfare. Nobody. It's kinda like, why wouldn't you? If they're givin' free money down the street, you go get it! Specially if you're comin' from a single-parent family. It's not like you have a dad and a mom who say, "We're here to work with you, and we will support you. We'll take care of your needs." If you had a single mom, like my mom, it's not like she was going to get an injection of money just because I was pregnant.

There's no shame. You just go get welfare. Nobody would look down on you for going to get welfare. You'd be more ashamed not to! If you didn't, everybody'd be, "Free money? Girl are you crazy?" You'd look pretty stupid if you didn't go get it, especially if you weren't workin'. Why wouldn't you? You're not crazy; so you go get your check! You're basically better off. You're seventeen, you're pregnant, and you got money coming every month.

Of course, you always had a man. But same as it is now, men didn't have no money. And if we're lookin' at when we were seventeen, then they're still livin' at home with their moms like we were. They had to contribute to their mom's house if there was any money at all. If they do anything, it was maybe to buy a little something for their kid. And, maybe being on welfare gave you a little better status 'cause you had a hold on your man. When you got your food stamps, he could come eat. Opposed to a girl who didn't have a kid. Plus you had that bond with your kid, so that gave you the added edge of keeping your man a little longer.

In the day, welfare was a way out. You could get an apartment. You could get in a project. You could get your own food stamps. You could get your own checks. You had money. You could go shopping. You had your own baby. It was a way out of your mom's house. Or it was a way out of childhood. Or it was a way out of nothingness. It gave you a status. You moved from not having an identity to being a grown-up mom with your own life.

But you don't get pregnant in order to get on welfare. Hell no! All fifteen-year-old girls—black, white, or Mexican—have a boyfriend. They're sixteen, they're seventeen. Not all of 'em, but a good amount of 'em have been sexually active. You're not thinkin' that you'll have more money if you have more kids. White people think you're having more kids to get more welfare. You don't do that. You just have babies 'cause you like 'em. They're fresh, they're pretty. They give you something to do all day. Give you something to show off. I mean, if you got one baby and you're on welfare and your house is clean, people just say that she keeps a nice house. It's not that hard to take care of one kid. But the girl with five! Hey, if you've got five, you're doin' somethin'! You are a helluva woman! You are a helluva girl! So that's somethin'.

And you been raisin' kids all your life, so you know how to take care of 'em. And it's not a "wanna." It's just something you do. You don't sit around wanting to be saddled with a baby. A crying, kicking, screaming, throwing-up thing. But they're mostly cute. So it's not all the time that they're a pain.

In our community, there's not that many women who decide not to have children. Honey doesn't have kids, and I feel sorry for her. But that's not common. And that's another thing, Honey couldn't have any kids, so Honey always had to work. She didn't have any choice.

After Dolly was born, I went back to work pretty quick. When she was four months old, I got off of welfare. I wanted to work. I never didn't want to provide for my child. Welfare people want to work, and I could get a job. Like I said, I worked for the state. It was great. I loved it. I grew up in that job. I loved the people. It enabled me to widen my world. I think that was something I wanted to do before I had the terminology or was conscious of it. I learned a lot there. I learned how to talk. I learned how to seek. It maybe just planted a seed in me of wanting to know more. I learned that there was a bigger world outside of my world. I learned how to deal with people on other levels. I mean, here I am, this nineteen-year-old girl, but there were college-educated people, there were people with only a high school diploma—just a big cross section of people that I had to deal with.

There was a lady by the name of Etta Dermitt. She was a sweetheart. She was a little old white woman, and when I came in there for that interview, it was painfully obvious that I couldn't type. And she gave me the job anyway. She would let me stay after work to learn how to use the typewriter. I just loved it. I was like a baby.

And so, I was quite the little worker. I got an award there for being just an all-around good girl, 'cause I had been real helpful and willing to learn. They gave me a $500 cash award and gave me the day off. Honey, I was in seventh heaven! I had my first apartment then. I was paying $125 a month. I bought a little table for my house. By this time I had Tina, so I bought my girls some little things. I loved that job. I was at the job five years.

After that job, I went to the Post Office. I could make way more money! I went from making $5 something to making $11 an hour. So I was outta there. But it wasn't worth it. I was sorting mail and boxes and parcels. I hated it. I was there about a year and a half. Then I quit.

Why? First, I was makin' all this money and hopin' to buy clothes and stuff, but you couldn't wear 'em. 'Cause when you start, you work at night, so I never had any time to wear the finery that I was able to afford now. And it was pissin' me off! So, I'd go in there with, you know, these green shoes matchin' my nail polish. And I had these long nails, and I'd wear wigs and be all coifed up. And I'd be walkin' around there all fine. And it'd get dusty and I'd be breakin' my nails, and I was like, "Look, I'm not doin' this bull work! I'm a lady!"

They tried to kill me at that job. They wanted me to lift heavy boxes. They wanted me to do bullshit work. Maybe it's this welfare thing, but these people don't care what you do as long as you do something. If it was their wife or their mother or their daughter, they'd go, "Honey, don't lift that." But since it's you, and you've been on welfare, you gotta lift eighty pounds!" We had to sort, we had to lift, we had to push.

Plus, I didn't like the management, the way they are trained to treat you. And so I'd get into it with the little supervisor. He was about two feet tall, and he'd point up at you and tell you to go into his office. So, eventually, I'd see him comin' and I'd just go, "In the office! 'Cause I know you and me gonna get into it, so we might as well just go now!"

So I quit. Everybody thought I was insane. For black people, the Post Office job is a dream come true. Who quits the Post Office? They go in there for life. They buy boats. They buy homes. They can't leave! The day they retire they have a heart attack and die. They're in bondage to the Post Office. Gosh, they thought I was crazy. They thought I wouldn't make it. They thought I would fall off the face of the earth. Because they're in such ruts, they don't see a future beyond the Post Office. They're slaves to the things they have been able to buy from getting these big fat paychecks. But they are just zombies and slaves.

I remember when I first started, I wouldn't want to tell the men that I would meet that I was workin' at the Post Office 'cause I know they'd go, "That woman works at the P.O.!" And they'd wanna get at me just for that. I wanted them to think I was just a babe. I didn't want them to think I had money! Get out!

But there's something else that people don't see. Something that money cannot buy: there's a value being home with your kids. I had more money than I'd ever had, and I was spending it like heck. I lived in an apartment and I had to be at work at eleven o'clock at night. I used to take my kids out to the baby-sitter. It was horrible. For a time, I packed my kids up and sent 'em to live with my mother-in-law, Grandma, because it was just too much of a chore. I remember that I would come home and I'd be dead tired. Well, I had these toddlers that I couldn't deal with because I had this job at night. And I didn't have a whole heck of a lot of help.

There were times when they would call mandatory overtime. After working this hard-assed shift all night, they'd tack on two to four hours at their discretion. If you got young kids, maybe your baby-sitter has to go to work. You don't have the luxury of two to four hours. You gotta go. If you tell 'em you gotta go, they're goin' to get rid of you. So, it was slavery.

I'd be so tired after working the night shift that I'd just fall asleep when I got home. Grandma got the kids off to school, but I would have to go get 'em in the afternoon. Several times the school would call and say, "Tina is sitting here in the office." I'd have forgotten my child! I slept through. And I'd just think of Tina sitting there thinking, Where's my mom? Everybody else's mom had already come and got them. I couldn't say, "Well, baby, I'm making $11 an hour, so it should be worth it for you, even if some days I'm gonna forget you." They don't understand that. When all the other kids are leavin', happy to see their mom drive up, pull up, walk up, they wanna go too. I decided these were important, formative years and that's *not* gonna be my baby's memory of her kindergarten years: how many days she sat in the office and waited for me to come in all groggy after I had forgotten her! So I quit. Got the hell outta there. It wasn't worth it for my child to be at school feeling abandoned.

One of the other things about the Post Office and why I didn't think it was worth it was that Grandma would talk about me behind my back. And she doesn't care, she'll talk about you in front of your kids, to your kids. There was one time she told my kids that I wasn't at work, that I was at home in bed with some man. I love Grandma, but she's bitter. That's her thing. But that right there wasn't worth it.

The money I was making wasn't important enough for me to miss my kids' formative years. Those are the years that you bond. Those are the years that you instill in them the values that's hopefully gonna keep them from bein' some horrible person. Society should value that work, 'cause the son that I don't raise right is the boy that's gonna hit you in your head, steal your stereo, break in your house. You should be glad that I want to stay home, if that's what I'm doin'. There's a lot of parents that are not doin' that. And maybe they are just simply welfare leechin', but I was tryin' to raise my kids. So, no, I didn't think it was a fair trade.

So I didn't always wanna work. In 1980, I went on welfare again when I got pregnant with Tina. It was during my maternity leave from my job, when I didn't have any income. So I went on welfare for a while. Then I went back to work. The next time I went on welfare was in 1986. But by then I had also lost some of the impetus to go to work because I had started bein' on drugs, and I knew I could survive and hustle just as good without gettin' up and goin' to work. So, I thought, hey! I could stay home and lead the same life! And somebody else could be slavin'.

There was one time a few years after that I got off because I didn't want to keep hustlin' the welfare system. I wanted to see if I could make it just doin' hair. So I quit. I just stopped sending in my status reports, and, of course, they cut you off. But I ended up having to go back on. Number one, I couldn't make it on hair. It wasn't steady enough. It wasn't organized enough. I didn't know anything about running a business, promotion, marketing, bottom line, cash flow, getting loans, nothin'.

Number two, housing wasn't going to help me. I was thinking, if I had a house, I could probably hustle up the rest. Or I could try. But I didn't really get a chance. I couldn't go down there and say that I don't want a check; that I want to see if I can do hair; that I just need housing. The housing people wanted to know how you were supporting yourself if you weren't getting a welfare check. I couldn't tell them about the hair. I'm not licensed. It's basically illegal. I needed to keep my housing, but I didn't have any legitimate income to report. So I had to go back on. But my desire was not to continue bein' a welfare fraud. I'm a good girl. I desire to do right. The system just wouldn't let me.

It's like if a whore wants to whore, and she's making good money enough to feed her kids, and all she needs is housing, let her do that. But you can't. It's a judgment thing. Being a ho may not be bad to her. But if you go to them and tell them that, they'll take your kids from you. Rather than helping you with what you need! Maybe she only needs a house. She doesn't want the rest of your money. But you have to take their values in order to get their check.

"YOU DON'T WANNA BE ON WELFARE FOREVER"

The thing about goin' off of welfare is the risk, weighin' the financials and everything. It's scary. It's scary to even think of the prospect of it because you're so secure at home. But you don't wanna be on welfare forever. And you wanna get off by yourself. You don't want them to kick you off.

Once I was talkin' to my girlfriend Patty. She couldn't believe it. She's like, "You would give up your food stamps?!" Patty's like, no matter what comes up, she can always figure out how you need to stay on welfare rather than tryin' to do more. I wanna be self-sufficient. I wanna make a contribution. I want to show my children a good example.

I've always wanted to be legitimate. I've been blessed with a lot of skills and talents, and if I can make 'em work for me, somebody else can get my check. Because I am able and there's a lot of people that's not able. I want to break the generational cycle, to show my kids a different example of how to succeed in our life. I don't want to see two more welfare mothers come out of this. I want them to see some college. I want them to see some knowledge. I want them to see some successes that are unlike my successes hustlin' the system (though they will be *based* on my successes). Each generation is supposed to be better than the last generation, and I've seen too many families where that is not the case. Families with another fifteen-year-old mother of a fifteen-year-old mother of a fifteen-year-old mother. I want to see a change. I want me to be the last hustler. I want me to be the last schemer. I want them to be able to do things legitimately.

I don't dream too big. No doctors are gonna be drivin' through the hood in their BMW's lookin' to marry my daughters. But they're not gonna be screwin' the dope dealer either! My kids will be different, and it will spill over into all areas of their life, even to their relationships. Maybe because I've always been a hustler, had a hustler mentality, done hustler types of things, liked hustler type of men, maybe they will be exposed to legitimate men with legitimate concerns, with legitimate interests.

It's like, I want them to know that they can want a man, be a part of a team. If you stay married to welfare, you can't even think about marrying somebody else. A man don't do for you what welfare does, but you gotta give up somethin' to get somethin' else. If you find somebody that you're sayin' you wanna marry, in fact, what you're sayin' is you gotta let this welfare stuff go. You can't have both pieces. It's either/or. And I want to show them what married people do, that they get out there and they make it.

"I DON'T KNOW THAT WORK GIVES YOU THIS GREAT HIGH"

The whole thing about the system is it's not necessarily about welfare versus work. I don't know that there's any incentive to want to work just for the sake of work. Unless you make so much money that it makes a difference. It's about who that person is. Take me, for instance. The curiosity about the world outside my neighborhood is what I've always had, not some desire to go to work. Okay, if I hadn't worked, I would not have been as exposed to the world. I enjoyed bein' around people. I enjoy words, reading—and those are things that I know my mom instilled in me. But the work itself, it ain't no big deal. I enjoyed what I was doin' at work. I enjoyed working on the computer, the filing, the interacting with people that I knew were college educated and had a different life than me. But I'm no different just because I worked.

It was easier to get jobs back when I was in high school. Schools were real good about helping you find employment. They don't have the same programs now to help kids find decent-payin' jobs. I worked in movie houses. I worked for the telephone company. I thought I had a pretty good job there. I felt necessary. I had my own desk. I had a phone. I had my own little Rolodex. I was about fifteen then. I felt good. I was making minimum wage. I made my own money. I was able to help my mom.

Even with all those jobs I never made very much money. I didn't have any better clothes than other kids. There wasn't that big of a difference. I remember kids that had stuff that I wanted, but I couldn't get it. I remember the money that I saved to get a pair of boots, and they were like the generic brand of the boots that were in fashion. They were like the cheapest "pleather." Lots of those kids were probably getting a welfare check, and they had better clothes than I did.

I remember that the most obvious badge of a welfare kid was free lunch. If the kid in line in front of you had one of them cards— welfare! Outside of the lunchroom, you didn't know who had two parents and who was on welfare. But there was a lot of 'em. I'm pretty sure my mom got welfare. There's no difference between welfare and a low-income kid whose mom is working and slaving her ass off. They're eligible for free lunch too. We were all in that lunchroom together. You're the same.

I don't know that work gives you this great high that the white man wants us to have from it. The high comes from being able to do for your kids. It's being able to have the things that you need and want, however you can get 'em. The satisfaction comes from that. It ain't from some damn work! If you can get those rewards some other way, it's just as valuable. I remember working—I felt good at work, but when I came home hauling my ass, I was living at the same level as girls who didn't work.

There was a time when I lived in this low-income apartment complex. All my girlfriends lived there. That was the time when I worked for the state. I loved my job. Meanwhile, most of my girlfriends were gettin' a check. But they didn't think it was silly that I was working. They don't look down on working women, 'cause some of them worked too. There were times when they worked and when they didn't work. Bernice didn't work. Gina didn't work, she sold dope. Sheila didn't work. Angel worked, but she didn't have kids. Suze didn't work. The girls that didn't work, they'd kick it, watch soaps, keep their house neat, dress their kids, hang out with their nig.

I was making $6 an hour working full-time. So what's that? Eight hundred a month in my check? I paid $350 rent. I paid day care. I had to buy a bus pass. I bought work clothes. My girlfriend Gloria had two kids. Her welfare check was about $350, and maybe she got $250 in food stamps. Section 8 back then would have been about $30 rent. Anyway, we were both just scraping by.

I had to get my kids ready before I went to work, so I had to get up early! I would catch four buses a day: I would haul these two kids out there, I would wrap them in blankets, I would feed them on the bus.

The funny thing is that even though I'm up hauling my ass out every day, I'm livin' the same low-income existence as my girlfriends on welfare. My house was clean and theirs was too, but I had to clean up when I got home from work and pickin' up the kids. On Saturdays, we'd pack up and go to the laundromat, me and Gloria. We shared a shopping cart. We weren't different. Our kids looked the same. On Easter we bought the same kinds of clothes. We lived the same life. My work didn't make a difference. On the Fridays when we went out, we looked the same. None of us drove, 'cept Gina, who was selling dope. There's no difference. The biggest deficit was not in cash. It was in the time I spent with my kids. The quality of my life. The energy that I would have. How I felt. And you can't bank that.

When I stopped working and got a check, I felt better not having to get my ass out in the cold, catch four buses. I felt better stayin' at home, scrubbin' my kids, makin' sure their hair was combed neatly, sending them out, being there if the school called, going to all the school programs, being able to applaud my children as they played whatever vegetable in the school play, going to be a room mother. I felt better doin' those things. I've seen it from both sides.

Each month whenever you get your status report, there's one form you fill out that says, "Would you be interested in jobs? And if so, what types of jobs would you like training in, etc. And if not, why not?" So I've filled those out. And there's been times I filled 'em out, "No, I wouldn't be interested." For instance, when I had a newborn infant. Or I remember filling one out when I just got my boys, two new kids. I didn't want to go to work. I wanted to stay home and get them acclimated. So there's been plenty of offers of job training, but sometimes I wasn't seeking a job. I wanted to stay home with my kids. My kids needed me. I needed them. I liked the security of being a major player in my children's lives, not being gone at 5 A.M. and not seeing them again until seven at night. I didn't wanna be throwing dinner at them and fallin' into bed. I wanted to be a bigger part in my kids' lives. I've seen that that has had an impact. I don't have any comparative studies that say my kids are better off than somebody else's kids, but I think I got a great group of kids. And I think a large part of that is me bein' home and bein' in all aspects of their life. So bein' home was cool!

Of course, I never told my technician I was a hairdresser. When you go in, you just fill out the paperwork. It's just like machinery. I can fill out the papers so fast. I'm in and out of there like clockwork. Boom. You don't tell and no one asks you. The only way that people get in trouble is if somebody tells on them. A disgruntled lover. A jealous neighbor. Or somethin' of that nature.

Another reason I never went to the job readiness class was that if I did, I knew somebody would say, "This ain't no dumb welfare broad. Put her to work today." There would be no way I could say no, 'cause I been workin' all my life in pretty damn good jobs. I didn't need the job training. And I didn't want to give myself away. I didn't want to have to go talk to these people and they'd go, "She's smarter than the average bitch! She's pretty damn articulate! We need her to be our receptionist right now!" I wanted to be with my kids. So I tried to stay away from situations where I would have to really talk to someone in person there 'cause it's hard for me to shut up and it's hard for me to conceal that I got a little bit of sense. So I didn't go. I knew if they peeled off ten people outta a hundred to get jobs, I would be one of the ten.

Welfare's there for you. Look at it this way. Say there's this distance we have to go. Either you could run it or you could get in this rickshaw. It's free. But you have the choice. I choose to get in the rickshaw. At the end of the race, I'm not sweating. I still have my energy. I'm looking just as composed. You choose to run it. You're sweatin', you're red in the face, you're huffin, you're puffin'.

But if we took that same distance and now added two kids, would you choose to run the race carrying those kids? Or would you say I'm gonna let my kids ride in the rickshaw with me? You'd surely give 'em the ride. Why should they get to the end of the race huffing and puffing? They've done no wrong. They didn't choose to run the race. That was your choice. Why, when I get to the end of the finish line, should those two kids be askin' me, "How come we didn't ride?" And if you're carryin' those kids, you're gonna end up way behind. You're gonna be last. Way last! The race officials have all gone home by the time you get your ass over the finish line.

And your kids are still goin', "Why the hell did we have to do that? The man said we could ride?"

And you're goin', "Honey, it's the principle."

And they don't understand one bit.

TBE   You once said something about every woman being just one man away from welfare. Remember that story we read about the Saudi woman whose husband abandoned her in New York, left her with five kids? She couldn't get any help from the welfare system, and she was so desperate, she ended up throwing some of her kids out the window. And she was a middle-class woman.

ST   Oh God, it was so sad. Her religion played a big part. She didn't have the option of selling her body. I was gonna say, "Why doesn't she just go and get her another man?" At least her kids would eat! But like they said, everything is a ritual and has to be prayed over and gotten permission for. Duh!

TBE   So that was out! Yeah, she was victimized by her religion, her culture, this guy who left her. What did you think about him?

ST   I think he's trash! Here's this guy that's supposed to be a Muslim, has beaten this woman over the head with religion, from covering her head up to covering her feet up, to raising her kids a certain way, to not eating pork. She now is starving and can't even eat a baloney sandwich at the welfare office! Because he's indoctrinated her with all this total crap.

TBE   That poor woman, I can't stop thinking about her.

FIELDNOTES: *From the first day we met, Sugar talked about getting off welfare. She wanted the Coretta King Center's small-business training so badly that she made a fuss when she heard the program wasn't starting until the following week. I liked her attitude and one day at her house I asked her why she wasn't comfortable on welfare. She explained that if she were indeed the person she thought she was, she had to get off the dole. She recited one of her favorite sayings: "All of my help comes from* the Lord." She quickly added, "I can't be sayin', 'All of my help comes from the welfare office!' On Sundays, I go to church, I don't go to worship at the food-stamp office."

"WHY ARE YOU WAITIN' FOR SOME WHITE BUREAUCRAT TO COME SAVE YOU?"

To be seen as a welfare mother says "I don't have control." And it's demeaning to have to say I have no control. Welfare says that and more. It says you're not grown up and taking care of business. The only business I can take care of is on the first, when I get my allowance from "daddy."

I wanna have some control. Like when the government shut down a couple of years ago. It was jeopardizing whether or not your check was gonna come on time. Chaos! Gosh, they had one woman on TV who was sayin', "I need my check. I gotta have my check. I got this, I got that to do." Well, what do you do when there's no check?

Me, I got a hair hustle. But what do I do when there's no hustle? Pawn! There was times when I was down to pawning my last trinkets, after I done pawned everything of real value. It was to the point where I was thinkin' I could probably go get $25 for this ring, maybe $15 for that one. I was that far away from bein' broke; everything else was already in the pawnshop. But I stayed calm, even though I hated to be broke. I really hated it. 'Cause it showed I didn't have no control over my own life! And all the time they're tellin' you to go out and get a job. But I can't take just any job, 'cause minimum wage is bullshit. You know I can't work for $5 an hour. I'd go crazy. It's not worth gettin' offa welfare for $5 an hour. You can't do nothin'. You'd kill yourself for nothing. Five dollars an hour is shit.

I read this story about a welfare mom in New York. She was living in squalor! A horrible place with rats and no furniture. And she was so depressed! All she was doin' was sitting there waiting for her welfare worker. To me, squalor would be a motivator, not a source of depression. All I could think of was, why did she only have a cot? I just didn't understand that because I know how I am. We would've had something, if only a box, a vegetable box, covered up with a rag, that would've been a little table. A bedstand, orange crates, milk crates, two bricks and a board. A lot of times, kids don't know that they're poor. Her kids—she had two—would have seen that their mom was tryin' to make it better. And those little things almost would have looked like furniture to them. Here she was waiting all day for this welfare worker to come bail her out. I just woulda done more. I didn't understand why she didn't have anything in the midst of her poverty.

I imagine there are places like that in Springfield, but Springfield has so many resources. You can go down two alleys and furnish your house. You can have a mattress. Why was there only a cot? She was on the first floor, she could have dragged anything in there. You can be poor, you can even be relyin' on welfare, but there's things that you can do to make it better for your kids. Why are you waitin' for some white bureaucrat to come save you? Try to save yourself. Maybe they'll see that and maybe they'll feel a little more compassion, and you'll get your check quicker. I don't know why some people don't use everything that is within their power.

I've always said if I was homeless, I'd go to one of these boarded-up houses and I would pull up a board and I would go in. I wouldn't be out there on the streets. And I'd stake out about seven houses and go to a different one every night and go in and sleep. I would be sheltered. I remember saying that if I couldn't feed myself or my kids, I would go to the grocery store and eat. I would go down the aisles and eat in the store. I would take my kids. It probably wouldn't be enough. Maybe I'd get arrested. Maybe I'd get some publicity. Maybe somebody would give me a meal. But I wouldn't sit and tell my kids, "There's nothing to eat, babies. Mommy doesn't have anything." I would get it. I would just get it. So a part of me just doesn't understand that total hopelessness.

FIELDNOTES: *Sugar doesn't like to cook, and she hates to shop for food. Nonetheless, I think a visit to the supermarket represents an exciting challenge for her because it allows her to put her coupon system to the test.*

Look, you know I am the coupon queen. The last time I did coupons I saved $49 on my groceries. And that's not even with double coupons! I got people who stare at me in the store! One girl said, "Tell me how you do that!" It's my scientific shopping! You gotta remember that I'm buyin' what's gotta last for a month. Next month I'll have more food stamps. So I got my method. If I got a coupon for fifty cents off any size, I buy the smaller, cheaper size. It don't make no sense for me to use my coupon on the big size even if the unit price is better, 'cause I'm on a limited monthly budget. My girlfriends laugh at me. They just go in and throw stuff in the basket. They don't clip coupons, so their shopping's done in thirty minutes. I spend one hour per $100. I got it figured to a science.

Back when I was on welfare, I got $469 in food stamps, and, of course, I'd tithe. I'd give away 10 percent of those food stamps to whoever needed 'em so they'd bless somebody. I'd give 'em to my sister or I'd send 'em to my mom; I'd give 'em to Gloria, the man on the street: whoever was in need. So then I had $400. I'd buy two newspapers every Sunday to get my coupons, plus I'd get them from my mother-in-law if she had any. And I'd clip 'em out of mail things. I'm still a coupon clipper. It takes me almost an hour to do my coupons. Usually I save 10 percent every time I go to the store. I figure I'm savin' $49 per hour of clippin'.

I always shop at Safeway. It's the best place for me. I know the Safeway like the back of my hand. So that's my store. If I go to another store that I don't know, it will take me twice as long. The people at Safeway know me when I come in the door. They know I'm getting two carts. I already have my little sign that I tape on to the first cart when I park it—it says, "Please do not remove, customer still shopping." All the checkers hate to see me comin'. Cabdrivers hate to see me too. But I take my time, and we eat to the end of the month.

We basically eat anything and everything that we want. I plan a few meals, like if I want burritos or we're having Tuna Helper. I buy a lot of cereal, fresh produce, cans. I buy a lotta fruits and vegetables in cans so we can get our five fruits and vegetables per day. We eat real good. That's why I feel bad when I hear a child sayin', "Mom, can we get Applejacks?" And she says, no, those are too expensive! Bullshit. Cut a coupon and let that baby have Applejacks. He's already in a welfare mind state, thinkin' he can't get nothin'. You get food stamps once a month. This is supposed to be the payoff, and he can't even get Applejacks. We got Applejacks, Pops, Snaps, Cocoa Puffs. And why? Because I'm a hustler.

It wasn't always like this. Before I got my hustle goin', we struggled like most poor folks. I remember when me and Gloria used to live near each other. Gloria would never buy paper products. You can't use food stamps for nonfood items, so she'd hold off buyin' 'em. I remember times when she'd be down to one roll of toilet paper, and she'd be doling it out sheet by sheet. It's a welfare mentality thing. But she was so used to it, that it wasn't even somethin' that she thought about.

People on welfare, you gotta ration. You go without paper towels.

You go without napkins. You don't buy cleaning supplies. Your non-food items, you just can't get 'em. You don't buy Ajax. You buy bleach. It is a multipurpose cleaner. You may think about nonessentials, but you know you can't have 'em. You don't buy shampoo, so you wash your hair with soap.

But eventually, you have to break down and buy some things. Somehow you find the money for deodorant. You buy stuff for your period 'cause you gotta bleed. But it's a sacrifice. And you can't necessarily always buy *good* stuff, so you buy something cheap that's gonna chafe you between your legs and feel like a damn mattress.

I don't know if it's still like that today. When I go to the nail salon, it's full of welfare mothers. I can tell 'cause their kids are with them and they're unruly, and it's the first of the month, which is a telltale sign. And I see 'em payin' anywhere from fifteen to twenty-five dollars, more if you get your nails decorated. And they're gettin' their hair done. And they're getting their toes done. But they probably ain't buyin' paper napkins.

My mom says they should learn to do their own nails. But, hey, the way I see it, these girls deserve it. If day in and day out you been doin' nothing for yourself, you wanna go and spend twenty dollars; you want to peel it offa that check on the first of the month and go do something for yourself. The rest of the month you ain't got shit, you ain't gonna get shit, ain't nobody gonna do nothin' for you. You won't have no more money comin' in. So you gotta find your pleasure on the first of the month. God bless 'em.

"POVERTY DOES NOT MAKE YOU DIRTY"

There's a welfare stigma. Like, say I go to a club. Well, on the first, there's more women in the club. It's almost like the regular customers can pick 'em out: "She's only here on the first, must be spendin' that check!" If you only go out on the first, that says something about you. You live off of a check! It's kind of obvious. You got on a new outfit. Your hair is done. Your nails is done. But the regulars know they won't see you no more this month.

I don't want to be perceived like that. People won't see you. They don't talk to you the same. I want 'em to know Sugar. And I want my opinion to count if there's a discussion goin' on and I have something to say. I am smart and I am knowledgeable. And I don't want 'em to go, "Welfare broad, shut up! You don't have nothin' to say." I do have somethin' to say.

I don't disdain welfare people. They are me. They are my cousin, my sister, my girlfriend. But it bugs me if a woman keeps her kid dirty. I don't see a reason to be nasty. Poverty does not make you dirty. Poor, rich, I wouldn't care what your financial status, but if you're not takin' care of your kids, that I disdain.

I know that I'm armed with some things that a lot of people aren't. And I know that some of the things I am armed with, even rich people don't have. The peace that I have, the faith that I have. I don't worry. I know the Lord's got me covered. That's not a rich or poor thing. But it helps me deal with a lot of the issues that poverty brings. But then again, it would help a Rockefeller deal with some of the things that their money brings.

I think somethin's wrong about makin' people feel bad about things they can't help. I think there's something wrong in judging people because of their circumstance. I think there's something wrong in thinking you don't have something to say because you eat off food stamps. I think that's unfair, it's stupid. And it's another reason why you don't want people to know you're on welfare.

It's like Dolly with this club she was in at school. It's like a high school business group. One time she couldn't get the money to go on one particular trip, and the other kids were all wonderin' why she couldn't get the money. It mostly seems like it's a rich kids' club. She was one of only thirty kids that got into that club, and I didn't want her to let them know she was on welfare because from then on they'd go, "Well, count Dolly out 'cause she's on welfare." They didn't have to know that about her. She deserved a chance to try to prove herself just like they did. She worked hard and earned her own money, and she went on the trip.

FIELDNOTES: *I love to ask my students to debate a controversial theoretical model of peasant reality called "The Image of Limited Good," made famous in the 1960s by the anthropologist George Foster. Foster's idea was that peasants see the world as a pie. Everybody gets a share of the pie at birth containing all the "good" they will have in life, for example, money, land, happiness, and so on. And, basically, you have to be content with your piece because unless you win the lottery—or something equally lucky happens to you—you probably won't be able to increase the size of your piece.*

The problem with Foster's theory is that he doesn't take into consideration the larger world surrounding the peasant village. Who, after all, denies them the chance to improve their piece of the pie if not the rich and powerful for whom they work for pitifully meager wages? His critics wonder if we should blame peasant poverty on the way peasants think, or look to the society at large that has convinced them to passively accept their fate.

Several times over the last few years I've thought of the Image of Limited Good in terms of its application to the African American women I was meeting. As far as I could tell, many of them existed in a world almost as isolated as Foster's peasants. I got this feeling of people from the hood going nowhere—having the same problems, limited opportunities, and truncated possibilities generation after generation. Basically, their shares of the pie stayed small, but was it because they believed they could never cut a bigger one? I didn't think that was the reason. But if they did have this image in their heads, who had conveyed that message to them?

Sugar eschews my social-scientific political economy of the hood. She hates to fall back on what she calls "the white man did this to us" excuse for the behavior of her neighbors and friends. She prefers a micro-level model of analysis somewhat akin to the Image of Limited Good.

Welfare mothers dream just like everybody else. Some of their dreams are just dreams, and they don't expect them to become a reality. It's just a nice thing to do. They dream of maybe havin' more of a soap-opera life, of getting things. Everybody dreams of having a man. Some of the others, they're tryin' to hit the lottery, maybe play the dogs, occasionally play bingo. But they don't dream that big. A dream is a new dress, not a $100,000 home. You're not figuring out how you can save your money to get this dream. Your dream can be realized on the first of the month. Your dream can be realized by screwin' the right nigger. Your dream can be realized by borrowing $10 from your mom.

Sometimes you can escape into a kind of fantasy. I used to watch the soaps when I was pregnant at home. It lets you out the house without getting out of the house. So that's why women do it. I always say I like soaps because you can fuss at 'em and they never fuss back. So you can say, "Bitch, why'd you do that? Ah, you're so stupid! You're screwin' her man!" And she'll never say, "Well, bitch, get a life!" You can vent on them. You can live vicariously through them. You can be glamorous. All the things that soaps are that you don't get to do. Of course they eat up a large chunk of your day. By then your kids are coming home or your old man comes home if you got that. It's like a bubble pops, pooof! And you look around you. No glamour, I haven't cleaned my house, I haven't done any laundry, I haven't done a damn thing. End of dream.

When you're on welfare, you live from check to check. If you can make it with that, then that's cool. But you can basically die there. The only way you can see of making things better is to screw the dope dealer and hope he falls in love with you. And then maybe he'll kick you out some of his stuff, he'll do things for you, he'll help you. You'll have rings 'cause a lot of tweekers give him rings and jewelry for drugs. Stereos and TVs, too. So that's one way to get a higher level of status. Or you can have a supportive family—mothers, sisters, uncles, grandparents. That's another way. Or you can win somethin'.

"WELFARE IS A JEALOUS LOVER"

Welfare means there ain't no man buyin' your groceries for you. Welfare means you don't get to be married. You don't get to have successful relationships. The most successful relationship you can have is with welfare. Welfare loves you. Welfare gives your kids Christmas presents when your man won't. Welfare makes sure you eat every month. Welfare don't ask you for sex. Welfare don't beat you. Welfare doesn't cuss you out. It doesn't call you "bitch." It doesn't screw other women on the side.

But welfare is a jealous lover. If you have a man, then he's not gonna want to see you sleeping with another man. Welfare had the same mentality back in the thirties or forties whenever it began. They were comin' in to see if you had a man living with you, lookin' in your closets and all. Course if you did, they'd kick you off of welfare. So you got rid of your man 'cause you had to feed your kids. They're not in your face like that now, but if you got a man with you, welfare ain't gonna do for you. And that's how any man would be.

Bein' on welfare allows a man to tell his woman, "Well, you're gettin' a check, so don't be askin' me for nothin'." He's off the hook, financially. 'Cause if she asks him for help with the food or whatever, he'll come back with, "What do you do with the money you get from welfare?" It's like she has another man who's providin' better than he is, so he'll find his reason to not give you money, like, "Well, I can't be with my son, so I'm not givin' you nothin'." Welfare has driven a wedge between black men and women.

For instance, you could choose not to be with your man, to make a choice not to be married or whatever until such time as he can support five kids in the manner that you are accustomed. You can't go to the welfare office and say your man can't find steady work. That the jobs aren't really out there. That he works labor pools or he's a janitor and ain't makin' enough. You can't say you love this man, we want to work it out. We want to make something that will grow up these kids, that will be good for society. Will you help us out? You can't do that. You have to choose the system in order to eat. Basically, what all this boils down to is that you just can't afford to choose love.

"HEY, YOU KNEW I WAS A HUSTLER!"

FIELDNOTES: *When Sugar got her cell phone, I was jealous. She'd be chatting away on her phone when we were in the car, or her kids would track her down in my office. It looked so sexy I wanted one, even though I thought it pointless to waste money on what was essentially a toy. This went on for about a year. Then, the phone company turned off Sugar's phone because she didn't pay the bill. I laughed for five minutes. She defended herself with her usual rap: "Hey, you knew I was a hustler!"*

Legitimate people, their bills come in their name, as opposed to a ton of aliases. I have aliases because I'm a hustler. If you run up a bill, legitimacy and honesty will make you pay the bill off. Hustlin' will make you run up a bill in one name and start fresh in a new name. And when that one is exhausted, you will get another name. I've had a lot of names. There's Lisa, Misty, oh gosh, Sugar, there's Genny, there's Danny. And they're just for little things. So it's not like it's no real big-time hustle. But it's easy, for instance, not to pay the $50 that you owe for the newspaper. They cut off "Danny Barlow's" paper; you reenter it as "Lisa Jones." You get the newspaper for another six months. Like if somebody else's mail comes to your house. I've had times when I would start usin' that name. But I want that to stop. Now I toss stuff like that in the trash. I tell myself, "It's not mine, it ain't fair; do it the right way."

That's another thing. After a while, it's too much of a hassle. You gotta cover your tracks. You gotta remember the lies. You gotta remember who you are. When I write out money orders, I have to sit and go, "Who am I this time?" There's been certain times when I've written a money order and needed to go cash it back and couldn't! Why? Because I signed it Lisa Jones, but I've got no way to prove I'm Lisa Jones. That's one that kinda got me caught. That kind of thing makes me feel a little dishonest, but you get numb to it after a while.

I don't particularly like it 'cause I'm not a lyin' type of person, but it's a survival mechanism.

I want to go straight, but sometimes I still backslide. The other day I was schemin', I was thinkin'. I sez, "Ooh, Dolly, the side of our house is really 3400 Lexington, and there's a door. I could like paint 3400 on the doorjamb and then we could call cable and ask them to come hook cable up at 3400 Lexington, which never existed before, and get cable."

And Dolly sez, "No, mom, just do it right."

She's my little voice of reason, my conscience. But I taught her that.

I don't think honesty has a color. I don't think honesty has a class. But when you're poorer, I think maybe you're forced to tell a few more lies.

"I'M NOT SURE WHERE THIS ENTITLEMENT SHIT COMES FROM"

I think there's a concept that welfare should help people up, but in reality it's not so. They don't give you enough to do anything that would make you want to be better. Not enough money, no real job training. They only give you enough to sustain you where you are, so you become used to it. It's a myth that welfare is supposed to help you pull yourself up by the bootstraps. Welfare alone can't do that because welfare doesn't give you enough to buy any bootstraps! I see welfare as a buffer between you and the street. Take that buffer, add a hustle, and maybe you got your bootstraps. But without your hustle, you might be off the street, but you won't have a life. You'll be stretchin' your $300 every month as far as you can. You'll be existing, not living.

I perceive that I'm a little more literate than a lot of other typical "welfare mothers." They don't know that welfare is supposed to help you start helping yourself, that it's only a base. They haven't seen that happen in the generations before them, never seen anybody take that check and make something more outta it. So they're not aware that that's what it's for. And that's when it really becomes "the dole," when all they know is that if you sit for a month, a check will come. And so they're just sitting there, and somebody's dolin' it out.

A lot of people look at it as their just due: "Handout, nothin'! You owe it to me!" I've seen people in the food-stamp office goin' on like they just deserve it. Stupid Welfare Bitch!

I'm not sure where this entitlement shit comes from. I've seen a lot of it in my friend Patty. She'll go to the welfare place, and if the person is surly, she will inform them that "you are a public servant and I am the public, so you don't talk to me like that. And if you don't like your job, you need to get another one. Blah, blah, blah." I think that's silly. I know the power that that particular person holds over my check. If I cuss you out on a Monday, you lose my paperwork on a Tuesday. Or you press the wrong button and send my check to Timbuktu. So I would never be that brash. Those people are gonna do their job anyway. And so it's not like Patty gets anything extra or anything special from mouthing off. As a matter of fact, it may work against her. Just recently, she went to her technician and she was shooting her mouth off, something about school and finances. So now every month she has to get printouts, lists, all this rigmarole documenting her finances, and is seeing her technician more than ever. All because she couldn't keep her big mouth shut. When I was on welfare, I tried to see my technician as little as possible. I made damned sure my status report was in the mail and everything was cool, and I for sure didn't do anything to rattle my technician's cage.

Patty's like that 'cause she feels like she's entitled. One time we went down somewhere to get a free turkey. And the woman says, "Are you here for the free turkey? Okay, you need to go stand over there." Of course, Patty starts to get all riled up and everything. She's going on and on about how these people are supposed to be public servants and they're supposed to be serving her and all that. And I'm thinkin', "Look, you in here askin' for a free turkey. Get your ass over there with the rest of the people." The woman's dealing with people all day. She doesn't have what it takes anymore to go, "Well, hello! How are you today? Are you here to get the free turkey, honey? Could you please just go over there?" Patty just doesn't understand. The reality of it is that you want the free turkey for your kid.

Patty's on welfare because she's a student. And she has children. And she likes and wants to go to school. She doesn't see an end to school. She told me the other day that she plans on stayin' in college forever. She says white kids do it all the time. They just go to school and go to school and just keep on going to school. So she's gonna stay a student, too. She claims, "I make $33,000 a year between welfare and going to school and everything." She said, "I'm gonna stay put."

For me, everything I do leads to something else. Classes and papers, that's supposed to have an end result. For it not to is lazy, dishonest, and unambitious. I think my poverty is unending, in that I know I gotta keep on struggling. I don't really see a closure to it. I have no nest egg. I have no emergency money or safety net. If something major were to happen, I'd be in trouble. I would have to rely solely on my welfare check. And, eventually, that would take its toll.

FIELDNOTES: *The mundane constancy of grinding poverty is something most middle-class people know little about. To me, its reality is summed up in a well-known diary written by Carolina Maria de Jesus, a São Paulo shantytown dweller. Every morning when she wakes up, Carolina asks herself this question: "How am I going to feed my children today?" Sugar's been lucky and enterprising enough not to have to confront that desperate challenge. Yet, she recognizes that often she is one short step away from trouble. She is not a complainer, but "Broke again" is a common enough refrain of Sugar's to have become her theme song.*

Certainly, a growing number of lower- and even middle-class people are living from paycheck to paycheck or relying on credit to make it through the month. The threat of one day finding yourself with no money is very real to a great number of Americans, in spite of a booming economy. Being one illness or pink slip away from the street is a vulnerable and frightening state, one that is not reserved for Brazilian slum dwellers or welfare mothers.

When I left the Post Office, I moved out of the apartment I had and went to live with my girlfriend. I was waitin' for this retirement money that I would get from the government. I think I was getting a little depressed then. But, eventually, my girlfriend got tired of me staying there and we got into this big fight, and she told me and my mothafuckin' kids to get out.

I've thought about this. This might not have been her motive on the surface, but a lot of times when people find you in a position of needing them, it's funny, but they start to treat you worse. I didn't have any money. I didn't have any place to go. Of course, later she said she didn't mean it and I didn't really have to get out and all that. But when you tell me to get my mothafuckin' ass out, you don't have to tell me twice.

But then the Lord stepped in, and my retirement check from the government came. Oh God, that $5,000 went so fast! I loaned my boyfriend $1,000 that I'm sure he bought drugs with. I gave Grandma some money. My sister. Ernie T. And I found a place, paid up a little bit of the rent, bought some furniture, and the money was gone.

So I was broke again, but no big deal. My lifestyle since I was nineteen has been on a very even keel. The Post Office didn't make a big difference, and bein' on welfare didn't make a big difference. It's pretty much a straight line. You kind of play catch-up. You maintain mentally. Money doesn't bounce around like a ball for me. I am pretty stable in my own mind and with my own faith. That's why it hasn't fluctuated that much.

When I was workin' for the state, I was struggling. Move me to the Post Office, and I catch up. Now I'm able to get furniture. I'm able to get my kids good clothes. I just get to fillin' some of the gaps. I bought clothes, records, music, furniture—things I hadn't had. Now when I leave the Post Office, it doesn't really matter 'cause I've already taken care of the basics. So the money from whatever new job I get just has to go to maintaining this lifestyle. I still didn't have any savings, no bank account. So, basically, there was never much real difference from one job to the next, from working or being on welfare.

After the Post Office, I got a job at Prudential. I was making five somethin' an hour. I wasn't happy. I was a check resolution clerk—was tracing checks, basically—having to go through microfiche. When I left that job, I had to leave a closure notice that said why I was leaving. And I wrote three short words: "Too many females."

Strange. I'd worked with females before. I love females. But this particular area was a secured area, and there were seven women that worked in that area, and we were locked in. I hated it. Their lives revolved around their men. And not only their men, but also all these trivial little things. So come Monday morning, conversation was all, "Wallpaper—I changed mine. Found toilet paper to match." Or, "My husband, this, my husband that." And that was everything that they did! And they'd bring goodies, cheesecakes and everything, and everybody was, like, overweight and stuff. And it was just gross and I wanted out, so I left.

Maybe I worked there a year and a half, if that long. I think I was making $6.10 when I left. I think I liked the work, but I also had begun to dabble with cocaine, and so I was slippin'. I wanted to talk to some men, and not 'cause they were men, but for a different perspective. These women were so narrow in their lives. Do you ever watch sports? Do you all volunteer? Do you do anything outside of these men and this job?

FIELDNOTES: *I had noticed Sugar's references to drugs creeping more and more into her story as she outlined her work history for me. Her dabbling in cocaine seemed to*

be escalating. Finally, I asked her how much coke and crack had to do with her
deteriorating work scene.

It probably is the underlyin' reason for everything. The partying and messin' with cocaine was starting to get serious from 1982 to 1986, but not really steady enough at first so that you could look at it and see it was a problem. But now that I look at it in retrospect, I can see the pattern. You see this fairly steady decline if you look at the big picture.

It seems that if you start messin' with drugs, they start to consume you. Maybe not consciously at first, but you start to wanna spend more time doin' 'em, seekin' 'em, finding ways to get 'em. Soon the only thing that's important to you is partying and drugs and drug people. It's like everybody else is a square. Maybe that's why those females bugged me so much. Like these squares talkin' about their bathroom tissue and their boyfriends and their lives. You start to feel these people weren't about what you were about. I wouldn't consciously say to myself: I'm gonna quit this job so I can do more drugs more better. Instead, I'd say: I'm sick of these females, I wanna get outta here, this job is not for me. I may not have admitted it before, but leaving the Prudential gig was almost a drug burnout thing.

FIELDNOTES: *Our discussions about crack opened up the world of urban drug users as never before. Everyone, everywhere, it seemed, was getting high.*

There's more drugs than you can imagine at the Post Office. I got started at the Post Office. The night-shift people in the Post Office, I remember them bein' a whole subculture. They're isolated. They're night people. They don't get to do the things that daytime people do. And all of a sudden, they've got more money than they've had before, and drugs are this cool thing now: high-class and glamorous. I remember bein' friends with this guy, and we would go home to my house in the morning and start getting high on drugs. The night job finances that. And you have all day free. And you almost don't have to hide because normal people are at work, and your kids are at school, so we'd have this great party.

After that job, I went back to where I worked for a real estate company. One of my good girlfriends worked there. We'd have cocaine in the desk drawer and be snortin'. Duh! And by then we were gettin' more high because by then we had started smoking. To go from powder to rock, that's really a deterioration, even though it feels like escalation. But it was the thing. It was new to Springfield, and it was cool, and the rocks were huge.

FIELDNOTES: *By 1986, Sugar's world was defined by crack. The freebasing that she describes as "social, popular, and cool" had become a much darker force that directed her energies away from work and the family. She was living from pipe to pipe, supporting her habit with her welfare check and her friendship with dope dealers. What had begun as a "party thing" was now an obsession.*

This episode in Sugar's life is one she does not discuss easily. She was addicted to crack for a year and a half, and only stopped smoking it after a near-death experience. Today she talks about the horrors of crack with the zealousness of a reformed addict, and she is very judgmental about drug abusers. At the same time, however, her negative commentary cannot hide the obvious pleasure she took in the drug and in being a well-known partier in the Springfield crack scene.

Like Valium among white housewives, crack has become the drug of choice for many black women, particularly welfare mothers. The mundane and insidious nature of crack addiction is reflected in Sugar's experience as a "tweeker." The scenes she describes may suggest the disordered, pathological nature of the lives of the poor, a factor often utilized by the popular media and conservative critics to explain multi-generational impoverishment. These analysts feel justified in focusing attention on the misbehaving drug addicts themselves rather than on the larger socioeconomic context behind their self-indulgent behavior. However, since we now explain white women's drug and alcohol abuse of the 1950s and 1960s as resulting from suffocating suburban domesticity, should we not look to the fundamental constraints of racism and poverty as reasons for self-destructive drug use in black welfare mothers?

CRACK—A TWEEKER'S STORY

I smoked weed from the time I was fifteen up until I stopped in 1990. One of the main reasons I stopped smokin' weed is that my kids were embarrassed by it. I wanted them to be able to bring their friends home, but they could never come home certain that the house wasn't goin' to smell like a tree, or that their mom's eyes wouldn't be all bloodshot. By that time I wasn't even gettin' high. I chain-smoked the shit. I would have coffee and a joint, over and over, all day long. People smoke cigarettes. I smoked weed.

The other reason I quit was that it was getting costly. I was spending $20 a day to support my weed habit. And I'm thinkin', well, what else could I do with this money?

When I became guardian to my cousin's boys in 1990, I was still smokin'. My own kids knew, but I didn't want the boys to know 'cause of the court hearings and all. So, after I got them, I would smoke in secluded little places, and I would open windows and burn incense and all that. So I was now hiding what I used to do freely. And one day I decided that I either had to tell 'em or stop. And what would I tell 'em? "Okay, boys, sit down. Now this is a joint. Now I smoke it and I get high." I couldn't see that. At the same time, in elementary school, your kids go through this DARE program, Drug Awareness Resistance Education, and I didn't know exactly how far DARE would go. I had this vision of some counselor saying, "Okay, now if your mom smokes one of these, come to me after class." And I end up in jail. So stopping was basically the easiest way out.

Crack was different. Crack first hit big in 1986 or '87 when the gangs started. They brought the drugs in. In those years, I don't think America, or at least Springfield, had seen the real horror of crack yet. We still hadn't begun to see the vampires, as I call 'em. Why vampires? 'Cause when you're on crack you're up all night and you sleep all day. And another thing that makes 'em vampires is you don't see yourself. I remember lookin' in a mirror and I could see that I was emaciated, but I didn't *see* that I was dying.

So, you know, I'm a trendsetter. A new drug? Okay, I'll try it. It was a party thing. Gates was my boyfriend then. We were celebrities because we were throwin' lots of fashion shows. We had the best parties. We prided ourselves that we kept the cleanest pipes, the best rum. We kept our tables clean, everything laid out. We was just rollin'.

And it wasn't costing us nothin'. Gates was a "runner." See when you're in the drug culture, there is a dope house where they sell the dope. Not just anybody can go to the dope house. You could be a narc, you could be the police, you could be anybody. So you gotta know somebody that can go to the dope house. So that was Gates. So you give him your money, and he goes and gets it. This dealer might kick him out some dope for bringing customers. And the customer has to kick him out something for picking up his dope. And in between this door and this car, he done pinched off their dope too! Not only that, but my house started becoming like a dope house. We had the party atmosphere. Gates worked in a bar and was stealing liquor, so we had plenty to drink. We were popular. So people wanted to come smoke. So if you come smoke, you got to give the house somethin'. And then, later, the house gets the first hit. And that was me!

I say "party" 'cause we'd have liquor, and we'd attempt to play cards. That was just to make us think we weren't hooked, that we were doin' somethin' like a party. But we couldn't complete a card game 'cause we were too distracted by the need to go get high.

"I TRIED TO LOOK HUMAN"

The feeling you get when you actually smoke we called a "blast." It feels like you're strapped to the space shuttle. You can almost feel the acceleration of the engine. And then, you hear bells. And you feel . . . I almost can't even remember now . . . strange, and wired, wired, wired. Mostly, it makes you not want to be bothered.

I enjoyed it for maybe the first six months. After that, you think you feel good, but you don't. You're an addict, a tweeker. I got to the point where I didn't want to go out anymore. I began to sleep in my clothes because I knew that at 2 A.M. I'd have to get up because now the party's gettin' ready to start again. When the sun came up, we were all tired and outta dope. That's when we went to sleep.

During the day you just maintain. I'd sleep all day while the kids went to school. Then I'd get up and pretty much do what I had to do to feed and take care of them. I tried to look human. And then it's party time again. I'd get them settled and we'd go in the room we used just for dopin'. We smoked almost daily for at least a year, probably a year and a half.

What was really goin' on was we were deteriorating, we were dyin'! We were crack addicts. But we couldn't see it! We weren't like the addict down in the alley with the dry, cracked lips, beggin' for a hit and smokin' out of cans, got a metal pipe burnin' their lips. But we were thinkin', well, hey, we have a nice house, we have all the dope we want, we aren't scroungin' and scrapin'. Our pipes were coated, our lips didn't get burnt. So we'd tell ourselves we weren't like them. We aren't tweekers. We thought we was "high rollers."

We had our ritual, and we would almost take pride in showing someone else how to do it. Course, lookin' back, we was getting other people addicted. But it'd be like, "Well, hold it like this." And we'd show 'em how to hold it. And, "Hit it like this. And hold the flame just this far from the bowl." So it was this whole ritual, this method that you had to do to get it right. "Here, let me help you, let me help you."

Even the way you would have to pull on the pipe, I remember it's just like, "Well, pull slow, and then pull fast." Then you'd hold it in your lungs. Then we'd hold our nose and blow like into our head. Sick. First you cook it up from powder form and you take it down basically to what is its purest form. You cook it in a vial, with fire, like on your stove, and you put baking soda in. You gotta have precise amounts. The baking soda removes all the impurities, and what you have left is a rock of cocaine, and that is like pure cocaine. 'Cause when you get the powder, whoever is selling it to you has stepped on it, broke it down, put in all these other different things, which could be like laxatives, all sorts of things. So the baking soda and the fire cooks that off, and then you got your pure rock to smoke.

We would have maybe three different pipes or even four—like a straight shooter, this glass pipe that was long and thin, kinda like a pencil only thicker; and then one with a bowl that kinda looked like those things they have in science classes; and round ones that you see in the mad scientist movies, which is totally what we were—mad scientists.

FIELDNOTES: *Crack has worked its way into the hood's subcultures and classes. Sugar's analysis points to the more well-off tweekers as role models for poorer folks aspiring to some of the signs of relative affluence. Working people, welfare mothers, and bums all partake. It is a rare friend of Sugar's whose name is not associated with crack use, either currently or in the past.*

CRACK TEARS EVERYBODY DOWN

Absolutely *everybody* who tries crack will become a tweeker in one way or the other. It's the nature of the beast. Now if you have the means where you don't have to go sell your body or you don't have to beg or you don't have to wander the streets because you've lost your home, then no one will necessarily *see* that you're a tweeker, but it's the same. They think it's glamorous because people with money are able to do it. So poor folks are gonna want to get up to that level, even if doin' the same drug is the only way they can reach it. It makes for a nasty type of equality.

You find the money. And dope dealers will take merchandise to a degree. But most people will get the money 'cause they work. They're already established. By the time you get to a point where you want glamour, you're already at a point where you can get glamour. You already have bank accounts, been on your job for ten years. Glamour is just a further step to the American Dream: "I'm workin' every day. I got the nice car. Now I wanna party pretty too." So the means were there. They don't have to sell their body. They don't have to sell their TVs. They have enough of a buffer between them and poverty for them to believe they're different than the crack addict in the alley—initially.

But crack tears everybody down. Very quickly. Like I said, six months after I was doin' it, the glamour was gone, and I was way addicted. I have pictures of me that look like this coffee stirrer. When I got offa drugs, I wore like a size zero. A size one was too big for me. Now how glamorous is that?

Back then, $300 would get you a good amount of dope. And it'd be gone in a night. If you had seven people with $100 each—and you'd expect them to bring at least $100 if they were comin' to party—that's $700. It's mind boggling. And the average welfare check for most people then was $356. Gone in a night! Then your food stamps are gone the next day. And the rest of the month you just spin around. Your kids get nothing new. They get the bare minimum. You'll sell your food stamps, so you don't have any food. And then you start moochin' off your family. If you have the wherewithal or presence of mind to even *want* to feed your kids, you may send them over your mom's. Or you may have a girlfriend who's also a tweeker. I remember I had a girlfriend who came and stayed with me. We'd buy food together, so we'd have more money for dope and still be able to feed our kids. I remember this girl ended up losing her home, everything. She got into dope too deep.

It's a whole subculture. In the scene, there are players who are pimps, dope dealers, high rollers, gamblers—but these people aren't really users. They have it to prey on weak people. Like I remember when I was at Bennie's Place one night, I met this old dude named Isaac. He says to me, "What do you like? I got whatever you want. You like a little weed, a little blow, a little smoke, anything for a pretty young girl like you." The thing was, he never did it himself, he just kept it as a come-on. It was power!

So a pimp might keep it 'cause if he got a ho that's usin', not only is she gonna work her ass off, but he can reward her. He's got that power, too. The people who *have* drugs have the power. They make lesser people—the ones who don't have the dope—do things. Like the girls who would do anything—sex, head, whatever—for drugs. We used to call them "strawberries." I remember hearing this story about a girl, somebody says to her, "You want this hit, lick that toilet stool." And she did it.

There's any number of women that's in prison now on a drug charge, and likely they're on a drug charge because of a man. Some women would do it on their own, but most often they do it for the glamour that they perceive to be there; and who tells you you're glamorous but men? Well, now we know there is no glamour in crack. Richard Pryor was doin' it, and all these glamorous people were doin' it. So it felt like a bit of the limelight for the rest of us. I think some women get into drugs by themselves, but most women get into it because of men, because of boyfriends. I think any girl who took her first drink probably was offered it by a guy.

Cocaine is supposed to enhance sex. I guess it's some kind of aphrodisiac 'cause it makes people do all kinds of freaky sex. Like there's no inhibitions. So if everybody's havin' a mad crack party, and somebody wants to do sex, get some head or somethin', it's like right there, with everybody sittin' around. If it's a joint thing, and maybe a lot of people have gone in, you're not gonna go in the room and miss your hit or risk somebody stealin' from you or pinchin' offa your dope to get no head. So you get these orgy types of things.

I don't know if I would have been doin' it had it not been drug-induced. When I think about it in retrospect, it's too much. You get sensory overload. I don't need that much sex. Do me once a night, maybe once a week, I'm fine, I'm cool. But if you got this cocaine in your system, you feel electric. Your nerves are raw. Like somebody's peeled off your skin.

FIELDNOTES: *After years of working among the close-mouthed Maya, I was delighted with Sugar's candor about her life as a tweeker. I felt like an ethnographic sponge, soaking up a cultural intimacy I had never experienced before. At the same time, however, the lurid and often frightening details of her deterioration were sobering.*

If you're too far gone on crack, you're a throwaway person. You're ugly. You're stinky. Your skin is gray. Your lips are chapped. Your hair is nappy. You stink because you don't bathe. You don't have time. You're on a mission. The mission is to get dope. The mission is to go get high.

I got to the point where I was scared to take a bath. Paranoia's the nature of the beast. Someone was always comin' to get me. I kept razor blades around my house to protect myself from this "ghost." I had razor blades in my pocket, in my couch pillows. My kids could have sliced their fingers off! I had more fear of somethin' that don't even exist than the fear of my children cuttin' themselves and then we'd have to go to the hospital and explain it. I was gonna cut the ghost. I mean I could see myself, slashin' at the air! So I wouldn't bathe because I knew that whoever was comin' to get me could kill me in the tub. Well, you've seen enough Alfred Hitchcock to know you don't want to die in the tub.

Tweekers are just scared. They peek outta windows. They pull back the corner of the curtain and peek, peek, peek. I used to live behind Burger King, and one night I'm hearing, "All right, everybody, come out with your hands up!" You know what it really was? Somebody at the drive-in sayin', "Two fries and a shake!"

I'd be scared of police comin'. And Gates was doin' so much dirt, pinchin' off of people's rocks, I'd be scared that somebody might come to get him. And he was never there 'cause he always had to run the dope. He'd come in, we'd hit off that piece, he'd have to go run some more. So I was always there by myself, thinking if somebody comes all pissed off for Gates, who they gonna kill? Me and my kids! So I was scared of *everybody*.

When you been so high so long there is almost no behavior but tweekin' behavior. You don't trust each other. You are paranoid. You argue with your man. If you go out with your girlfriend to the store and you take a little longer, he'll think you're getting high. A tweeker hates to think that there's some dope out there in the city that's not bein' smoked by him or her. So he might be mad that I went out and got high. He's not even concerned that I might be out screwin' with another guy. But was I smokin'?

And my kids knew about it. I remember one time, I cleaned a pipe right in front of 'em and smoked in front of 'em. Because I still didn't realize how serious it was. I didn't register how different this was than weed. Later, when I thought about it, I was appalled.

FIELDNOTES: *After more than a year on crack, Sugar's life was in a sharp downward spiral. It would take a brush with death to get her to quit.*

"ONE NIGHT THIS GIRL FELL OUT!"

The Lord saw fit to save me from it. That's the way He had to do it. I don't believe I had the good sense to give it up, but after I faced death, that's when I stopped. The Lord hit me up side my head. It wasn't no nice little coaxing. It wasn't that I saw what was happenin' to my kids, thought about it, chose to stop. No. It was almost dying that was the turning point for me: when I fell down half dead.

So I was a heavy hitter. I guess I'm always larger than life or somethin'. There wasn't a female that could hit like me. I'm always puttin' rocks on and then scrapin' up scoops of residue. Then this one time we were partying hard downstairs, and I take this big hit and I kinda feel myself fallin'. I just kinda felt like I was slippin' away in slow motion. They said that what happened was that I went stiff and fell back off the barstool I was sitting on. I remember wakin' to these faces kinda like in a circle around me, like somethin' you'd see on TV. Gates took me into the back room, and I was sittin' up a little bit, and I was laughin'! Probably my ass was brain-dead! I had this stupid grin, and I'm goin', "What happened?" And Gates has tears in his eyes, and he's, "Sugar, you passed out. And I saved you, I gave you mouth to mouth."

After he took me into the bedroom and laid me down in the bed, Gates went back out and continued to party. He almost watched me die and yet he could still smoke! Later on, I found out it was not Gates at all who had saved me but this guy named Joe. One day years later, after I had sobered up, this guy Joe the plumber comes over to fix my toilet. He's looking at my pictures I have on the wall.

"Well, these people right here, they sure used to party," he sez. "We used to party with them."

And I didn't say anything, I just kinda listened to him talk. And he started talking about these wild parties.

"One night this girl fell out!"

I just kinda looked at him, and I didn't let on, and I go, "How do you know about that?"

And he goes, "Well, I saved her! I gave her mouth to mouth. I saved her life."

I looked at him, and I said, "That was me."

And me and Joe hugged, we embraced. I could tell he was still usin'. He said he always wanted to know what had happened to me. So that was a kind of poignant little encounter. I told him, "Brother, whatever you ever need—whether you need a sandwich, five dollars, or somebody to go to bat for you, I'll do it. You saved my life."

FIELDNOTES: *At this moment in our work, I gave Sugar a long, hard look. She had said to me, "Drugs make lesser people do lesser things." And here she was, almost dying on crack, but even that didn't stop her from getting high. She was on a serious slide, no longer able to control herself. What finally reeled her in was a two-sentence conversation with her daughter. In that moment, she knew she was no longer honest, moral Sugar. She was a lying tweeker.*

Did I stop right then? No, I tried it again one more time. But my daughter came in. I thought I had cleaned everything up, but there was wax in the ashtray, 'cause you use candles. When you partying, you keep a flame goin'.

And she saw it and said, "Mom, have you been smokin'?"

And I said, "No."

And, I think the drug was part of it, but the worst thing was that I lied. Because I never lied about anything that I did, especially not to my kids. When people would go, "You sure are losing weight," I'd say, "Yeah, I'm on the pipe diet." I've always been an honest person. So when I told my daughter that lie, I knew that I could not continue. So that was it. And I never went back.

TOMMY ANDRE

FIELDNOTES: *Tommy Andre was a pimp I would have liked to have met. Sugar's loving description of this urban denizen piqued my curiosity. There was danger and glamour in this man. More than for any other moment in her life, I wanted to be a fly on the wall for their interaction. I wondered what she was like as reformed tweeker turned hooker. And what was so special about this man that she still dreams of him, ten years after his death?*

I been thinkin' a lot about my baby Andre. He wasn't really a hardcore pimp, more of a hustler. He was a dope dealer, not a user. When I caught him, that was one of my milestones that I was off dope, 'cause the dope dealer would not have a tweeker as his woman. And when I met him, I was on dope. He used to come sell drugs to us. And I remember seein' him over the top of a pipe. I remember takin' a hit and lookin' up and there he was; this gorgeous man came in the door.

And I decided that I was gonna get that man. So for me to get him, number one, I had to be off drugs. And then I had to catch him. I pursued him. I cleaned up my act. We used to go to this club, the Circle Club, and party all the time. I would just wait and wait until I saw him, and one night I went up to him.

I said, "I know you don't know who I am, I just want to invite you to dinner." And I gave him this long spiel. I was talkin' a mile a minute. He was the kind of guy who would just put his hand up in your face, like, "Be off with you, you peasant tweeker!" The fact that he just stopped and listened was cool.

Then he says, "Yeah."

It was so romantic.

He gave me a number, and I would call the number, and it was a wrong number. So I thought I'd never see him again, that I'd lost my big chance. But one day I was crossin' the street, 'cause I would go walk my kids to the bus stop, and this car pulled up, and it had these cool tinted windows. And I didn't pay any attention. Then all of a sudden this window slowly comes down and I look in and see him, and I just about lost it.

And I was like, "When can you come for dinner?"

And he came, and from then on, it was somethin' special. He used to come sleep at my house. I used to wash his hair. I mean these are privileged things. For him to trust you enough to sleep in your house and eat your food means his guard is totally down! To have a man who's a pimp give you money, is like, you special, 'cause the business is you give them money. I would give him money, but it wasn't like I had to go turn a trick to get it. I would do hair, make a little money. He might need somethin', and I would kick him out some money just like anybody would help their man out, so he wasn't pimping me. He gave me TVs and stuff. For him to be doin' those things for me, it meant I was different from his other women.

I loved that man, I just loved him. It didn't last too long. I got offa crack in 1987, and he got killed in 1989. So, basically, it was about a year and a half.

It was a different scene for me, bein' with Andre. Kelly was my wife-in-law, 'cause we went with Andre at the same time. That's what women in the life say. In some states they call themselves "stable sisters," but the common term is "wife-in-law." We were all married to the same guy. With Andre, you didn't mind. He was worth it. You just wanted to be his woman. He was fine and he was suave. He was charismatic, he was smooth, he was cool. He didn't take hisself as serious as I've seen a lot of hustlers do. He was younger than me. He was just gorgeous. He wore a size thirteen boot, and for years after he was murdered, I would ask men what their shoe size was, tryin' to find a thirteen.

We were three wives-in-law. Tammy was the mother of his kids. Kelly was the hard-core ho. I was the good girl. A lot of men will have those different distinctions of women. They'll have their studious schoolgirl, hard worker. They have the woman who bears their children. They'll have the ho.

At the funeral, women came out the woodwork. And I felt special there too because I was clean! I had on a nice black dress, a black-and-white jacket, and a black hat with a black veil. Like this classy broad. And I said my good-byes all alone. Very tasteful. As opposed to some of the other girls who went up and were all throwin' themselves on the casket, and all that whoopin' and hollerin'. Plus I had on black gloves. I was the best old ho in the house! When he died in 1989, I pretty much got out of hustlin'. Lost my impetus.

Sugar's Diary

May 1996

I dreamed about my baby Andre last night. You were the fun man in my life. You marked a milestone that I can never forget. You never took yourself so seriously, like other players do. They can't even laugh half the time. But you, baby, you, you were different. You wanted me to be a good girl. You didn't treat me like those other girls. A good heart you had, baby. A foundation based on Christ. Your birthday approaches, honey. Also your death day soon. I guess that's why I dream of you so vividly. I wake up wondering where you were, are. So I can hug and kiss you one more time. I love you, baby. No other man made me ever do what you made me do. You changed me. I'm working so hard, baby. You would be proud.

FROM RELUCTANT HO TO ENTREPRENEUR

TBE Tell me about this Sugar Daddy image. What did you have in mind?

ST Maybe it's me wantin' my father in my life or somethin', but I wanted to be taken care of. Maybe it's just the desire to be away from the struggle. I want to be soft. I want to be pampered. I want roses. I want nice gifts. I want somebody to surprise me with a big box. I want to open it up and there's something foo-foo in it. I wanted to be a kept woman. I wanted marabou slippers. Somebody that will drink champagne out of my marabou slipper.

TBE   What's a marabou slipper?

ST   You know, the feathers that go [*Blows*]. Jean Harlow, Marilyn Monroe, marabou!

TBE   Where did this image come from, girl?

ST   Growin' up in the fifties, we perceived the ideal woman to be like June Cleaver. She was Prell. She was Breck. You remember the ads. She was soft. She had on an apron. And she wore pearls when she cooked and cleaned. She never argued with her man. Dinner was ready. All that stuff. I want it. I want that peace.

We know now that that didn't really exist, but if you grew up on TV, as we boomers did, that's the image that we got in our minds. The man provided for his home. And he took care of you. Of course, you didn't see images of black people doin' this, but it doesn't mean you didn't want it nonetheless.

Intersperse that with my love of gangsters. Their women were taken care of. What does she have to do? She drinks champagne out of her slipper all day and had her little Fifi puppy and wore marabou feathers. Her makeup was impeccable and her nails were done and her skin was flawless.

TBE   You want both of these images?

ST   Yeah. The gun moll wants to be June Cleaver. Ain't I showed you by now? It's *hard* bein' hard!

FIELDNOTES: *Sugar remembers that my ears pricked up when she said she had been a whore. I was curious, yes, but not in a salacious sense. To me, prostitutes are simply female workers in a potentially dangerous service industry that has been misunderstood and unduly glamorized by the media. I've spent time with prostitutes in Guatemala and found them to be confronting many of the same issues other women do. They were trying to make a little money to feed their children while maneuvering around potentially abusive or irresponsible male behavior. Given this background, I was, of course, curious to see how this African American hustler fitted whoring into her game plan.*

As the story unfolded, I realized that the section on Sugar's approach to "the life" would be brief. My first clue that she was not a whore at heart was when she told me she had learned the business from a book, a well-thumbed volume from the sixties by a famous pimp called Iceberg Slim. Clearly, Sugar was not suited for this line of work. Not only is she somewhat prudish sexually, but, more important, she found the investment of her time offered only limited monetary rewards. Tricks provided some extra cash, but her other businesses were more profitable. She tried to apply an entrepreneurial eye to the business in order to develop a new kind of intelligent, efficiently run whorehouse, but that fizzled when the whores she knew proved to be too stupid to carry out her directives.

In the end, the key to the whoring business for Sugar was that it would help her find a Sugar Daddy. Men, she had aplenty. But through "the life," she hoped to expand her network to more elusive, wealthy, generous protectors. Sugar and I both saw this as more than an entertaining fantasy; it was a cry for help. She honestly wanted to be released—however temporarily—from the struggle of raising a family. This dream also failed miserably. As she soon figured out, her customers were looking for "pussy," not Pretty Woman.

I was in the life for three years, from 1986 to 1989. Findin' tricks was the easy part. I could walk out today and get a trick at the bus stop or the library. Tricks are everywhere.

I started thinking about getting into "dating" in 1982 when my first marriage fell apart. I was feeling so bad that I didn't want any more of "love." I opted to give up what little good there was livin' with a man, so as not to experience the bad. I thought, it's more honest to just be sellin' your pussy. No pain. No tears. No fights. Which is what I did. Here's this essay I wrote about it that kind of sums it all up.

Do You Date?

During most of my intimate encounters, I felt unsatisfied. Now, mind you, I may have experienced the greatest nut in the world, but my dissatisfaction is with the post-nut. After a few of these experiences, I began to think and wonder, "What am I doin' here? Here I lay on my back, let this nothin' nigger screw away, and all I have to show for it is a wet spot on my sheet? This screwin' is not gonna pay any bills. I can't eat it or use it. This nigger's layin' up in my bed, and when he's finished, he'll want me to give him a wet towel and a glass of water. Maybe even want a sandwich! Now, what am I doin' all this bullshit for? This is my house, and this nigger expects me to do for him. He should be doin' for me."

Now if I have these thoughts, I thought, why not date? It's a more realistic way of givin' away your pussy. I mean, it's honest. The parties involved know what's to go down, how long, and for how much. Besides that, you made a little money on the side. I know a whole lot of people would probably raise their eyebrows at this, but so what! What's wrong with a little honesty? Why not make some money off your assets? 'Cause you're just gonna be givin' it away anyway.

The first time somebody asked me "Do I date?" I was nineteen and pregnant. And still possessing a bit of childhood innocence, I did not realize the guy was trying to purchase my womanly wiles. He wanted to know if I was hookin'. And even after he offered me $25 and a new dress and a bag of weed, I never fully understood what he was askin' me! Talk about being stupid!

Well, I must admit that I've always been pretty hot. I am aggressively female. Probably from the womb, who knows? What I do know is that I have been interested in males from a very young age. I remember umpteen prepubescent kisses. I liked them and initiated many, many of them. I recall the gropings and rubbings, the smacks and feels. I can visualize torrid games such as "Hide and Go Get It," "Boyfriend and Girlfriend," and "Blind Man's Bluff," all of which were naughty variations of otherwise harmless children's games. Now, in retrospect, I see they were just watered-down versions of games adults play day in and day out.

I have been through several relationships with men, intimate and otherwise, though I can honestly say I have only been in love one time. Once was enough for me. (I'm jaded at twenty-two years old, already.) I prefer lust. Lust is so much more truthful than love. With lust, it's a situation where two consenting adults realize their need and fulfill it. It's honest in that there are no delusions of love. We both realize what we're here for, so let's go get it. I can dig lust.

When love enters in, then you have problems. It makes you so intense. Everything is magnified, even to the point of being distorted. The magnification is okay when it's a good thing under the lens of love: happiness, fun, sex. But throw the lens over your problems and they grow so big you can hardly contain them. All your hurts and tears are that much greater. Basically, if you stay out of love, you don't have to worry about dealing with pain.

"NO HELLUVA PRO"

I had this girlfriend who was a hard-core ho. If her guy told her to go, she had to go out in the snow. She had to get her ass out there. He was pimping her, though mostly he was just a dope dealer.

Now, I didn't have a pimp. In the life, they would've called me an "outlaw." And there's a lot of places where if the life was thrivin', they'd of never even tolerated me. I'd of had to have a pimp or I'd of been killed or run off or somethin'. The reason I got away with it was because Springfield didn't really have any real "underworld." The pimps here were "tennis shoe pimps," not the hard-core kind. A decent pimp wears alligator shoes and nice silk and leather clothes. So if you've got this guy runnin' around in tennis shoes, he probably got some poor cheap ho's who don't even make enough for him to buy decent alligator shoes. He drives a little hoopdy or probably takes the bus! And they don't even exist no more, gone by the wayside. So you could be an outlaw if you wanted to.

I never really got that into it. Sometimes some trick would call, and I'd go, "Nah, not today." Maybe I could do one or two a week. And it wasn't all the time. You know, for instance, I might be busy doing hair. I'm not gonna mess up a $100 head to go screw some dummy for $50! But if I didn't have any hair, I ain't doin' nothin', and somebody called me, I might as well go make fifty dollars. It could end up taking an hour. But the hour wouldn't be sex. The hour would be the process of come get me, pick me up, we go get the hotel room, small talk real quick, screw, get me back home. There's your hour.

It took me a couple of years and I still wasn't no helluva pro. I was always a prude! I wouldn't do oral sex. I certainly wouldn't do anal sex. The guy is thinkin', "If she's a hooker, she should do whatever." Wrong! People got this concept that a hooker is someone walkin' down the street, doin' all this stuff. But it wasn't like that. I ran my own little show. I remember one time when this guy took off the condom, I jumped out of the bed and cussed him out. He threw me out, of course, but no big deal. They gonna do this my way or not at all. And no way I'm gonna stay there all night! I gotta get home. I got kids. I'm a mother. I got a life!

FIELDNOTES: *I like to think of Sugar's foray into prostitution as a journey in search of love. Maybe it represented a kind of bizarre ghetto fantasy, but nonetheless, being a whore was Sugar's attempt to find Prince Charming. I don't believe her that it was only a Sugar Daddy she was after. She was just stepping out a little further than normal, hoping that the man of her dreams would magically appear.*

For a while I was doin' some modeling, working in this seedy little lingerie shop that was basically a front for prostitution. So I'd model, they'd come to me. Lingerie, with my little skinny ass! I did it maybe a couple of times a week, if that. I'd spend the money on the things I spend money on: buy a pizza, go shopping, buy some shoes, get my kids somethin'. Of course, I did hair, so I didn't really *need* the money. So I wasn't really doin' it for the money. I guess it was the excitement and, of course, the cultivating.

I wasn't like the average ho. See, what I really tried to do was cultivate some Sugar Daddies. I *wanted* to be a kept woman. There was a time when men would set their women up, and they took care of them. You didn't have to do nothin'! That doesn't exist anymore. I didn't want some bunch of tricks comin' in and out of my life. I wanted to be able to call a guy and say, "Yo, I need $50"—even if I wasn't havin' sex with him. So I was really trying to cultivate these kinds of friendships.

I rarely did strangers 'cause I wouldn't pick up guys. I would meet a guy, and we would exchange phone numbers. And if he didn't wanna give me his phone number, then I couldn't be bothered. I had to have a way to reach him 'cause I'm tryin to cultivate. And also, I was trying to find out if he had as much to lose or more than I did. That way, I could guarantee myself that he wouldn't beat me, kill me, or anything like that.

I eventually got into the Sugar Daddy thing, but not to the degree that I would have liked. The closest thing I had to it was Ben. And even he wasn't near what I was lookin' for. Let me tell you about Ben.

For some strange reason, whatever it is, men fall in *lust* with me. I can't take a cab ride from downtown to my house without the cab-driver being like, "Don't get out. Can I see you? Don't get out yet. Let's just talk." So, anyhow, Ben was like that. Crazy about me. He was my landlord. He started just hangin' around all the time, like cuttin' the grass at all hours and everything, trying to get me to notice him. After I moved out of Ben's place, I went and started doin' some work for him 'cause he had other properties. We became friends. And, of course, by this time I had already started hustlin', so I wasn't gonna give no pussy away. He had to pay. But then, he would still fix things for me. We'd go out, and he'd take me to nice places, restaurants.

He was into stereo equipment, so we'd go to stereo stores. And we'd go and eat vegetarian sandwiches, all these things totally new to my life. He'd say he was goin' to the bank, and I'd go, "Get me a little somethin'." He'd help me now and again, but it was never of the magnitude of what I believed other women to be getting. Whereas I might be able to talk somebody out of $50, how is it that some women can get $500 or $5,000 out of a man? But that's what I was gunning for.

I definitely didn't do it for enjoyment, because you was a sorry ho if you was in there enjoying sex! You're not in it for your pleasure. Almost like, to be experiencing pleasure, you've gone over the edge, and you're not doin' your job. When you're workin', you're turning off your brain, turning into a machine, switchin' on your work mode. You couldn't enjoy it. I guess if you had the kind of trick that wanted you to like it, you could fake and act, but that wasn't even what you was there for. It was a business thing.

If somebody went, "Say I'm your baby," I wouldn't. "You ain't my baby. You's a trick. Pay me. Let's not get into that love stuff, okay?" That was my attitude. Of course, when I wanted to raise my price from $50 to $75 they started getting indignant. "You won't call me baby, you won't give me no head, you won't do nothing right, and you want $75!" So I wasn't even a good ho!

It was the power I dug! The power I got from having control over this part of my body that I had never had control over before. I don't have any problem being orgasmic, and in prostitution that was somethin' I had to control. But the tricks were in it for themselves, so it wasn't like they really spent a whole lotta time making me come. If I could just hurry 'em up and get 'em finished, then I didn't even have to worry about it.

It was always, "Oh, Shugie, Shugie, Shugie." Boom.

Or, "Oh, you're so wonderful. You're so sexy." Boom.

I tried to keep it to more straight-laced guys, not kinky freaks. Though I did have the one who called me "Mistress Shugie." And he was an exhibitionist. All I'd have to do was say that people that we knew were looking at him, and he would like totally get off. He loved it! Strange guy.

FIELDNOTES: *I asked Sugar whether she was ever concerned about getting AIDS from her tricks. She said she didn't recall being concerned about it when she was hustling.*

ST   It's like you're gonna die, but you certainly don't want to die like that. I don't know, maybe I was just numb.

TBE   What about now? You still don't use condoms. Are you still numb now?

ST   Does it mean that I'm reckless with my life because I don't use a condom? Sometimes I think we get too preoccupied with stuff. Yes, it is a real concern. But maybe I just can't make it of utmost importance in my life because of what I'm dealing with every day. Hey, I could be dead tomorrow! Maybe dead from the sex or not, but there are days when the shit I'm dealing with almost makes you want to go out and do something reckless. I don't know. It's hard to make condoms and shit so important when one of these guys could bring you a moment of pleasure. It's hard to deny yourself that moment of pleasure 'cause you're about to be right back out there in the mix. It's gonna be real. The real deal is just gonna be in your face.

TBE   Weren't you afraid that one of these strangers you slept with would hurt you?

ST   None of those guys ever took from me. It was fair exchange.

TBE   What about the pimps? Weren't they threatening?

ST   Well, there was Harold, this evil pimp from Las Vegas that I got caught up with. Harold's a scary freak that wants to see women together. So he would always ask Mina if we were screwin'. And to appease him, she'd tell him all these freaky things 'cause otherwise he'd beat her up. But we never really did anything.

"HOW TO MAKE MORE MONEY WITH LESS WORK"

After a while, the entrepreneurial me emerges, and I'm tryin' to figure out how to make more money with less work. See, what I had envisioned was this cool whorehouse I was gonna have. They would come in the door and I would have these pretty, knowledgeable girls who were up on current events and everything. Smart girls! I wanted them to actually read the newspaper. You may never even have sex. You talk. So I wanted them to come in the door in this nice place, and they would have hors d'oeuvres and champagne. For prostitution, you gotta have your front. So, basically, the front was gonna be lingerie modeling. So the ladies will model for you. After, there would be a series of things you could go through. You could choose massage, a hot tub, but the thing is, you didn't pay for any of these services with the girl.

What you did was you bought a pair of panties for $500. So that's how you got around the law, and, of course, the police would have gotten onto it eventually.

Well now, we would want these old goats to be clean, so first you give 'em this nice bath, and you oil them down and they'd get a massage—like an assembly line. And then finally, the girl models the lingerie that they chose. If he wants it in private, then they go to a room. And what I wanted was a green room if her lingerie was green. A pink room if it was pink. And you could do whatever sex act you had previously paid for. And out the door you go. Bring in another one. Give him some cheese and some bon bons and send him through the assembly line. All day long, we'd do this. But if you really wanted to do this, you'd have to retain a lawyer. You'd need to have enough money to get your whores outta jail. You'd have to make an investment. You would have to treat it like a business.

I could never afford such a setup, but I *was* a madam, very briefly. There was only maybe two girls that I could really say I turned out directly. I didn't take innocent girls and turn them out. I took girls who were already givin' their pussy away and showed them that if you're gonna give it away, why don't you come over here with me and get paid for what you're already doin'. But see, they were *stupid!* I guess they were the wrong girls because they were so busy fuckin' anyway. There was Crystal and there was Mina.

One time, Mina did this freaky guy. I took her over there and turned him on to her. She'd have to kick me out some money so that way I wouldn't have to work. He gave me some weed, and I was sittin' in there smokin' and drinkin' champagne while they're in the room. I'm making money and don't have to do nothin'. After a while I go in, and I hear these smacks. Well, I know he likes to get his ass whipped. I go peek through the crack, and I had to go in there and snatch her out. She's in there getting her butt spanked! Stupid! I had to explain to her it's not her pleasure we were there for! and if his pleasure is to beat you, he's gotta pay extra for it, duh! Crystal was the same way. They weren't very bright, but those two stupid whores were all I could get.

FIELDNOTES: *Among welfare mothers, prostitution is often described as a survival strategy. Welfare checks are not adequate for all the bills and expenses, so women on assistance have to resort to any number of scams to make it from check to check. Mostly, they have boyfriends who give them a little money, hold jobs where they are* paid under the table, or manage surreptitious home businesses. Less often, women deal drugs, shoplift, or sell sexual favors. In short, a considerable variety of legal and illegal money-making activities go on behind the back of the welfare system.

In Sugar's recounting of her stint as a prostitute, the focus is on the mundane details of this small business and how Sugar integrated it into the broader family economic strategy. She entered "the life" not only to supplement her welfare check but to undertake a futile search for a Sugar Daddy, or what we social scientists would call male-centered financial security. What she sought in a trick is what she needs in a husband: a good provider.

Her frustration with being a whore stems not only from her failed Sugar Daddy search but from her inability to apply entrepreneurial skills—her hustle—to developing an efficient whorehouse.

SUGAR, THE ENTREPRENEUR

FIELDNOTES: When I first met Sugar, she was supporting the family with income from her welfare check and from doing hair. Ever the hustler, she kept her hair money secret, always refusing to actually tabulate what she was making, even for this book. What I did learn was that without the extra few hundred dollars a month she produced in her back room, she would have been in dire straits financially.

In fact, to Sugar, the meaning of the word "hustler" involves using your brain to improve upon the bare-bones lifestyle a welfare check provides. If you're a hustler, you are doing whatever you have to do to provide your kids with a decent life. It was the hairdressing business, therefore, much more than her brief foray into prostitution, that kept Sugar's children from ever suspecting they were poor.

"LIKE EVERYTHING WE DO, HAIR IS FOR MEN!"

I been doin' hair for twenty-five-plus years, since I was a little girl playing with my dolls' hair. Of course, braids is old as Cleopatra. When braids became really in, especially extensions, it gave us black women somethin' that we never had and that's hair that moves. White women have always had the monopoly on hair that's long, hair that you can pull up in ponytails. Here we are walkin' around in little itty bitty Afros, and who are the men lookin' at? Women with hair that moves! Hair is not really a fashion statement. Like everything we do, hair is for men!

Doin' our hair right is one of the best things that happened to us in terms of self-esteem. Our men and our society have been conditioned to this white Barbie doll ideal, and though we say we don't want to be her, this allows us some of that beauty. You've told our men that that's what is beautiful, so we're like, "I'm gonna get me some of that. Where they keepin' it?" It's like, we're not gonna keep fighting it.

When we were little, our mom gave us Afros, 'cause my mom was a radical. She wanted to be a Black Panther. So she cut our hair off, and what little girl wants to walk around lookin' like that? We would put pantyhose on our heads and the two legs would hang down, because we wanted long hair.

Outside of these black power people with their Afros, there were still these conventional people that pressed their daughters' hair and wore ponytails. But unless you're mixed, your hair is not growin' very long. If you're mulatto or mixed with Indian, you might have long, silky hair. In the black community, they call it "good" hair. Still call it good hair! Such a throwback to slavery. But we all have been told that long hair is beautiful. So if you don't have enough mixture in you, like I don't, you end up with kinky, nappy hair. Of course, there's really nothing wrong with that if you like kinky, nappy hair.

TBE I always thought a lot of the women with braids were making statements about being African.

ST Oh, gosh, no! Don't nobody care about that! [*Laughs*] It's ease.

Because my hair is short, I'm ready to go. I can concentrate on getting that lash on! There's times I haven't gone places because I've fought for hours with my regular hair and it refused to act right. If it wants to, it will betray you at the most inopportune moment. With extensions, you don't have to forego any parties because of your hair. You don't have to be late to work because of it. That's another reason why we like it. It's predictable. I always know my hair is gonna work.

Another thing, as far as romance is concerned. I can come out the shower looking beautiful. Just like they do on TV. On TV we see white women, they're shampooin', they're rinsing; they're coming straight out of the shower and getting into bed—"Honey (sigh), I'm ready for you." We have to braid our hair in these knots and go to bed looking ugly. No wonder our men leave us. Black men are hair struck!

So, doing hair is pretty good business. I only accept a certain amount of customers. When I need to get an injection in my business, I will tell all my customers that they can send me one well-chosen, hand-picked customer. I tell them to only send me someone they love and trust, because if the customer fucks me, if they don't pay me, or if they are somebody that's comin' in only to take my technique and show it to their beautician, I'm not only gonna fire the customer, I'm gonna fire the person who sent the customer. I require a certain amount of customer loyalty, and I get it.

If I went to one of them uptown places, I could probably command $300 for a braided hair weave or $100 for a streak and a perm, maybe more at a really upscale place. But I did some research, and they're not really offering all that. Springfield has its wealthier black folk who are payin' those prices—yes, they must exist—but I don't know that they're into braids or extensions. Maybe they get it straightened.

I'm doin' one, maybe two heads a week. And that's not every week. It just rotates. Sometimes people change. Or sometimes they fall on hard times and can't get their hair done as much.

Hair's a good business, but it ain't enough. With the hair this past week, I had all three of my heads cancel. Hey, they do whatever they gotta do. Don't have the money. They gotta live their life, just like me. They're broke out there. If you have bills comin' due or whatever, the first thing you gonna do is postpone my hair. That was approximately $250 that didn't come in. So if all I'm lookin' at is doin' heads each week, I don't really know if those heads are gonna come through.

I could give it a boost if I wanted to advertise, but I don't really know how much longer I want to pick up in this area. That's one of the reasons that I went to college. I wanted to start nurturing whatever else I'm going to be doing, 'cause I'm not goin' to be doing hair for the rest of my life. My legs will give out for one thing. My legs already get tired in the back of my knees.

THE FASHION SHOW BUSINESS: "SUMMER COOL"

FIELDNOTES: *One spring evening, early in our work, I went to see one of Sugar's fashion shows at Lucille's, a black nightclub in Springfield. Being invited to such a venerable local institution—Sugar talked about Lucille's all the time—got my ethnographic juices running, so when Sugar handed me her homemade flyer, I immediately accepted. Sugar had already impressed me as a kind of magical woman, but I was unprepared for "Summer Cool," the compelling, sophisticated production she had put together.*

Lucille's is made up of a comfortable series of big rooms, with a large, busy bar, tables, and a dance floor. The customers that night—mostly women—were impeccably dressed. The dominant theme was pastel or black chiffon worn with or without a hat. Some women wore smart tailored suits and stiletto heels. Everyone, it seemed, had just had their nails done. In short, it was a sophisticated crowd taking advantage of the opportunity to show off their finery.

There were six acts, each with its own music, décor, theme, and, of course, fashions. The models were of varied ages and sizes, each one exquisitely made up and coiffed by Sugar Turner. Sugar herself appeared in each act, looking every inch the diva. Between scenes, a pop singer did his best to make women swoon, and they gave away lots of door prizes.

"I KNOW WHAT MY PEOPLE WANT"

From 1983 to 1985, I basically modeled, maybe once every six months, for all these people that I call the "Intermittent Production Company." They come and they go. They're people who just say, "I want to do a show." Like Andy Hardy and them: "Let's do a play." And they do 'em. So those are the people that I've worked with over the years. When I worked with Gates's shows, I did everything from picking the clothes to writing little commentary cards that the emcee would use. I would help pack the clothes, haul the clothes, carry the clothes, unpack the clothes, anything that it would take to produce the show. Other people were actually in charge. It was their money. Then in 1985, I began to produce. That's just like me. I'm not gonna be satisfied just with the superficial crap like modeling. I began to work behind the scenes. Even though I continued to model, I started to produce, I wrote, I did hair, I directed.

These productions take place in clubs and hotels. They're not really about fashion. It's just another form of entertainment to offer to black people. In my community, there is some kind of show every weekend. If it's not some sorority, a church, or a beauty shop, it's one of these independent producers, or the club itself, that puts it on.

There's quite a few people doin' these shows. And they're doin' it mostly for fun. It's not for business. It's all done with volunteer labor. Nobody ever makes any money.

It's all done because everybody wants to be a star. Everybody wants that fifteen minutes of fame that Andy Warhol promised them, and this is their way to get it. By bein' in the spotlight, by gettin' made up, dressing up, bein' a star for a minute. Everybody likes celebrity, and everybody likes celebrities. So everybody wants that glamour, even if it's a flash, even if it's a weekend's worth, and even if they have to put in two or three months of rehearsal free, on their own time, to get that fifteen minutes, they will do it. But the thing is, they wear out, so you have to keep gettin' new blood. Pretty quick they see that the fifteen minutes of fame is all that it is. They see that it don't pay no bills. When they come down, they still got all the same problems at home.

It actually cost me to do this, what with all the volunteer work that I've done, especially since I didn't have a car for a long time. I caught cabs. I paid people gas money. You wear your own clothes. You buy your own makeup. After it's over, the photographer will sell you pictures or a video, so you spend money on that. Basically, it costs you. But you do have a record. So if you do want to say, "Oh, way back when I used to model," you have a record of it. But it doesn't help the bills. Hell no!

I know what my people want for entertainment. A black woman like me, I can't afford to go to Vegas. What I can afford is five or ten dollars to go to a fashion show. That's my quick high. So I know that there's a market for this, because we want a little escape and we can't afford the Bahamas. This is our little escape where we get to dress up in our fancy clothes, be glamorous, and hob nob—"Hey girl!" and that type of thing. We like styling. We wanna dress up. We wanna feel good, 'cause, after it's over, we come home, and it's all still here.

What you see at a show is pretty standard. Six scenes that include business wear, casual wear, dressy wear, evening wear, lingerie, and maybe swimwear or furs, dependin' on the season. They're almost always the same. There might be a little change, so that you might have a hat scene. But basically, that's it.

I put my own shows together by the skin of my damn teeth. I basically financed them by doing hair. I'd do a head, then I'd print the program. I'd do another one and pay the singer. Fortunately, I was friends with a couple of people that had some clothes. Lots of organizing and figuring how to save money goes into it.

These shows, it's in my blood. I'm just a little entrepreneur at heart, and I wanted to do shows. I like the flash and the lights, bein' in the spotlight. I also like the business part of it. I feel that it builds esteem. I feel it kind of pulled together several of my goals, my loves: helpin' people, makin' people feel good, dressin' up, makeup, hair, beauty, fashion, men (ha!), all in one activity. I could address all these different things: bein' a businesswoman, bein' able to direct people, running things. So I get to fill all these different areas of my life just by doin' a show.

ST   Even afterwards, you are still high! You still done a good thing.
        People are revved up and wanna see you do more.

TBE   How much money did you lose?

ST   Well, gosh, I lost $1,800! That's basically what I spent.

TBE   Here I was thinking how entrepreneurial you are, putting all this
        stuff together! Getting people to donate the clothes and everything.

ST   I am!

TBE   But I had no idea that you had lost all that money. I'm gonna smack
        your face.

ST   Please, smack me twice!

FIELDNOTES: *As part of its plan to move women from welfare to work, the Wisconsin Department of Family Assistance offered clients two-year business training programs. Sugar enrolled in a course at the Coretta King Center for Women to teach her to run a small business. This pilot program met daily for eight weeks to teach women business basics. In order to graduate, they had to write a business plan. The capper was that upon completion of the course, trainees would receive a $2,000 loan to be used to start up their businesses.*

Sugar was full of ideas and schemes to perfect and launch her fashion show business. Her concept was to automate the fashion shows, to have an inventory of clothes and models and sets in order to lower costs. In addition, by mass-producing her shows she wouldn't need extensive lead time to put a production together. She'd just have to plug in the appropriate season and theme, thus enabling her to book many shows quickly.

Although I was very impressed with the fashion show I had seen at Lucille's, I was skeptical about her being able to ever make a profit in this business in which everyone, including Sugar, had lost money or gone under. How was she going to turn an amateur fashion show into a finely honed production company? It was a stretch. Her enthusiasm, however, was contagious. Her Coretta King Center stint was a purposeful step toward fulfilling her entrepreneurial dream. She had a plan, and it was far more realistic than her previous plan for a high-volume whorehouse.

TBE   Okay, answer this: If nobody's ever been able to make money from
        these shows before, what makes you think *you* will?

ST   Mine's gonna be better, more creative. The models are gonna be
        trained better. The level of style is gonna be better. The level of
        entertainment is gonna be higher.

TBE   And that would translate into what in terms of money?

ST   More money! Because I would be doin' 'em more frequently, which
        would give me more recognition. Which would make more people

come out more regularly because they would see it as a regular alternative to the club scene. It could be, "Well, it's Friday. Do you wanna go to the Circle or to Lucille's?" "Well, let's go over to Sugar's show."

TBE   Like a regular thing to do?

ST   It's a good concept. My idea is what I call "Electric Fashion!" I coined the term years ago. Electric Fashion is automated fashion shows. Actually, it's a very similar concept to what I had dreamed of in my little whorehouse. I wanted people so trained, so precise, and so ready to go, that on a moment's notice they would be ready to perform. I would have a roster of themes. For instance, the opening theme at my "Summer Cool" show was we were all in white, and we used fans. Valentine's Day: dress 'em in red, give 'em roses. Halloween: dress 'em in orange and black, give 'em witch hats. Same scene. So I thought if I could put the initial work into gettin' these people trained and get 'em so polished, then all I need is to book some dates.

Training is crucial. I need to train models in the way of Electric Fashion. Just like I wanted to have the little ho's all trained up. I want models with polish that can come out and pose, and maybe do scenes, interact with each other. Basically what you got now is eight ladies who parade on stage, turn around, go off stage. Those are the shows. I would rather see a Valentine's scene, a man and a lady interact. You see 'em crossin' across a park, a few props that make you know that this is a park. Let them be trained in eye contact, things that I know how to teach people.

TBE   Those women did seem pretty damn confident up there!

ST   Right! 'Cause at the same time of bein' trained, you're building esteem, getting your fifteen minutes of fame. Your family and friends get to live vicariously through you. All this self-confidence rubs off on everyone around you. It has a rippling effect of all these touchy-feely good things that I wanted to spread in my community. All these noble things, but it just needs somethin' in the way of money to git goin'! If my business head was as good as my heart, I would probably be a helluva businesswoman.

TBE   Give me an example.

ST   I would like to *pay* my models. I know I would have better shows 'cause I would be able to command better people. After somebody's done six of Gates's shows, they're about burned out. You're a volunteer, so you start lookin' a little stupid! And then, people start talkin' about you, 'cause they know you ain't gettin' paid, you ain't doin' nothin'. If somebody can say that every time I model, I make fifty to a hundred dollars, you get a better-quality product.

TBE   What else would the Coretta King Center loan go for?

ST   I need capital for sets; costumes; better, slicker promotions—which is, of course, the first thing that the public sees. It could provide a decent flyer. Flyers are the way the people learn about fashion shows, plus the weekly newspapers, the neighborhood circulars. Now, having gone to this class, I know that your name needs to be out there nine times, so if you're gonna do radio spots, you need to do a lot. Two spots don't do you nothing. You need more recognition.

I would change up my format. I would like to see more theatrics. I would like to see more skits, more variety of music, more different models: sizes of models, types of models, colors of models. I wouldn't stay with standard procedure. So I just need the capital to do this.

TBE   But I thought you wanted to buy a car.

ST   If I had a car, I know that would shave off at least half of the time I spend on these things. I know that time is money. If my rehearsal's at six o'clock, normally, I gotta leave my house at four or five to catch the bus or a cab or whatever. I can't leave at a quarter till six. So how much money am I wastin' in time? It's totally takin' when it should be puttin' in. If I could just govern myself and learn how to make it click. I mean you're carrying clothes, tons of that shit you're carryin'. A car would just make a big difference.

So it could work. But I got other ideas too, like widening your horizons, workshops, seminars, things that I could do. Say a luncheon, a tea. Black women love to go to teas and luncheons. They love to wear their hats. They love to wear nice clothes. Where we gonna wear 'em to? They're sitting in our closets. I would pay $10 just to have someplace to wear a nice dress to. To go out to sit with other women. Serve 'em tea, have a speaker. Have fifty women, ten dollars apiece: $500. Spend a hundred to pay the speaker and maybe make $200. Not a lot. But if I did 'em every week, and began to get a following, that's how the money would be made. I just want to hit 'em enough times in my community with enough positive things that it would begin to make money.

FIELDNOTES: *Sugar never did implement her plans for Electric Fashion. In spite of her zealous determination to make a go of this business, she faced too many obstacles. Mostly, there was what seemed an impossible jump from ghetto impresario to Springfield businesswoman. She became frustrated at how naïve she had been about the demands of the "real" business world. There was so much to learn, so many rules and regulations to adhere to that she would have had to completely abandon the approach she had developed over the years. This felt awkward and, to her mind, ridiculous. For example, she couldn't understand why she would have to pay taxes on the small amount of money she paid her models.*

And the $2,000 prize at the end of the Coretta King Center course quickly seemed insufficient. As the course progressed and she learned to tally her costs, she realized that she needed more than five times that amount to adequately capitalize Electric Fashion.

The course itself was a disappointment. Although Sugar bonded with the other students, they had as few resources as she did to mount small businesses. The Coretta King Center itself came in for a fair share of Sugar's criticism, especially when the pressures of home made it impossible for her to do her homework or complete a project. However, she stuck with the course both because it was a welfare requirement and because she liked expanding her world by going to the sessions.

The real prize turned out not to be the $2,000 loan but the new world of learning that the King Center offered to Sugar. She hungrily soaked up the materials they provided, loving the exercises, the readings, the intellectual challenge she had longed for since high school. Although she didn't start a business, Sugar used the King Center as a springboard. Just one year later, she enrolled as a first-year student at Springfield Community College.

3 THE MR. LESTER CHRONICLES

TBE   For all the changes you have made in who you are—getting off crack, quitting prostitution, moving away from welfare, going to college—you still insist on maintaining this open-door policy for these frogs to come in off the street, hoping that you'll kiss them and turn them into Prince Charming. The problem is, the damn frogs come in your door one after the other, you kiss them, and they stay frogs!

ST   Find me a good one, my Jewish mother.

TBE   Why haven't you got a better plan for meeting Prince Charming? After all these frogs, why haven't you learned something?

ST   What makes them frogs?

TBE   None of them have loved you, taken care of you.

ST   Where am I going to find 'em? Where? These guys come from all walks of life. What makes them frogs?

TBE   I'm using this as a metaphor. You want these guys to be the man who's gonna sweep you up and love you forever, and that ain't happening.

ST   Then I guess it ain't never gonna happen.

TBE   You said to me last week, "I'm not changing. I'm the woman from the hood and I need to be with a man who appreciates that in me." That particular strategy is ending up with you crying.

ST   I'm *gonna* be crying. It's not gonna change.

FIELDNOTES: *Saturday night, 10 P.M.: I get a call from Sugar. I had just come home from a ten-day trip. My last words to her before I left were, "Don't get married while I'm gone." I was kidding around with her 'cause she was being so silly and teenagerish about Mr. Lester, her new boyfriend. So, she's on the phone (somewhat sloshed) announcing that now that I'm home, she's getting married—on Wednesday. She wants to be part of a team, and the "Mr. Lester Team" looks like the one. He's good to her kids, he cooks, he's sweet to her, he's a wonderful lover, a Vietnam vet, etc. I immediately register shock and disbelief. She shuts me up. She had already heard from all the naysayers in her family, she reports. "Why can't you just say, 'Go, girl!'" I respect her enough to be quiet. They get married. Her daughters are totally against it and make that really clear. In fact, one of the wedding snapshots shows a visibly upset Dolly sneering at the camera.*

I feel really, really bad about this decision. I went over there yesterday afternoon. I met Mr. Lester, who ignored me until I actually asked him a question. He was affectionate with her and attentive to the kids, but . . .

My concern about this quicky marriage was, I felt, well founded. Yes, I knew she had been having a fun time with him. And, I knew that she felt they had a lot in common. Unfortunately, their bond was based on the fact that they both had lovers who were drug addicts. The mother of one of his kids, Mary Ellen, was a tweeker who was just getting out of jail. There were all kinds of rumors and accusations from friends that Mr. Lester had beaten her and fed her the crack till she was a goner. To me, the guy didn't seem to have any redeeming characteristics.

Sugar ignored her initial suspicion that Mr. Lester was a smackhead: he was nodding in her bedroom, he had tracks on his arms. He was just another street hustler as far as I could tell. Yeah, he was going to school, but I sensed that it was some kind of a scam. Plus, he lived with a bunch of junkie friends in what Sugar described as "the world's most stanky apartment." For all the romantic giddiness Sugar expressed at the mention of his name, Mr. Lester had "loser" written all over him.

Okay, so they're married. Mr. Lester goes home to Boston for a while. He's gone more than two months—wanted to get a job at a car dealership but had some kind of criminal record following him around, so no dice. Then, supposedly he hung around for family reunions and tried to make some cash, painting the house, whatever.

It all seems so predictably familiar to me. I was worried. But when he comes home, Sugar and I get together, and she's all Miss Pollyanna Turner. She's sooooo happy and insufferably optimistic in spite of what seems to me a dire situation. The conversation begins with her saying she's not going to badmouth her man anymore, like she's done with every other man she's had. This time she's going to be positive in her thinking about him, no matter what. She's going to get into compromise and not confrontation. It seems she tried yelling and screaming the first time he came home at 4 A.M. without giving her any idea where he had been. He became angry and resentful that she thought she had the right to ask. He sees no reason why he has to tell her anything. But she's understanding. He's a hustler says she, and he has to go out to do his thing, such as selling drugs or whatever, so she just has to accept that.

What else? She's asked him to cook three nights a week as part of his responsibility in the house, but the cook won't cook anymore. He thinks it's unmanly of him. We'll see what happens there. He wants to get a dog. This is a biggy. The kids are scared to death of my golden retriever, Alma, the world's gentlest dog. Of course, Mr. Lester wants to get a big dog. Thinks if they have it from when it's a baby, the kids will be okay with the thing. Yeah, right.

Lastly, and the one thing you knew was coming, he's not giving her any money. So the guy who started out being a poet, a war hero, and a college student now turns out to be a hustler, a drug dealer, and an asshole. On and on.

I said to her, "Look, you know I love you. I was negative on this guy in the beginning, but you shut me up. But you gotta know that if you want to complain about him, if he disappoints you or whatever, you can come to me. I promise I won't say 'I told you so.'"

She laughed it off and said, "Well, he'd just be another one anyway."

I've told her that I just cannot figure out why she makes these bad choices when it comes to men. She puts her own happiness ahead of her kids' peace of mind. She picks one loser after another and teaches her kids a sorry message. And she always ends up crying. Funny, she sees this. She really does. But it's the one major area of her life where she has no power to turn things around.

"I THOUGHT HE WAS KINDA CUTE"

Reggie got his fifty-two days in prison for domestic violence. That's when me and Mr. Lester had our little tryst. It was about a month. We were courting. We were talkin' on the phone. We ate. We had drinks. Happy hour. We rode the bus together. I'd help him with his English papers. Stuff like that. Oh, I wanted a man. But it wasn't even that. I was just lonely and feelin' pretty downtrodden after two years with that tweeker!

I ran into Mr. Lester and we started talkin'. I thought he was kinda cute. Curly hair. He had these huge, deep-set bulging brown eyes like Reggie's. He was the same golden color as Reggie. He's the same age as Reggie. Taller than Reggie. He's even from the same place as Reggie. He's just a bigger facsimile of Reggie. And my kids say he has a mouth like Reggie, nice teeth, but a nose broken once or twice.

Nothing really attracted me to him in the beginning. I'm not a "love at first sight" type of girl. Because, first of all, I like everybody, and I talk to everybody, and it doesn't matter. So there was no attraction, but he was witty, smart, articulate. Then all these little things came up. He's a Capricorn, same sign as me. He's a Vietnam vet. And he's articulate as hell! And poetic. He writes me poetry. And he's got a sense of humor. He's not afraid to laugh. He's concerned about me. Just little stuff like carryin' my books. I think the main attraction was that he was attentive. I was lonely. He was gentle.

He's been a hustler, a survivor. But I gathered that, unlike Reggie, his survival was not on women's coattails. And then I got a good report. My girlfriend came over, and she and Lester knew each other. Just the way her face lit up when she saw him.

And then she was sayin', "Well, where's Mary Ellen?" His ex-woman.

I sez, "Well, he brought her over. She's outta jail." She sez, "Yeah, because when she used to disappear for days at a time, he'd take care of them kids."

My friend gave him a good report and that makes me feel good. I know men that if the woman went out, "I'm not taking care of no fucking kids. You better tell your mom to come over here and get these brats!" Or whatever. So he was a family man. I was gonna take a chance, because I knew that he was a Christian. That he was substantial. That he had good fiber.

If you spent some time with Lester, there was just a difference. He laughed. He cried. He talked to all my kids. He knew my kids' names instantly. And I appreciated somebody who comes in and makes it a point to know my children's names. He never asked me twice. I know they appreciated it.

Since Vietnam, he'd been hustling. Selling dope. Being on drugs. Raising kids. Being a handyman. He'd worked at the Post Office. Just livin' this life that we have to live out here. What he really wanted to do was get his electrician's license to be an apprentice. He wanted to buy and renovate houses. I saw in Lester a man that was tryin'.

I met Lester at college. Actually, I met him crossing the street going from school. I was going somewhere, and he was going wherever he was going. We just spoke and that was that. "How ya doin', brother?" A general greeting. And then we crossed the street.

About a month later, we were on a train together. Well, then, we struck up a conversation. I was askin' him about the significance of the necklaces he had on. He was telling me what they meant. One was like an African fertility goddess that represents women and represents his mom. He had one that's a peace sign in a cross. So that represents peace and Christianity. And then he had another one—some beads—that represents harmony. So he was talkin' about his beads. And I had my camera that day, so he asked me about it. General stuff.

We just started talkin' after that. But he knew I had a man and all that, but that my man was treating me so shitty. I was tellin' him about Reggie. See, we had it in common, 'cause his woman was in prison. Or his ex-woman or whatever she was. She was in prison for bein' a tweeker, too. So then we have this common bond: "Oh, your woman smokes? My man smokes!" We could lean on each other. At the time I was choosing him, he ain't low-life scum. The guy that I met was a student who was tryin' to do somethin', who had an interest in our English papers. We both had addicted partners. We'd both been healed of drugs. So we were two people that was tryin' to come up from these horrible situations, tryin' to better ourselves. He was taking courses in the Veterans' Upward Bound program, attempting to want to do something—versus "asshole" Reggie, who just wanted to sustain his drug habit.

Then we had one little affair. Well, I went over to his house to help him with his English papers, 'cause I'm an English whiz, so "yeah, I'll help you with your homework." And, as they say, it just happened. We made love! No, we screwed. It wasn't love then. It was horrible. Shitty. It was nothing to write home about. I thought he was joking, but I didn't laugh. Actually, I was a little pissed. I don't think it lasted five minutes.

He asks me if it feels good.

And I lied. I try not to play it up too much because I'm not a good liar, but I can eke out a "yes." I guess I was just lookin' for an extension of the affection. We'd go out, he'd hold my hand. We'd walk arm in arm. Really, I was lookin' for an extension of that. And as far as the "extension," it didn't extend! I didn't plan on ever bein' there again. I wasn't gonna give him another chance! Hell no!!

But then I got it figured out. First of all, his place was creepy. A poor bachelor pad. There was no ambiance. I like home. I don't like being other places doing things. I like my place. I like to know where my bathroom is. I don't want to have to ask you for a towel. I'd rather get you one. I'm uncomfortable on other people's turf, especially in vulnerable positions like that. Probably a part of it is a question of control, but I don't like creepy places. I don't like flop houses. I don't like bachelor pads. I don't like stuff like that. Bedrolls and no furniture or raggedy old furniture. Ick!

I didn't exactly know it was a dope house then. But I was suspecting. When you walked in, it was like disgusting. The carpets hadn't been cleaned in like forever. It looked more like a storage room. And there were all these cats that came in and out. And it was like dusty and dark and dank. Horrible.

One time I went over there one Saturday, and little did I know he was in jail for what he said later was some kind of traffic charge. Old traffic warrants or something. I went past there, and these guys were there and there was obviously drug activity. But he wasn't home. So the next time I saw him I told him, "I'm not comin' back to this dope house."

I wasn't blind. I knew Mr. Lester was a junkie. I knew, but I didn't know. Basically, I didn't want to admit it. But, shit, he always wore these long sleeves. His apartment was a gross, fucking drug den. Not only that, but there was that fresh fat track sittin' on his arm that he told me was old. But isn't that typical of me to get some cad? I feel bad about that, too. 'Cause I can't find nothin' but a junkie.

People kept tellin' me I needed to look for different types of men. Where might I go? Why, the university, of course. It figures. I would find a junkie at the university. It's so strange. I could find a junkie in the grocery store. I could find a junkie in church. They find me!

TBE   Why do you think you attract tweekers and junkies? Here you are in college with people who are supposedly trying to improve themselves, and who do you end up in bed with?

ST   Some junkie! Of all the people I can meet on the college campus, how come I can't meet a college man? You know why? The devil sent Lester to discredit God, to throw me off the track. God can turn anything around, make a lesson out of it. So I am learning.

Since Reggie, I been sayin', "I don't want another Christian man." Well, there's a victory for the devil 'cause he don't ever have to worry about her gettin' with another Christian man.

TBE   Why did you say that?

ST   'Cause Reggie soured me. I don't want no damn Christian. He is the first one I've had, and he broke my heart and sent me through hell. Why would I risk another one?

TBE   Then don't go out with any blue-eyed men either. So tell me, how long after you met Lester were you in the sack with him?

ST   The sack?

TBE   It's a white expression for sex.

ST   It was about a month. We were courting.

TBE   I can't get over this. Not only is he old and a junkie, he has no money, he's riding the bus.

ST   See, that's part of the discrediting. I had promised myself to not deal with another man walkin'. Well, make a liar out of me. Walking means you're just as poor as I am. What the hell am I doin' talkin' to you on a bus? I vowed I would never talk to another man on a bus besides hi and bye. Out the window! The devil wants to make a joke out of me. As long as I'm doin' what I say I'm gonna do, I'm gonna stay in right, then I'm a credit to the Lord. The devil's business is to discredit God. So, here's your sainted Sugar. Watch what I send her—a stankin' junkie, ridin' the bus. Watch her jump.

TBE   So he's not a former junkie?

ST   He says he's been bein' a junkie since he was sixteen. But you see, he's supposed to have been off for eight months.

TBE   So what was this nodding behavior?

ST   He was here one night. He couldn't keep his eyes open. He was sittin' right here, and I was sittin' on the bed. We weren't talkin' that much because I think at that point I had told him that, you know, I'm breaking up with you. He was kinda quiet, and so his eyes were closin', and he had his head in his hands, which is sort of typical of somebody who just got the boot. (Of course, I changed my mind.) But then, he started nodding. And I never seen it before. I've seen it on TV, and I've heard enough about it.

TBE   He's a smackhead.

ST   Then he kind of comes to, and he tells me he had been walking in the sun and that kind of drained him. And that he had a couple of drinks. But see, we've been out before and he's had a couple of drinks, and he didn't act like that.

TBE   No, no, no. Nodding is specifically associated with opiates.

ST   If they nod, it doesn't necessarily mean they're sleepy? And so, they can still function and do things, because he was up playing music till one or two o'clock in the morning.

TBE   Exactly. Opiates actually invigorate you so that you have a lot of energy.

ST   I don't know enough about heroin. And I said, "Baby, you was noddin'." And he sez he wasn't. But I saw tracks.

TBE   Did you ask him about the tracks?

ST   He told me he was a heroin addict since the time he was sixteen
years old until eight months ago. With the Veterans' Upward Bound
Program, he says we're all recovering something or other. But it's
the recovery part that I like. Reggie was dedicated to the cause of
being a crack addict—at all costs. But it's the recovery part that
attracts me. Because in my world, everybody's a recovering something. Or they are on something. I would rather align myself with
the recoverers because there's hope. I guess the others, their hope
is further off. I don't wanna say there's no hope.

"I WANTED TO BE PART OF A TEAM"

We'd been talkin' about getting married since early on in the relationship. My desire to get married was nothing new, just the partners change.
But I thought I got a better man this time with Mr. Lester—more of a
partner, less of a pariah. I had been wantin' to get married. That hadn't
changed. I wanted to be part of a team. I like bein' in love, doing
things the right way. My faith dictated that I go ahead and do this. My
social situation, too, as far as Section 8 and all that—you couldn't
have a live-in boyfriend. What I wanted was us being together, living
together, and I don't mean *residing*, but having a life together.

So I told Tina, "Me and Mr. Lester's goin' to be gettin' married. I
want to be a part of a team."

She sez, "Oh, Ma, you are part of a team, the team you *made*!"

That's all they see.

"Baby, wait till *you* get to be thirty-seven!"

And she was laughin'.

I sez, "I deserve to have somebody."

"You got somebodies! Us!"

It was difficult for her to see how he fitted into the family. In this
community, you never see a good marriage. I know in my generation
if you had a dad, it was strange. In their generation, it's still true. I
can't think of a friend of Tina's who's got a dad. Shalina has like an at-
home father. I don't know anybody else. But then one time we had a
slumber party and they invited all these girls. And there were some
twins. And they were Shalina's *sisters*. I don't know if they had met
them before. It was awkward as hell. They were her dad's children
from an affair. So even the one dad is tarnished. They haven't seen a
success story. Where would they?

Normal is moms and the kids. I won't say like I speak for all blacks. But in my world, that's normal. But I knew my girls could accept another type of life. They could see that life with Mommy's not the only happy life.

And with Mr. Lester, we were happy, at least for a while. They loved me bein' happy. And they had seen so much of that other with Reggie—totally unproductive, nothing, stinky, horrible, mean, making Mommy cry. So they were cool with it. Which told me they could like being married. They could like having a "normal" type of family. They probably thought, of course, that it wasn't gonna last.

FIELDNOTES: *Two months after she broke up with Reggie, Sugar married Mr. Lester. This hasty decision marked the beginning of a new life for her as a married lady, and a change in our relationship too. I realized that she wasn't being forthright with me where Mr. Lester was concerned. And I figured she was probably kidding herself as well. In spite of all our discussions about his being a junkie, she told herself that he was in recovery. Consequently, she had convinced herself that it was okay to go ahead and marry him, have him live in the house with her and her children. Whenever I asked her how things were going, she was so overpositive that I became suspicious. Honestly, it is unnerving to look back over the transcripts from that time. There are so many lies.*

TBE   So tell me about Lester. What does he have going for him as a husband?

ST   Mr. Lester's in the development stages. He's a hard worker, even though he's not employed at this time. He's willing to be part of the family, in contrast to a lot of others. He loves my kids, interacts with my kids. He's not just in the bedroom all the time smoking, in the kitchen eating, in the bathroom shitting, or in the bed sleeping. And he cooks. And we actually have conversations where, like, two people talk. Not monologues where I'm talked at. So that's refreshing. And we go out. And we party. And we do like a normal thing, whatever normal is.

I've always said, "I don't ask for much." Some of the things I tried like hell to get Reggie to do, Mr. Lester does: he wears clean clothes, he washes his body, he brushes his teeth, little things. He cries. He writes poetry. He's tryin' to better himself. He goes to school. He loves his family, and loves and respects his mom. That's pretty cool. Lester does anything and everything he can to help, and Reggie did nothing. This is what I desired in Reggie, to do what you can do. 'Cause you can't do anything in the area that I already got covered. Like Mr. Lester will cook. He cooked lasagna yesterday. He's been cookin' since he came. You know what I'm sayin'? Do what you can! Don't try and compete with me! Together we can be a team. 'Cause I can't cook worth anything. So you pick up that portion of it, instead of trying to tear me down, trying to *make* me cook.

TBE   How is being married to Lester going to affect your life? How's it going to change things?

ST   Bein' married to Mr. Lester means things *are* going to change because I won't be single in spirit. I don't have to make all of the decisions. So that's one thing that'll change. Course, the dynamics of my family will change in that there'll be a man livin' here. The newness of havin' a man living here happened with Reggie. That was not something that we had experienced in a very, very, very long time. The most shocking part is that Mr. Lester participates in the *living of the life*. He's a proactive part of this family. Like he's taught Terrell how to put on his underwear. He actually talks to him.

TBE   It's still *your* house and he's living in *your* house, right? Is that going to change?

ST   I gave him a key today. And Reggie James never got a key to this house. It's more of a feeling of our house because he's living here. He's not merely *staying* here. He's not living on me. He's supportive in however he can be supportive. For instance, I was doin' hair the other day, and I sez, "Honey, can you get Terrell some gear?" And I don't have to ask twice. He'll get up, he'll get Terrell dressed, face washed, hair combed, clothes on. That's helpful to me. In contrast, I could've said, "Reggie, could you get Terrell dressed?" And he'd say, "Oh, what do you want him to wear? Well, what do you want me to do? Well, Sugar, how come *you* just can't . . ."

Like the time when Reggie claimed he was tryin' to buy me a car for Christmas. "Oh, I wanna get you this and I wanna get you that." And he's got his eyes set on some big Cadillac. Never did see that car! Mr. Lester said he was gonna get this *little* car, a little Chevy. Some girl's gonna sell it to him for $100. Mr. Lester gets the little junkster. It doesn't work. Mr. Lester says he gotta do some clutch work on it. *He does* the work on it. A "hoopdy" is what it is. It's nothing more than a little get-around car, but he said he was gonna do it, and he did it. And that means a lot to me, people that keep their word mean a lot, no matter how small the thing is. Big

promises don't impress me. If you say you're gonna do something,
do it. I value that. That's cool. That's honest. This man does what he
sez he's gonna do. And he don't promise you the world.

TBE   How's this gonna affect your financial status?

ST   Financially, life around here won't change much because he's a poor
man. So it shouldn't change it very much in that our standard of
living probably won't rise or fall.

TBE   Having him in the house won't impact your welfare check?

ST   It will not really affect my check that much. Now if he becomes
unpoor, and very rich, very soon, it would cause a lot of cutbacks
and whatnot. But I don't see any major change right now. We'll
have to go apply for some other type of program. He's said that
he's interested in him continuing some form of schooling for as long
as we poor people can take advantage of schooling. He wants to go
to school to be in an electrician's union and get the education to be
an apprentice. And, of course, I got to keep going to school. That's
not an option. So right now, we're just poor with one more family
member. Just a poor couple.

Right now Mr. Lester's not working. He sez in essence he's a
handyman. He ain't workin', but I'm willin' to work with him. We
can make some fliers. I made fliers one time for Skip. Skip took
those fliers around to real estate places. He worked and would be
still working if he was any good. But he's no damn good—can't
read and won't learn how to read. So eventually every job Skip gets,
he loses it. But that ain't gonna happen here. Lester could take
those same fliers around to single women right now. We need nails
hammered. We need our filters changed to help our gas bill go
down. He's just doin' things that, as far as a black woman, that's
what we want. No biggy.

FIELDNOTES: *In the beginning of the Mr. Lester era, everybody had something
negative to say about him. Even Reggie contributed some rumors he had heard about
Mr. Lester beating some woman. Sugar's close girlfriends were particularly vocal,
because they knew something about his previous woman, Mary Ellen, who was just
about to get out of jail.*

*It was interesting how quickly this brouhaha about Mr. Lester quieted down.
Sugar's passionate support of him as a real husband deterred any lingering suspicions
as to his character. And, he won over the family with his charm and his cooking.
Sugar noted how comfortable the children became with her new husband: "They'd
come, sit, lay out on the floor. They'd laugh. He fed 'em, cooked for them. He set 'em*

plates aside, made sure that everybody got to eat. He was concerned about everybody, and they loved him."

I liked him too. We always had comfortable conversations when we met. He found a job with a contractor, and from Sugar's reports, was a reliable earner. Moreover, he jumped right into the role of fathering Terrell. He bought an old van, and they played basketball together, and he bought him the appropriate kid's gear. But I noticed that he was stoned a lot. Sugar didn't see it, but I knew.

TBE   Okay, let's start chronicling the naysayers here.

ST   Oh, gosh, everybody's a naysayer. It started with my mom. My mom was down here, she was talkin' about, "Well, you know, it's just as easy to marry a rich man . . ." I sez, "Mommy, if you don't stop with that lie. That is a crock of shit! And I'm not gonna tell my daughters that nonsense. And if it was true, you and all my aunties would've married a rich man." I asked her, "When's the last time that Prince Charming was riding through the ghetto in his Mercedes? You know it ain't happenin'!" Everybody's sittin' around waiting to exhale. They got their eyes set on this prize of this brain surgeon, and they're overlookin' the mechanic. But if you think you're a good person bein' a poor woman, how come a poor *man* can't be a good person?

She's sayin', "Well, you know, at the age of forty-three, I really wish Mr. Lester were a little more stable." What she's really sayin' is, "He don't have a job." Well, he's also not kickin' my ass either! So it's a trade-off, Mom. Thank you.

TBE   Who else?

ST   Then there's my sisters Paula and Kathleen. They're giving me all the "what ifs." What if he does this? What if he hits you? Have you prepared yourself for if he wants to fight you? See how people think?

Paula was sayin', "That Mary Ellen woman is gonna be part of your life. Do you want that, Sugar?" He has family. He has kids. And he has Mary Ellen, his ex-woman, his youngest daughter's mother, who is just out of prison. But I've met her, and I feel that I can touch her life. So call me crazy.

My sisters are sayin', "This man has baggage."

Hey, don't *I* have baggage? I have five kids, two adopted—in a family full of loonies. So why would I think somebody's gonna come in my life and not have baggage?

TBE   So what's the baggage *he's* bringing?

ST   He says he's got eight kids total.

TBE   Eight?!

ST   But only three are the ones he has birthed. So he's been with other women—of course he's been with women—and their children he still calls *his* children. And I respect that. You still love 'em. Just because you're not with their mama, whatever.

My sisters are sayin', "Well, will he be able to tell your boys what to do?" Why wouldn't he? He's gonna be my *husband*. I mean within reason. Like if he sez, "Why don't you boys get this trash out?" That's one thing. But if it's, "Why don't you little fuckers get this trash out," that's wrong.

Paula says, "Well, there are some things my husband doesn't tell my daughters, and he's their father." Kathleen says, "Ain't no man who can tell *my* kids what to do. If there's anything going on, then *I* tell my kids."

But see, I'm looking to relinquish some of that. I'm a student full-time now. I'm lookin' to relinquish shit like the trash, the dishes, or things that Mr. Lester may see that I don't see. That's why two heads are supposed to be better than one. That's why you have a partner! I don't wanna be Superwoman any more!

TBE   This is so totally different from your friends tearing down their men all the time.

ST   I don't want a man to castrate. I want a man to come in my life and be a man. And I can't really define what that all is 'cause I'm learnin'. And that means I have to let some things go. I know that I don't want to duplicate what I grew up with. We never had no men in our home. I've seen so many times over and over again where you got, basically, a human dildo. You can fuck me, but you can't tell my kids what to do. You can't tell *me* what to do. You don't have no say-so in nothing that goes on in the family life.

I guess what everybody's sayin' is that by virtue of the fact that I have these kids, that basically ı have an obligation to set my life aside until these kids are grown. FUCK YOU! 'SCUSE ME! HELL NO! I AIN'T DOIN' IT! I got my own life I gotta live!

With Mr. Lester, your house can smile. Your kids can smile. They don't have to tiptoe around. Lester is patient. He is willing to do little things like cook, spend some times with my son, chill, be part of the family. He's not looking for me to detach myself from my kids. He'll talk to my mom. Talk to my sisters. Introduce me to his friends. Introduce me to his family. I talked to his mom and his dad in Boston. He even brought his ex-girlfriend, Mary Ellen, over. She just got out of prison. They came and barbecued. They brought groceries.

TBE   Wait a minute! This is the girl who was going to come over and kill you when she got out?

ST   Well, I didn't know what was goin' on, but Mr. Lester said that it was cool. He says they've been broke up for a while now. They have a daughter together, and I've seen her a couple of times since then. White people do it all the time. You see these extended families. They spend time with their stepparents. The parent that has the child drops the child off, and you don't have to be out in the street fightin' and killin' and all that. It can work. See, I know how to have a wife-in-law, but she's not my wife-in-law. I don't have to share him with her. Their chapter is closed.

FIELDNOTES: *Despite what Sugar said here, the Mary Ellen and Mr. Lester chapter wasn't quite closed yet.*

"YOUR SHIT IS RAGGEDY!"

A couple of weeks later, Mary Ellen came to see me. She claimed she's been with Mr. Lester for ten years. She says he brought her from Boston. That was well before my time. She came by looking crazed. A month outta prison, and she's already back to crack.

So she comes by my house. She was sayin', "Well, where's Lester?" She was jonesin' and trippin'. She was agitated. She was pacing. She was talking fast. I hear that she used to be a very pretty girl, but she was a crazed-lookin' bitch right about now. She's not quite emaciated, but she looked really thin to me. And one of her eyes was kind of cockeyed. Maybe Mr. Lester dotted that eye. I know he used to beat her up. I don't know how much, but my girlfriend says he used to whup that ass.

There are certain circumstances where maybe the people that will read this cannot understand a man whuppin' that ass. White people say, "Oh, how can they hit their kids?" Just two different worlds, totally. But we can understand certain ass-whuppin's. And in this context, it was that this girl was druggin', would leave the home for anywhere from three days to a week at a time, leavin' him with the kid, takin' the money. You do that, when you come back, you get a ass-whuppin'. I can see it. I don't really condone it, but I understand.

So she comes over and she wants to know where is Lester.

And I sez, "Well, he's gone to Massachusetts," almost like, "Didn't you know?"

Anyhow, she's surprised that he left, and sez, "Why didn't he take me? He knew I wanted to go home!"

"Well, he didn't take you, 'cause, Miss, you ain't his woman! Sorry!"

She didn't get it. But I can understand her not lettin' it go, because this was her life.

And so she's sayin', "Well, he brought me down here. He's the one who got me on drugs! Now he done got a woman who don't *do* drugs, and I'm supposed to be happy for him? I'm not happy for him. I'm gonna go tear up all his shit! You can tell him I'm goin' to tear up everything—all his papers, everything."

She's sayin', "I'm gonna make you guys' life miserable. I'm gonna cap that ass. I got a razor!"

And I'm thinkin', "No you're not, bitch! You will go back to jail."

FIELDNOTES: *Mary Ellen died of AIDS only a few months after this interview. For me, her entry into Sugar's world symbolized the decaying layers of heroin lurking beneath the veneer of this marriage. At first, her coming around had been a statement about the successful blending of families. By her death, it was clear that Mr. Lester's baggage contained some unpleasant surprises that were about to be unpacked.*

Mr. Lester had all these drug friends that were very prevalent at the beginning, like all the people with no names. I would tell him, "None of your friends have names." I knew what that was. They would call him: "Man, this is Blue. Meet me at the Queen's Inn." The Queen's Inn's a fucking drug motel. Get out of here! "Pops needs a ride to work"—all this code language and shit. The hangin' out all day, the hangin' out all night. It was all too much.

He would go out and do it. Then, he would come home stoned, and he'd clean—be up all night. He'd cook. He'd scrub the kitchen and the walls. He was doin' dope! And then there was the time he said he saw Reggie. I'm sittin' there figuring, thinking out loud: "You saw Reggie, and Reggie doesn't do heroin, and you guys are in the same circle, close enough to see each other, that must mean you are on crack too."

"No," he sez, "I told you crack is not my drug of choice."

He said that Reggie basically was a crack addict and him and his people wouldn't really even associate with Reggie and his type. Like he's in a lower caste. Reggie wasn't usin' heroin. He was just a straight-up crack addict. Mr. Lester and his friends—they're smackheads, a higher echelon of junkie.

That's when Terrell found that needle in the glove. There were some brown gloves in the back seat of the car, and Terrell's playin' with them, and he says, "Mom, look what I found!" And he pulls out an IV needle, a syringe.

And, of course, Mr. Lester's defensive.

I'm sayin', "Your shit is raggedy! You're not even a good junkie! Nobody would expose their kids to this shit! You act like you all that, and you ain't even got the decency to protect your son from your nefarious funky-ass habits!"

He really was just quiet, so it got turned around on me. I'm the one that's emotional. He's cool. I'm the one that's ranting and raving. He's quiet. He doesn't say, "Oh man, that was so damn stupid of me! Oh baby, I'm sorry! I don't even know what I was thinking!" He's just silent. So without sayin' anything, it gets turned around on me.

That's just about when he got his prisoner ankle bracelet that he tells me was about "traffic," but I knew it was about drugs. Of course, he tried to put me on the defensive and make me think that I was crazy, that I was blowing it all out of proportion, 'cause it was just about traffic.

And then, I finally figured out that what he had done was he had an overdose in the back of his van! Can you believe it? I got all this evidence—stuff that showed what was goin' on that I didn't know was goin' on. Which really kind of pissed me off, 'cause I think a couple should be able to talk to each other, and if you can't, you're not a couple. And you don't have any business bein' married.

It started about the thirteenth of October. I came home and he was layin' across the bed, and he told me that the van had been impounded. This was not long after the van had been repossessed. In order to get it back, because his license is so fucked up, I had to go down and put my license on it—basically be a co-signer—so he could get his van back. So I did that. I had second thoughts, but he needed his van, and he's my husband.

After that, I remember sayin', "See, honey, you do need me."

And he told me, "I needed your license. I don't need you, I needed your license, bitch. And I got that, and so I got my van."

So a matter of days later, I come home. There's no van. He's there.

"Oh, honey, where's your ride?"

"It got impounded. I was in the Park lookin' for a basketball game."

Middle of the day, you supposed to be at work, you're lookin' for a game? Yeah, right.

"Why would they give you a ticket for lookin' for some hoops? I don't understand." I never was like nosy, but when shit doesn't make sense, I ask questions.

"Because I had an expired tag."

"But you just went and got your new tags, why didn't you put them in the window?"

By now I'm trying to make sense where there is none, 'cause he's covering up this bullshit.

A whole other month later, I'm talking to my friend Jerry. I'm tellin' Jerry about this irresponsible bastard. This is December. I'm tellin' him about getting the van impounded in the damn park.

And Jerry looks at me and says, "Did he go to the hospital?"

And I say, "I don't know, did he?"

And Jerry's tryin' not to get in my business, but he's tellin' me volumes. Now it's startin' to make sense. My husband overdosed in Central Park on heroin! Him and some of his other drug buddies. I imagine that his buddies called the ambulance and bailed out. Then I started opening mail, and it was all there: ambulance bill and oxygen bill and heart-starting-machine bill and doctor bill and hospitalization bill. All these reviving-your-stupid-black-ass bills!

So I went to him one morning, and I says, "I either want a divorce or I want a separation. I want us to do somethin'. I want you to get help for your problem."

"What problem?"

"Honey, your drug problem."

He looked me in my eye and says, "I don't have a drug problem." Knowin' that two months ago he overdosed!

He was an addict. That was enough! Shit, I had just came off of Reggie. I remember thinkin', *I'm not getting ready to go through this again!* And not only that, I was concerned. Hell, he was pickin' my son up from day care, and he'd have three or four of these *niggers* in the car. I was scared. At home, Terrell would be tryin' to crawl up on his lap and talk to him, and he'd be in a stoned nod. *My kids are in the house and you're nodding.* No way! I couldn't do that. I couldn't go, "Hey, kids, I traded Reggie in for Mr. Lester. I traded crack for smack. Yay!" I owe my kids more than that.

I told him if he wanted to be in my life, he had to clean his shit up. I told him that I was trying to get to the point where I didn't have to judge as much, and I didn't have to be right all the time. That I didn't have to make him make choices for his life. But I told him I could make choices for my life. I told him that I wasn't judging, or that using was wrong. All I was sayin' is, if he *chose* to use, then he couldn't be in my life. Pretty simple. I wasn't sayin' stop usin'. *Go on out there and use to your heart's content!* But I choose not to have it in my life.

I was prepared to go down and file for a separation very early on. And he sez, "Don't go. I'll stop."

And he began to change. I saw the difference in the first year and the second year! He wasn't nodding. He stayed home. He went to work. He paid his bills. You could hold a conversation with him. He wasn't walkin' sideways. He wasn't talkin' out of his throat, like his throat was constricted—when he would be high, I could always tell because his voice was different.

I think he really wanted a change. He knows the family that he comes from. He grew up with a mom and a dad and brothers. And I think he knows there's more to life than sticking a fucking needle in your arm. So I think he wanted to change. And I think I might have represented some of that change to him.

I figured he was really tryin' when he stopped doin' crossword puzzles. Crossword puzzles, I figured out, are tedious. You have to study them, and so you can actually nod, and you can use it as an excuse. He did things like that a lot. There were times when he'd come home and pretend to be writing something, concentrating real heavy, thinking real hard, or else he'd fake like he was reading. This motherfucker read *TV Guide* like it was a novel. And I'm going, "What the hell is taking you so long to find a program? But he's sittin' there and he's gone, though he could always pick up if somebody said something to him, "Oh, yeah, *Gilligan's Island.*"

He'd also come home late and would not get in the bed. He would get on the bed, leaning half on and half off, and put a *TV Guide* in front of him, and then he'd nod.

Now he stayed home at night. He got a job. I didn't think he was using. But it was the whole other extreme. He stopped doing almost everything. Once you lose that addiction, what do you do with all that time you spent feeding that addiction? So he lays up in bed and watches TV. He could watch TV for twelve hours. That nigger had no motivation, no ambition. Happy with the status quo, as long as I got cable TV.

But he was still pretty good with my boys. Malcolm and Will listened to him. I don't want to say they "obeyed" him, 'cause it's not like he was givin' out a whole lot of orders or anything. But if he told them to take out the trash or help with the yard or somethin', they'd do it. They had a good relationship, I think. The dirt that he was doin' they weren't really seein', because he was fairly quiet and subtle about it. I think what they did see was the inactivity, but that didn't faze them any 'cause they're out busy being teenagers. Malcolm was out workin' two jobs. Just bought a car. Will was workin' hard night and day. So Mr. Lester's laziness fortunately didn't rub off. But Terrell, who was under him all the time, could pick up on the quiet, subtle stuff that was goin' on, like talkin' to me disrespectfully, barking at me, not saying "thank you" to me, being basically an asshole. But the older boys weren't around for that. They had their own lives.

He never gave me nothin' for bills. But I was doin' everything by myself. However, I didn't even, like, require it. 'Cause me bein' me, number one, I made more than him. And so the bills that were my bills just kept bein' my bills. It's not like I would say, "Honey, I want you to pay half these bills." First of all, he didn't make that much. And second, I wanted to help him get his life together.

Did this for two years! For him it was a great improvement over livin' in a fuckin' dope den and chasin' heroin.

He paid the cable, which was his. He paid his car. He paid his Ward's. He paid for the phones for a while until I got my new phone. And I go, "Well, honey, I want you to still pay my phones, since you've been payin' 'em." Never happened.

FIELDNOTES: *Many of Sugar's complaints about Mr. Lester were familiar to me. Hadn't we been through the Reggie Chronicles already? I thought I knew the pattern by heart. But now, two years into the relationship, lots had changed. Our friendship had matured, and we trusted each other enough to share our concerns on a more intimate level. We were no longer simply mocking Reggie for being a fool liar. Mr. Lester was her husband. He was close with her son. She had committed to him, wanted to make this marriage the real thing. When she reflected on her life with Mr. Lester, she was certainly angry, but most of all, her heart was breaking into a million Sugar pieces.*

Yeah, my crib was a wonderful place for Mr. Lester to rehab. There's nothing there that I want to go back to besides the fact that I loved him. For two years, whenever I'd say anything about love, one of his standard jokes was, "What's love got to do with it?"

Duh, Sugar!

I loved him, but I didn't want to return to the way he treated me. Once the heroin cloud lifted, he was to the point where he had no regard for me. So then I've got this asshole that doesn't respect women, who says that all women are bitches.

He hadn't separated himself from his street mentality. No, there was nothing I wanted to go back to. So basically, in order for us to stay together, I said, "Okay, You gotta change. If you wanna stay as my husband, we're gonna turn the TV off twelve hours a day, and you've got to tell me I look pretty at least once a month." And I didn't have that right. I could ask, but I couldn't enforce it.

Obviously, he didn't want to *do* it.

I don't know that things were that bad. If he had never put his hands on me, I could've probably dealt with the lack of communication. I could've dealt with him bein' an asshole probably for a little while longer, but the thing was that the times that I said he was an angel and a king and whatever, I believed it. It was him who didn't believe it. He didn't believe that he's a king, that he was worthy to have great things in life. Not only that, I believe in the energy and speakin' truth and speakin' a life. The Bible says you *speak* life. I believe that. So I'd a been *worse* off if I'd have said he's a rotten, funky, lazy ass every day. I'd have been doin' the same thing he was doin' to himself by sayin', "You're stupid and lazy all the time." I said what I needed to say: "You're not stupid, you're great! You're great!! You're great!" And I believe in that. I've seen it work with kids. I saw it work for him for a long time.

I've been hopeful since day one. But that's just my mode. I'm just a hopeful person. I can't afford to dwell on the bad stuff. But my life was so full with everything else. And there were some good things with Mr. Lester. There were times he would compliment me in his way, even though his way is very crude. I enjoyed the relationship that he had with Terrell. And that's probably one of the most hurtful parts. He had a good relationship with my son, but my son was learning to have a bad relationship with me. He was seein' that it was okay to speak to a woman in these horrible tones. That it was okay to bark at a woman.

There were lots of those times. The last time was when I was ironing Terrell's stuff for school, and I came to the back and Terrell said, in this little big voice, "Hey! Where's my clothes?" But there were other times during the two years, times when he would start making disparaging jokes about me. But I can't blame him, 'cause he heard Mr. Lester do it. It would kinda be like, "We're the guys," and it's okay to say Mommy was stupid.

My baby-sitter said she had noticed that since I got married, Terrell was more aggressive at day care. There was one little girl. They would be playing like husband and wife. And Terrell would stare her down. I know it was because Mr. Lester was teachin' him all these men things: to fight, and stop cryin'—*Don't be a crybaby.* I would try to say, "Mr. Lester, don't play these games with him just before bed." There was never any quiet time, time to settle down. They'd go toe to toe. They'd wrestle and they'd fight. And Terrell might end up cryin'. He'd go, "Oh, Daddy, ow, that hurts!" And whenever he'd stop cryin' and get away outta the headlock or whatever, he'd go back in. It was playing.

He taught him how to play basketball. They were doin' all these *man* things. But it was makin' my son more aggressive. Do I want my son to grow up to be a sissy? No. But no way I want him to grow up disrespectin' women and thinkin' it's okay.

And the violence Mr. Lester filled his head with! He'd watch these movies over and over and over again. I couldn't do it. I can watch *Come Back Little Sheba,* okay, but not *The Terminator* and all those other Arnold Schwartzenegger movies. Titties and stuff. I'd go in there and say, "No, Terrell, this is not a kid movie. You gotta go." Terrell's sittin' up there watchin' the TV with him while he's smoking cigarette after cigarette. And they're hanging out. It's wonderful that they hung out, but it got so that I had to remove him from it.

Another thing about Mr. Lester was that he was always right, he always had to be right, and even when he was wrong, he wouldn't admit it. He would go to extremes to prove someone wrong. Is that just a male thing? Well, that was him. He didn't value women. I think that might be what it all boils down to. He didn't think women are worth anything. And that's that old pimp mentality: pimp's up, ho's down.

When I got my job at the day care, Mr. Lester thought I just played with kids all day. He called me *lazy!* Like after a long day of work—I worked two jobs—and at the second job, I would bring Terrell to work with me from the baby-sitter's. My request would be that Mr. Lester would come get Terrell after he gets off work. That way, Terrell would be able to go home. And I'd be home two hours later. So he did that a few times, and then one time he didn't. And I called him and said something like could he *please* come and get Terrell? He hung up in my face. He said he doesn't see *what* I'm doin' that's so important that I can't keep Terrell with me.

"But, honey, I told you I have a lot of paperwork and stuff that I gotta do that I can't do with him here."

"Well, make the little nigger sit down!"

"That's not fair! It's not fair for me to make him sit in a chair—he's four years old—when you can just come get him!"

"Well, I drive all day! And don't you know after I drive all day, I do not want to get back in the car and come out and drive just 'cause you want me to jump at whatever you say!"

It was all about him not having any power. It was about him not wanting me to have any power either because it further underscored the fact that he didn't have any power. It was all about him being a black man in America and not having nobody to lash out at or not knowing how or not having enough *balls* to go out and really fight the enemy. So everything was a competition. *Everything* was a dig at my intelligence.

I could do smart things all day, and I'd come in the room and ask, "Honey, have you seen my glasses?" And they're on my head, and he'd be like, "Duh!"

And then he started to do the same thing to Tina, calling her stupid or calling her ugly in different ways. I told him to leave her alone. I sez, "Okay, I'm toleratin' shit, but Tina is not your fuckin' wife!"

When you perceive yourself to be only an inch high, then everybody else has to be a quarter of an inch for you to feel tall. Sayin', "Hmm, maybe I oughta grow ten inches" is too hard because it requires more of you than it takes to sit and pull everybody else around you down. And so, that's basically what Mr. Lester made his unconscious or conscious agenda.

One day we was havin' a conversation and I sez, "Look at you! Rather than challengin' yourself, you pick on me about tryin' to widen my world. You surround yourself with the likes of Billy, who's borderline retarded, with Mr. Rio, who's an alcoholic and heroinhead." He surrounded himself with retarded people so he could feel smart.

I just feel like this: we just had different agendas, we had different goals. I don't want to say that he was wrong or he was so awful. Because like I told him, I didn't want to judge him, not even for hittin'. For me, it's not okay. But, believe me, there's a woman out there that wants to be hit *every Friday*. For some sick reason, she wants a man like him.

I don't want to be made to feel stupid. So I spent a large part of my time reminding myself that I wasn't stupid, doin' things that said I wasn't stupid. All my validation had to come from outside my home.

FIELDNOTES: *I'll admit that I considered it laughable that this street junkie would disparage Sugar's accomplishments. With all the work she had done to expand her world and learn something more about it, it enraged me to see how easily he could make her question her own capabilities.*

I saw it happen one night when Sugar came down to Las Callas for a meeting on urban poverty. She spoke on a half-dozen panels—about welfare, being a single mother, ethnicity, and the African American urban experience.

There was a reception the first night, and Sugar brought Mr. Lester along. He was all duded up in a three-piece suit, nice tie, fancy shoes. We hung out together, they talked to lots of participants, seemed to be having a good time, although I saw his eyes were pinned. He was stoned.

Later she reported to me that on the way home, he angrily accused her of "kissin' white ass!" He said he'd seen her "park her nigger ass" at the shrimp bar, where she stood for a long time eating "white." When she said that, as far as she knew, liking shrimp wasn't a color thing, he pointed out that she had repeatedly refused to eat the pork parts he ate at home! So it was a color thing!

It was clear to me that Mr. Lester put down Sugar whenever possible because he was jealous of her wit, her confidence, her ability to make her own way. These were all the things I cherished in her. But in Mr. Lester's mind, her success diminished him, reminding him of how peripheral he was to society at large. So while I was incensed that Mr. Lester behaved this way—and there are dozens of similar instances—the anthropologist in me could see the bigger picture, and I knew where his resentment and sense of impotency were coming from.

Despite all of Mr. Lester's emotional abuse, Sugar was determined to work with him, to try to work it through. It wasn't until his abuse became physical that Sugar could bring herself to leave him.

"DADDY LOVES YOU"

It began with him bein' an abusive man who's been tryin' to keep it under control for a long time and just couldn't do it no more. He's a brutal woman beater. He told me. And I know it about him. He's told me things, of like friends who are fightin' with their women, how he would have dealt with it. How he would have kicked her ass if she was his woman. How he's punched people out. How he's knocked people out with one punch. How he'd dealt with his life like that, growin' up. So then I end up with him!

He'd been wantin' to hit me for a long time. After he finally did, he tells his friend I attacked him. What I did was I batted him across his stomach with a potholder! I had been sleeping in the back room. Now, mind you, I slept for a year and a half with earplugs in my ears so this motherfucker could watch TV, because he wouldn't compromise. I couldn't sleep with all that noise. I finally ended up moving out of my room into the back room. So I was already mad. Me and Terrell were sleepin' out there with the door closed. It was ten o'clock at night, the TV blaring so loud you can hear it all over the house.

So I go and I say, "Honey, could you turn the TV down a couple of notches?"

And he sez, "Nigger! If the TV is too loud for you, go back in there and close the door!"

I had made up my mind that he couldn't continue to talk to me in that tone of voice, especially in front of my son. I had made up my mind that every time he talks to me like that, I was gonna back him down.

"Look," I sez, "don't talk to me like that!" He just barks at me and talks to me like I got a tail! I went in the kitchen and thought about it. I had the potholder in my hand, and I went back in and I "hit" him.

I went, "Motherfucker, you not gonna keep talkin' to me like that."

And he came around the bed and hit me in the head. Then I got up and I hit him. Then he hit me a couple of times. We were by the bed. At one point I remember bein' on the floor. I hurt my wrist. And I went and called the police.

When I went to call the police, he accused me, said, "Yeah, you like all the rest of 'em."

That is so typical black bullshit!

I said, "I *am* all the rest of 'em!"

I dialed 911. He pulled the phone outta the wall. Typical nigger shit!

And, of course, I got a cell phone. So I dialed again, and he lays in the bed like he's big and bad and he's not gonna do anything.

And I go, "Leave, nigger, 'cause if the police come and see this phone pulled outta the wall, you know you going to jail."

So he sauntered out.

When he came back two days later, I was working at my computer, and I looked up and I said, "Now you know you have to go."

Nobody can hit me and not go. He was kind of smirking and thinking I was kidding. Then I got a little, I guess, hysterical. I was cussin' him out. He was so calm; I looked like this crazed fool. Terrell was there watchin' it all. Once again I'm carrying the brunt of everything, and him comin' up smellin' like a damn rose! So that pissed me off.

And he was also indicating to me, "Well, I'll be back."

And I'm like, "No, you've got your car. Start getting your shit now."

So I packed up a lot of his stuff. And he let me. Ask me, did he help me? He just let me haul all this shit out to the street, and then he placed it neatly in the van. I wasn't throwin' it or anything.

I did cry! And I did cuss him out! But how many days can you spend like that before you and your loved ones say "Enough!" I'm just not a dweller on pain. But I did cry, especially about my son. My son was hurt and he was crying. And I cried because he thought I was the bad guy. Because when Mr. Lester came, and I was loadin' Mr. Lester's stuff up, I was cussin'. I called him a "fat fuck!" because he was leaving, but the truth is he's been fat for a long time and he's been a fuck for a long time. He was gonna drive off, and he hadn't said anything to Terrell.

And I sez, "You fat fuck. The least you can do is come back and tell this boy somethin'! Say somethin' to him!"

That's when I started cussin' him, and, of course, he's deliberately very, very calm. So what Terrell sees is this crazed, deranged woman, who, yes, she must be crazy. Thinking, *everything my dad said about her must be true because look at her, she's goin' off, and she's throwin' my dad out, she's packin' his clothes.*

Terrell was so angry at me. And that hurt me like hell.

FIELDNOTES: *A few days passed. Things quieted down. Terrell was kind of moody, but they talked, and his anger seemed to dissipate. Meanwhile, Sugar was in knots trying to figure out what to do. Her boy needed a father, but she wasn't going out on the streets to find him a daddy! She had her own life to lead. Her kids' needs were a constant concern, but they weren't going to redesign her life to suit themselves.*

Mr. Lester called and left a phone message for Terrell. He sez, "This message is for Terrell. How's everybody doin'? Daddy loves you, and I'll call you again later." Terrell must have listened to that message about fifteen times and he came in the bathroom where I was, and he said, "Mom, it's like I'm gonna cry." And I said, "It's okay to cry, honey.

I know you miss your dad." Then when he knew it was okay to cry, he went back and listened some more, another fifteen or twenty times. And cried. He cried the whole time. It was heartbreaking.

You know that first day, he was so mad 'cause I was cussin' Mr. Lester out and stuff. And I held my hands up and let him hit. I let him punch my hands, and just get it out. And then we hugged. After that he was pretty much cool.

He still talks about Mr. Lester. He wants a male in his life, but I can't afford to have just *any* male. *Okay, here's a male in your life, you grow up to be a misogynist motherfucker.* You think that'll be okay, long as I'll be able to look back and say you had a male in your life? No! So he may be desperate, but I am not going to get him another daddy. I'll have to fill it in other ways. One day I'll have somebody, but not while he's young.

And I can't say what I want to say: "Well, honey, look what your dad did to me last night! He hit me upside of my head! He busted my lip!" I wasn't goin' to go to that. He was only four years old. So I ended up bearing the brunt and lookin' like shit in my son's eyes for throwing yet *another* daddy out. So later on, I'm explainin' to him, I'm sayin', "It's not good for dads to fight moms, and if they do, then sometimes the mom and dad just have to be apart. Bottom line."

FIELDNOTES: *In the midst of all the tears and anger, Sugar did something that had to make you laugh. Terrell told her that when his daddy came, he was going to go with him and not come back. Although this really hurt Sugar, she somehow got it together enough to use a retort familiar to the boy, "That's cool. I'll get me another little boy. His name's gonna be Pete. And he gonna play with your toys."*

When I told the older boys about Mr. Lester leavin', Malcolm asked, "Did that nigger hit you?"

And I said, "No, son, I'm fine."

And he said, "I'll kill him!"

And I said, "No, you won't have to kill him."

He said, "Well, I'll hurt him."

I sez, "Really, honey, I'm fine. I'm cool."

And he took my chin and he looked at my face, he turned me to the left and to the right, and then he said, "Okay."

Of course, he *had* hit me! But I wasn't gonna tell Malcolm that! I didn't need my sons to be fighting Mr. Lester behind my situation. That's my doing. I had to handle that. My son could have got killed. And a lot of people do drag their kids into that. Like Gloria. Her and

Danny will fight, and her kids will be in it! Felicia hit Danny in the face. There's no way my kids are gonna be hittin' my husband in the face. And I'm not gonna put them in a position where they have to fight. It's up to me to handle it. Do whatever you have to do, but don't get your kids involved. And so, thank God, there wasn't any visible evidence to tell Malcolm that I was lyin'.

It's not that they didn't care about Mr. Lester leavin'. But they just love me. And what I say goes. Everybody else is incidental. So you can come or you can go. We don't have a problem with you comin'. We don't have a problem with you goin'. I had told Malcolm, "I really am prayin' that my marriage will work out. And hopin' Mr. Lester will come home." What I was trying to do then, as opposed to what I did with Reggie, was to keep them posted in a realistic way. I didn't want my kids to think, "I hate that nigger! I hate him! And if he comes around here, we're gonna blast him!"

No, I told my kids, "I'm hopin' that my marriage will work out. But right now we're goin' through somethin', and I don't want you guys caught up in it. But you guys need to know that this is goin' on."

I would sit and think that he was somewhere pining and trying to figure out how to get back in my good graces and come home. However, the reality was he wasn't doin' that! He was movin' on with his life and tryin' to figure out what else could he do for himself. So don't flatter yourself, Sugar, thinkin' that he loves you so much that all his every waking moments while he's away from home he's thinkin', "How do I get back? How do I get back?" He didn't give a damn!

Anyway, he took his stuff and was gone for like thirty days. Did I see or hear from him? No. Heard rumors of him out doin' drugs while he was gone. I guess he was kind of like a kid runnin' away from home and stayin' for a while and getting to do anything you want to do, 'cause now you're free. So then he came back. And that's when we had a long conversation where I did most of the talking. It's kind of like he liked me to chastise him. So he would listen very attentively. And I could tell, some of it he took to heart, just like a kid.

I told him then that this was either the beginning of the end, or the beginning of a new beginning. And it was the beginning of the end. Nothing really changed. That was mid-September, and by mid-December he was gone for good.

FIELDNOTES: *There have been many tears shed in the recording of Sugar's life. Every session, I find myself handing her tissues. It may seem odd, but when she cried over having her own checkbook again, I cried too. Because a checkbook of her own testified to the fact that she had not achieved her goal. A joint checking account was all the proof she needed that she and Mr. Lester were a union. They were not one, and never had been. So she opened her own account again and got a brand-new checkbook.*

Why did it make me cry? Because it's bittersweet. It's a victory. But once again it shows how strong I am by myself. It's good that I'm strong by myself. It's sad that I have to be strong by myself.

I like bein' married. I like bein' part of a unit. I like bein' part of a couple. I would like to have someone strong with me. I'm not gonna say I can't have it 'cause I can. But once again I didn't. I haven't been able to attach myself to someone that's strong like me. And I can dream about how if there were two strong people, how that checkbook would look, and what we would have in savings.

MR. LESTER'S GONE

Mr. Lester came by last week. It was strange and interesting. We hugged and we kissed. I thought he was in Boston and that he was outta my life and that I'd never see him again. I was telling people, "This has been so easy. This is so seamless I keep waitin' for the other shoe to drop. It was almost as if that three years of my life never existed. My house was as peaceful as it ever was.

So anyway, out of the blue, Mr. Lester drives up, and I go, "Hmmm . . . Terrell, there's your dad." So I let Terrell go out and greet him. And they hugged and hugged and hugged. And he came in. And he was sayin' that he wanted to hang. Would I mind if Terrell hung out with him today? No, that's fine. He's dressed, but he was gettin' ready to go get his hair cut. Can you take him to go get his hair cut?

"Well," he's sayin', "If it was up to me, I wouldn't cut his hair."

And I said, "It's no longer up to you. Would you get his hair cut? If you want him to go with you, cut his hair."

So he took him to go get his hair cut. And that seems like about all he did. And he came back, and I started to say, "Well, that was quick." But I didn't. He was then sayin' that he had a headache. And the second thing he came for was to get some of his stuff out of my way.

First of all, he knows I'm not goin' to let his shit stay in my way! He knows every nigger's shit goes in the back of the basement: Reggie's, Gates's, Jerry's, and Mr. Lester's! It's nice, it's neat. I put it where it won't get wet. You can come back ten years from now and get your shit! He comes back upstairs and says, "My head is hurting, and I don't feel like looking at the stuff. Can I take Terrell to church tomorrow?"

I say, "Sure."

I guess I was trying to read a lot into this and trying to figure out what he was doing. On the one hand, I'm flattering myself thinking he's just tryin' to see what I'm doin'. And on the other hand, I'm goin', *Sugar, don't flatter yourself! This man don't give a damn about you! He's got some kind of strange motive. He just wanted to get into the house to see if you'd moved another nigger in, quick, like you moved him in.*

I think he was waiting for me to make some move, some silly move, wanting me to say something like, "Well, I'll go to church with you."

But I'm not makin' another silly move. I told the Lord that I wanted a new husband, and Mr. Lester's gone.

I won't see the lesson in this decision to marry Lester until I'm further past it. But one of the lessons that I *can* see is that I've been doin' a lot of studyin' and tryin' to stay in tune with God. And I feel confident with my decision, however it ends up, I get to make my own mistakes. I get to make my own victories. I get to make my own choices. And I would have liked it to be the happiest, most blissful thing, and that we would ride off into the sunset and live happily ever after. But, however it ends, I always come out on top. I never lose. I have no regrets for Mr. Lester. I'm wiser. You can't pull the same games on me anymore. But, hey, marriage ain't forever, so nothing to worry about.

For Mr. Lester, I had to make a choice. I had to say, "I don't love your world. I don't love drug addiction." Which meant I had to sever my love. You can't take the person without their world. I love my life. What's wrong with that? I keep makin' those rotten choices. But my life is secure and I love it. And it treats me well for the most part, except for these assholes of men that I keep choosin'. I mean, somewhere in this life, there's got to be a nice guy.

4 MOTHER, DAUGHTER, SISTER, WOMAN

TBE   I'm such a worrywart that sometimes it's hard to believe the level of optimism that you bring to everything you do. Is this something you got from your mom?

ST   You can't be who you are without getting somethin' from your mom, your dad. But some of it is just so *me* that I can't explain it. Maybe it's just a defense mechanism. But my mom was so awesome, had all these kids, and this man was kickin' her ass on a daily basis. You had to have some kind of optimism!

FIELDNOTES: This is one black single mother who belies the stereotype of generations of welfare dependency. Until she was six, Sugar's life was relatively stable and somewhat middle class. Unfortunately, what Sugar has called the family's "Leave It to Beaver" existence was undermined early on by domestic violence and alcoholism. Eventually, Sugar's breadwinner father left, throwing the family into an unpredictable financial and emotional tailspin. Her mother bore another child by him, even though he had gone on with his life, and the entire family suffered because of her persistent depression and alcoholism.

What is amazing about this story is that through adversity, abuse, and abandonment, Sugar managed to grow up optimistic, persistently honest, and with a strong moral code. Sugar believes herself blessed. She later admitted that she believed she was spared the agonizing traumas of sexual abuse experienced by other siblings because God had chosen her as the family's emotional caretaker. Whatever the explanation,

these early memories set the stage for appreciating Sugar as a survivor, a woman
heading down the path to destruction who stopped at the brink and struck out in an
entirely new direction.

My parents were married, but I don't know anything about their life together before me. I don't really know the history of my own family. I feel jealous when people know their history and can talk about it. What I perceive is that our family history is so disgusting, so full of violence and abuse, that it's been erased. And so, we don't have one. I wrote my mom this letter one time, and I asked her about the woman that she was. I just wanted to know. How was your courtship? What was it you liked about Daddy? How did you guys meet? How was your first date? And she never wrote me back.

There's the story that they met in college and he was like Big Man on Campus. And she was into a lot of theatrical things. I don't see a picture of a loving young couple whose eyes locked across the campus lunch room and they ran into each other's arms. I see this womanizing, handsome man and a young woman whose esteem probably wasn't so high, and she got caught up with him. Basically, I think she probably did his homework and ended up pregnant.

I am the second of five girls. The first is Precious. She's severely retarded, has been most of our lives. And I suspect that my dad had somethin' to do with it. I just know that man hit her in the head or did somethin' to that girl, but the story has it that she was deprived of oxygen when she was born and that's why she's retarded. All this crap! I don't believe it. Then there's me, Kathleen, Paula, and Ronnie.

When I was little, we lived in a nice home on Langdon Street. My dad was in business at the time, and he had an office in the basement. The basement was clean. There was a file cabinet and a desk and a light, and he would be down there working. And I don't remember anything strange at that time, just regular family stuff. But one day, all the kids were outside playing, and I went to the basement and was lookin' in the window. He must've been doin' somethin', 'cause I got my ass torn. He came up and beat me with a two-by-four. And I remember being so puzzled and just crying 'cause I didn't know what I had done. And after that, my mom took us out for ice cream. She was covering for him, of course. But she always did. Anything to appease Dad.

While we were with him it was like a middle-class existence. Very poverty-stricken emotionally, but otherwise pretty middle class. We had this toy chest filled with the coolest stuff. We had one of those dolls that you'd flip her skirt, she's black. You'd flip her skirt, she's white. It was so cool. My mom wasn't working. Maybe that's why all I remember is her doin' housewifely things and getting her ass beat by my dad. I think she was the typical 1960s housewife. I remember when we were small they would have these great parties. They were literate people. There'd be all these African people and different white people. We were supposed to be in bed, but we'd be somewhere on the fringes, watchin' and pretendin' like kids do.

All this time, my sisters were my girlfriends. In spite of whatever was goin' on around us, we played, we sewed, we did each other's hair. We were close. We always had a houseful of kids—cousins and stuff—stayin' with us for the summer. We swam in the park. We were always going over in big groups. We would raid apple trees. We had some spending money, and we'd buy our little penny candy. We played as late as we wanted at night. It was a safe time then. You could play late, and the moms knew all the kids were safe on the block.

I have this little affirmation over my desk that says, "I am who I always was." I was a good girl then, and I still am. They used to say that I was the peacemaker, like in the Bible. I would always try to diffuse situations. I was always helpful and obedient for the most part. When I was in second grade, my mom and I did some kind of local soap opera here in Springfield. So I acted and I played a character named Becky. It was a short-lived soap opera, but I was a regular.

I loved elementary school. I was a good student. My favorite teacher was named Miss Collins. I remember Morris Emerson, Sr., bein' the principal at my school. And he would play the violin at Christmas, and we'd sing on the stairs. It was gorgeous, I still have dreams of that school. I can even remember how it smelled. I got good grades. I got picked for things. I won good-citizenship awards from day one. And I got President's Fitness Awards, a Cheerleading Clinic Award, and a couple of Optimist Club Awards. I was on the honor roll, and I got academic scholarship awards. School played a huge part in my being happy then, 'cause it allowed me to excel. People paid special attention to me. I was popular. I could stand out there. Like when I'd get an award, there'd be an assembly. You'd go on stage and get a bag of candy and your certificate. You'd get applause and get to shake the principal's hand. And I'd beam!

I don't remember my mom ever coming to see me get one of those awards. Maybe she did, but I don't remember her there.

"WE LIVED WITH MY MOM"

My mom drank Jack Daniels. She says she didn't drink, but I remember the bottle on the headboard. It's funny, I can almost pinpoint the onset of alcoholism in my mom. When we were little, our house was always clean. Mom would sew. She'd be up at night makin' us little matching dresses. I remember seein' her ironing. Our hair was always combed. Then the domestic violence started up. One time dad broke this chair over my mom's back. It was horrible. Me and my little sister were goin' in and seein' if she was okay, and she was throwin' up in this bowl, just retchin'. It was brutal. So that's when she started drinking. The house wasn't as clean, and the attention wasn't there as much. So that was the beginning of this much-abused woman tryin' to cope by turnin' to the bottle. He beat on her for years, and things continued to deteriorate.

One of my early memories is being in this shelter. We were little. I was maybe six. I remember goin' down and having meals, a real homey type of kitchen where women and their children were. And I remember a courtyard where we would play. That was when my mom first got the strength to leave my dad. I don't believe we ever went back. Right after that we lived in a house not too far from where I live now. We lived with my mom, my two aunts, and all the kids that were born then. So it sounds like three strugglin' young sisters and all their kids, and no men livin' in this little house. That was where I remember my little cousin would be goosin' the bed. She'd be humpin' the bed, simulating sex with the bed. How did those kids became so sexually aware so early? Maybe we were seven! I remember goosin' the bed 'cause she was goosin' the bed, and she would tell us "Goose Stories" and stuff.

After they divorced, we moved a lot! We lived on almost every block in south Springfield. In those days, it was easier to get a place. So you moved and stayed in the new place until you didn't pay the rent a couple of times and got kicked out. Or you left just before they kicked you out. Of course, my mom was also on the run, running from her life!

I remember when my mom would come home from "work," or wherever she was. Now when I come home, my kids converge on me; it's "Mom, watch this" and "Mom, do that!" They hand me the baby. I'm the center of their lives and the hub of the house. But when my mom would come in the door, it was a different story. We'd try to get her attention, but she'd be, "Just a minute, let me rest my head." Well, she'd go rest her head, and that'd be it for the night! But we just were thinkin' our mom was tired and needed a nap or something. Now I know that if you been drinking, and you go to rest your head, you're out. And she was definitely out.

Us girls were pretty much on our own in the house. Our mom would be gone somewhere. Moldy food and stinkin', dirty dishes were a common occurrence. I didn't realize somethin' was wrong with that till I was an adult. Now I know how long it takes for food to mold on the stove. So these things just weren't bein' taken care of.

My mom wasn't aware of what was happening in my life, probably 'cause of the alcohol. Like, I would tell my mom I was job huntin', and I'd go lay up with my boyfriend. Now, my daughter can't come home after sayin' "I'm goin' job huntin" without me askin', "Well, how was the job huntin'? Who did you talk to? Where did you apply? Did you get applications? Do you need me to call anybody?" But that didn't happen to me. So I was able to tell my mom, "I'm goin' to the moon" and she wouldn't care. I didn't have to do a whole lot of sneakin' because I didn't have a whole lot of accountability.

My mom was using several names, probably because she was dodging bills. I don't know what kind of work my mom did. She worked at the library for a while. And I remember a bar-restaurant-diner that she worked in. But I often wondered if my mom wasn't some form of a hustler. Matter of fact, I remember tellin' her somethin' like, "Well, Mom, if you was a hustler, you wasn't a very good one." 'Cause she would be, like, too proud to take things from men, but yet men would be around us and men would be preying on us. They might as well have paid! My sister remembers sittin' on these men's laps and bein' passed around. Gettin' coins. Mother would have these big parties, and after the parties, us kids, we'd have little parties of our own. We'd have chips and we'd taste drinks, the whole bit. But we'd have to step over these bodies. The people wouldn't go home. They'd just flop.

From when I was ten to fifteen, we lived in Milwaukee. My mom worked in real estate then, and we bought this new house. I like to use the word "carefree" when I think of those times. All I did was swim and play and go to school. We lived right across the street from an elementary school, so that was our playground. We played tetherball, climbed up on the roofs, ran all over the place. But then, we came back to Springfield for what was supposed to be a visit and never went back. My mom says it was because the car broke down, but I never believed that. Somewhere in the back of my mind I'm thinkin' there was something shady going on in that real estate place where she worked. We were confused: "Mom, we gotta go back! Our diaries are under our beds! We gotta say good-bye to our friends!" You know, we only brought a few clothes with us to our cousins' place. But we never went back, not even to pick up our stuff. Same way we went there, same way we left. Had to be about my dad. I got a letter from my boyfriend: "Dear Sugar: I went over to your house. I didn't even know you were gone."

When we were older, my mom would send us over to our dad's place. We wouldn't be sayin', "Mom, we wanna go see our dad." But she'd be, "Go see your father. He's still your father. I don't care what he does, he's still your father." She didn't want to badmouth him in the hope that someday he'd come back. Plus, if she said he was a dirty, low-down, sexually abusive sonofabitch, and then she gets back with him, she'd look stupid. And the truth is, she ended up losing him to a white woman! The man who she had given her young life to and who gave her five girls. He beats the hell out of her, and then this is the thanks she gets? They divorced and he married Marion, this white girl.

FIELDNOTES: *Having a "voodoo priest" for a father might go right over the head of any ordinary little girl who cares most about school, friends, and dolls. In this case, however, voodoo did not translate into ritualized prayer, but instead was a vehicle for sadomasochistic fantasies and the distribution of pornography. The impact on Sugar is unmistakable. The irony of the situation lies in Sugar's acceptance and even understanding of her father's bizarre behavior. It is her Christian mother who is the object of her continued contempt, because she did nothing to warn her daughters, nor did she ever interfere.*

The consequences of sacrificing young girls' emotional and physical safety to a dominating male show up repeatedly in Sugar's narrative as they echo through her life. Looking back on this period, it is clear she learned then that men are irresponsible and abusive, but as she says, "you know that comin' in."

"SMELLS LIKE VOODOO"

Marion basically infiltrated our family and took my mom's husband. Years before she became my stepmother, Marion was entrenched in our life. We used to play with her little daughter. She was a friend of the family! Marion is who introduced my mom and dad to astrology. My parents were in all these artsy circles, and they'd have all these parties and do the astrology and have all these otherworldly type people around. So they became devout astrologists, to the point that they had stacks of magazines: Linda Goodman's monthly, weekly, yearly, the century, lined up, stacked, till the piles would slip down. That's what my mom was really into. But Marion and my dad got into all kinds of weird stuff too, and I think this is what grew into voodoo.

My dad was this tall and handsome man, with a cool deep voice and long fingers. After he became a voodoo priest, he always wore black. And he'd wear a leopard hat and leopard earrings to match. But there was nothin' feminine about him. Later on, I met a guy who, when he found out whose daughter I was, took two steps back. He was afraid of me 'cause of my dad. The people really believed in his voodoo power.

He had a little voodoo store that was catty-corner across the street from where we lived. It was their first voodoo temple. Honestly speaking, they probably believed that voodoo was this religion, but I think it was a front for sex. Like, in this little temple, he sold oils, powders, candles, lotions, voodoo paraphernalia, all this ritual stuff. But he also had lingerie and dirty magazines in there too. You couldn't walk in and buy them though; they were for the followers.

They had this deity, this mannequin that was cut off at the knees, kind of like *Boxing Helena*. And they had strapped on this dildo, this mega-dildo, and it was *black*! And they had all these rooms with tapestries, carpets, and pillows that you'd sit on, or whatever. Marion is very artistic, and she would draw these posters of these gorgeous women and put them up in the temple. They all had these huge pointy tits. Their heels had to have been eight inches tall, the kind that make your feet look like Barbie, straight up. And they'd all have their breasts exposed, with whips and masks, hats and gloves, and garters. I remember candle-burning, and incense, and a sickly sweet smell that I can still smell today and go, "Smells like voodoo."

Mostly, I remember bein' over at my dad's and looking at pornography at a very young age. And this is where I feel a lot of the anger and puzzlement about what my mom was goin' through that she would let her girl children go and look through pornography. We'd get magazine after magazine and look through them—I mean hard-core stuff we had never seen. Somebody suckin' somebody's penis. What'd we know about that? And we'd sit and we'd look and we'd look. And we'd take another one off the stack and we'd sit around and look. When you went to the bathroom, on the wall are Polaroid's of all these people, women in various stages of undress, legs open. So you can sit on the toilet, and you can go, "Oh, there's Wanda, Sally, and there's Dora." And you're lookin' in her snatch! Get out! So it's not like my mom wasn't aware.

My younger cousin Marie, who was five, was living with us then. Her and this other little girl were caught doing oral sex on each other. Where does a five-year-old learn that? She had been goin' over to my dad's, and they had been doin' her. You see, Marie was almost made to go over there a lot, supposedly to play with my stepbrother. So she would go over there and they would prey on her. Finally, one time when Marie was seventeen, my sister Kathleen went over with a gun and pointed it at Marion and my dad, and said, "If you ever touch her again, I'll . . ."

I can't help but think that my mom had to know somethin', but then again, what does a person know if she's keepin' herself sedated?

Years later my dad went to the penitentiary for messin' with these young girls over at Washington Junior High School. I still have the clippings somewhere. Luring them in under the guise of modeling lingerie. Big scandal! Him and my stepmother. I think that all the women that were in that church of his, if they weren't bisexual when they came in, they sure was when they left!

I'm sure some of my sisters were abused when they were little. I know one thing. My mom had these five girls. Men knew she was vulnerable: low self-esteem, probably on alcohol. It seemed like they would come to prey on us. I remember my cousin Mikey comin' to live there, and he was on drugs. We lived in a one-bedroom apartment. We had no room for no grown man to be livin' there. Then my cousin George came and stayed. My cousin George is a pedophile. He may not be today, but he was then. He used to have me sit, like straddle his chest, and pick the in-grown hairs on his face for hours. And I'm thinkin' I'm a good girl, I'm doin' my cousin a favor. He'd be hard the whole time! I was eleven or twelve.

He had some child pornography in his room up under his mattresses. We went and found it. There were these prepubescent girls— they didn't even have breasts—in these sexual acts with grown men. One time, he was coming out of my sister's room, and she was almost hysterical. He was sayin', "It's okay, okay." Like, "Be quiet, I'll leave." We saw that and didn't quite know what it was or what to make of it.

It was not too long after that he was gone from our home, but that was the year we couldn't touch her anymore. She was fourteen.

FIELDNOTES: *A lot of Sugar's childhood is based on half-truths and missing information about her family, especially her mother's life while the girls were growing up. During her thirties, Sugar became so angry about her mother's refusal to talk about herself that she and her sister wrote their mom a letter demanding some answers. They got no satisfaction, only infuriating them more. At one point, Sugar was determined to make a movie "exposing" her family's secrets and lies. Since then, she has mellowed considerably. In fact, she wants to kind of set the record straight on her mom.*

Well, I love my mom. I think she's the greatest thing since sliced bread. She worked very hard. Now that I've had kids, and they've grown older and become teenagers, I know that there are certain things you have to keep from your kids when they're young. I don't know if you should still be keeping it from 'em once they become adults. So I still disagree with that piece. She wasn't a bitch. She was just a troubled woman. My whole thing with her is that now I'm grown, she should be able to tell me everything.

With my kids, I've shared some stuff with them that I thought they should hear. Like, when Terrell asked, "Back in the day, did you smoke weed?" It was time for me to address that. Should I be like my mom and say, "No, no, honey"? And then he'd grow up and then I'd have to fix that lie? I said, "Yes, back in the day, I smoked weed until I realized that it was not healthy for me to smoke weed. Because I did not want my kids to grow up thinking it was healthy to smoke weed, and so I stopped." And he was okay with that answer, and he has a piece that he can put together. When other kids are talking about it, he can say, "Back in the day, my mom smoked weed. But she stopped. She didn't think it was healthy." He's got somethin' he can use.

DOLLY

Well, she's her mother's child, which is all for the positive, but also the foolish. Her strengths and her weaknesses are that she's very much like me. Her strengths are that she's independent, she's forward-minded, she's outspoken, she's confident, she's beautiful, she's hard-working, she's loyal. She's smart as a whip. She's articulate. She is on the side of right, and she figures out what is right. So she doesn't necessarily go with the crowd just because they're goin'.

Dolly is the kid that brings home stray people. She is compassionate. She gave some homeless person her gloves. She's brought home runaway teenage girls like other kids bring home lost dogs. Once she tried to bring home somebody's kid whose mother was on dope. It was like, "Mom, can I bring her home?" *Yes, put her on the newspaper on the back porch and give her a bone!* So she's just very loving. She cries. Oh God, we were reading the newspaper or something about somebody that sodomized and murdered a two-year-old baby boy, and that girl just cried and cried and cried.

She doesn't drink. She doesn't smoke. She hates it and doesn't think it's cool. That's not very popular to say that, especially in the midst of all the kids who are saying this is cool. One time she was on the phone, and they were tellin' her about this party where they were all falling out drunk. She goes, "You guys is stupid!" They were sayin' how they all laid out on the floor, and she's sayin', "Oh, you guys are geeks! You are the geekest of the geek geeks!"

How did she get this nonconformist attitude? Duh! Probably from her dear sweet mother is the only thing I can think of. She's got elements of it that she's just refined herself. But I'm proud of her for it, you know? Not to be a follower.

She gets good grades in school; she's active, a leader. She has a little trouble with math, like I always did, but her grades are good.

I taught Dolly to do hair—a normal rite of passage. It's what you do. Mothers teach their daughters how to braid and do their hair. She's been doin' hair since she was eleven years old. And she is a little entrepreneur. I had to teach her the business aspects and how to do a consultation, which she can do with an adult client, and they'd think they're talkin' to a grown woman.

She started out doin' her little sister's hair. She would braid her own hair and do all her little friends' hair at school, her doll's hair. And she'd get better and better. I didn't give her real lessons. A lot of it might be through osmosis. You show 'em the basics of it, and if they watch, and just look and see and practice, that's how they get it. So you show 'em the minimum, and the rest comes just in the doin' of it. One night I heard her up on the phone, and she was sayin', "I be braidin' my ass off."

She wants to open a natural hair care salon. The salon is in the dream stage, but she just got through doin' the hair of a lady at the mayor's office. She commands anywhere from a hundred to three hundred and some.

As for her future, she's had various thoughts. A pediatrician is where she started. She likes workin' with kids and youth. But she decided she wants to be a businesswoman. She wants to be a CEO, the boss. I see her bein' pretty much an entrepreneur. Now she has said that she wants to go to cosmetology school. That would be good 'cause then she could go into business and be the CEO of her string of braiding salons.

I would like her to go to college, not far away from home, but to a school where she could get the college experience. I remember I used to turn my nose up at college-type people, because at college age I was a mother of two, and divorced, or soon to be. So I just didn't think they were as mature as me. That may have been the case, but then they had somethin' that I didn't have. And that was an innocence, a fun, and I would like my daughter to have that.

FIELDNOTES: *Sugar has described Dolly as a terrific young woman who has smartly carved out a promising direction for herself. But at the same time, when Dolly was a teenager, she had some sexual activity that gives us a sense of how foolish she's been with boys. Clearly, Dolly was not making good choices about sex and love. Although I've recorded her mother wringing her hands in frustration about all this, the model Sugar has presented of male-female relations is one that her dutiful daughter Dolly seems to have replicated fairly accurately.*

Even with the sexual thing, it's like her choice. It's not a wise choice, but it's not that she's being pushed, prodded, and doing this because all the girls are doing this. That's not the reason why. It's silly. She's looking for love. Bein' like me. Bein' very mature. Wanting to be special. Making the same choices like me: gangsta guys—not necessarily gang members, but those gold-teeth type of guys, just like her mama.

She *did* have one that was pretty straight-laced, Bobby. And they didn't last. Her and Bobby seem to be gravitating back together. Bobby's got a child, I hope not two. He's older. Dolly's a caretaker like me. Maybe she sees that she can make him better. She can make him more noble. She can help him.

When she was sixteen, she was on birth control. She just got over the clap—serious clap. She didn't get just a clap, she got applause!

And she knows about condoms! I found a bagful in her room. The problem is she ain't usin' 'em. I talked to her about condoms and everything. She just keeps sayin', "Whatever."

She has had so many boyfriends! Get a grip! I'm always goin',
"Dolly, if you gotta be in love, okay, but why do you gotta end up
having sex? Why can't you guys just date for a while? Why does he
have to be your boyfriend?" Duh!

FIELDNOTES : *To a certain extent, Dolly, a thoughtful, centered young woman, has*
replicated her mother's habit of using appallingly bad judgment when it comes to
men. Sugar has tried to set her straight. But no matter how many heart-to-heart
talks they have had about valuing yourself and "being a queen," Dolly falls back on
what she's seen of men while she was growing up: Sugar's bad habits and worse luck
in finding a good man. It's fascinating that Dolly has internalized this message about
men while her younger sister, Tina, has not.

TINA

I'm pretty sure that Tina hasn't had sex. Thank God! Tina is just a
different child than Dolly was at that age. And I'm thankful for that.
It's almost like it gives me another chance to try again at raisin' a
teenager different than me.

Tina and I have talked about sex, not as much as me and Dolly, but
a lot. And I believe her and Dolly have talked, too. And also, she's seen
what Dolly went through. So there's been a lot of different forms of
communication about it, and not just all talk. What she's seen with
her eyes, what she's heard, what she's seen with her friends. One of
her little friends is pregnant now, and she's just so fed up with this
little girl who's going along sayin', "Don't walk so fast, I might have
my baby right here in the hall!" Or, "Would you go get my lunch tray,
'cause you know I might have my baby!"

And Tina's like, "Look! Get over it!"

If she decided to have sex, I think she would tell me, but then I
thought that about Dolly, and she didn't. I believe she would come to
me because she's more of a girl—which could change overnight. She's
more scared of life, where Dolly was more daring. So before she did
somethin' she might want to know what she's in store for. She doesn't
have a boyfriend. She's not doin' a lot of boy talk. She's not doin'
makeup, although sometimes she'll put on a little lipstick.

We still hang out. We like to watch old movies together. We watch
all the crime movies. We watch all the movies of the week. And of

course, we comment and we talk about 'em, what we would do in this or that situation, and how if our baby was kidnapped, we would search for her to the ends of the earth.

Part of Dolly's and Tina's differences are that Dolly's older and was kind of the groundbreaker. Somebody had to do it. And Dolly has done that to make Tina's life easier. She established herself in the schools. She just broke the ground so that Tina doesn't have to. You know it's like when you're hikin' and somebody else is breakin' that trail, then your legs don't have to get as scratched up. And you don't come out with as many thistles in your clothes, because somebody went through there before; and that's what Dolly has done.

Tina has been able to be close enough to a lot of situations without bein' in 'em because of Dolly. Tina has seen the trouble you can get into with boys through Dolly. She's not awestruck by boys. So she has been able to take a different path. She can see, "Okay, this is what happens when you mess with boys, when you screw around, so I can choose to get into drama club instead."

Tina's on the right track. She's working. She loves her mommy. She's loyal. She's startin' to do the teen thing. Tina is active. She said she wants to be a star. What she really means is like a musical singer, a teenager that's gettin' paid and looks like they're livin' the life. Oh yeah, she wants other things, but she knows that she can do that too. But right now, what teenagers want is to be making thousands of dollars for looking cute and singing. She wants money and she wants the trappings. And she knows that being active and being involved in school is part of the way to get there. You can't jump up and be no overnight success. You gotta be rounded. And patient. These are things that I've told her.

FIELDNOTES: *It is just so fascinating how diametrically opposed Sugar and I are on some things. Take, for instance, the issue of running your kid's life. Sugar is confident that she's done a grand old job with her kids, and that they are therefore capable of deciding things on their own now that they're teenagers. She'll still give them the condom lecture or ask some pertinent questions designed to spiritually wake them up, but she doesn't steer them around. Since I grew up with parents who monitored my every move, it's always a shock to watch her operate. It's not necessarily a negative reaction, just a kind of cultural and personal double take.*

Sugar's response has been that she has to let her grown kids live their lives, especially to live her own. If she is ever going to have her own life, she can't spend all her time hoverin' over her children.

Here's an example of just how differently we approach childraising: Tina was a good student in high school. She was taking Advance Placement classes. And she was in drama club doing plays and musicals. She wanted to go to college. Although Sugar was very proud of her daughter, she did little about helping her choose a college or get into a good school, figuring Tina could handle it. Meanwhile, I can't stand to not backseat drive. While Sugar has no idea what the requirements are for Tina to get into college or when she has to have everything submitted, I'm madly strategizing to find her a tutor for her SATs, setting up interviews for her at nearby colleges, offering to help her with the applications. She basically indulges my attentions, but calmly sets about applying only to a community college.

Her mother appreciates this, but I'm bewildered. Why wouldn't she be opting for a better four-year school? Or try to get a scholarship? At least play the race card and see how far it gets her, no? They ignore me. My reality is nothing like theirs.

What I don't realize (until a year later) is that by going to community college, Tina can save money, buy a car, and move toward fulfilling her real game plan, which is to transfer to Spellman College. She doesn't have the grades for Spellman as a high school senior, but she can transfer in with only a 2.5 GPA. She does this. She gets in! She only asks me for my advice just before she's to hear about admission (I would have written her a letter if she'd wanted one) and only because her mother insisted she at least be polite to this rabid white professor and friend worried over her future. But she's her mother's daughter. She gets into Spellman all on her own. She starts next year.

Tina has been going to clubs. She a party animal. She par-tays! She goes to Las Callas. She goes to Madison. She's living the college life. She went to the "Big 12" in Las Callas, some kind of black college gathering that comes together during Black History Month to celebrate themselves, I guess. Her and her girlfriends had a hotel room.

She says, "Mom, I'm meeting people I never met before!"

Now she realizes that the mom who was trying to keep her home at first ends up having it together. She can finally see the benefits of it: She's able to get a new car. She's able to safely go out to things but know that she can go home. She's able to have money because she doesn't have to pay rent.

I said, "I'm so happy for you. You're just doin' the college experience!"

She says last night, "Mom, we have philosophy homework." What I do is I read it for her and I break it down into ebonics! Like, the thought of what makes a person a social-valued person? Is it because they don't cheat on their wife? And had no desire to cheat on their wife? Or is it the man who wants to cheat on his wife and doesn't? So, I'm breaking it down to, maybe, who is more responsible? The girl who goes in the store and wouldn't steal? Or the girl who wants to steal and then doesn't. I place it in settings that's right in our hood, so I put this hypothetical girl in Target. Tina enjoys it and she understands it. So she's able to go into the class and join the discussion and know what's goin' on.

FIELDNOTES: *I have always been concerned about the children seeing Sugar with men who mistreat her. This is a constant topic of conversation between us, to the point of nagging. I will ask something like, "Well, how does this problem with Mr. X (or Mr. Y or Mr. Z) impact the kids?" Sugar's response has always been that her kids don't pay attention or can't hear or don't care. But the children have been much more involved in these domestic scenes than she will admit or would like, as Sugar's talk of "the drill" illustrates.*

I'm tryin' to think of when I instituted the drill. It's so old. I'm tryin' to think in my life, did I institute it because of someone? I don't think so. It's just a preparedness drill, kinda like a fire drill.

I gave them the drill just in case some crisis happened, to get ready for it. If somebody was to come in here and try to hurt me, harm me, bother me, destroy me, we use the drill. Dolly comes and helps me fight, Tina calmly goes to the phone and calls the police. You don't ask questions, you don't ask what's goin' on, you simply go to the phone and you call the police. That's the drill.

I needed the drill because I've had a lot of men in my life. And all of 'em I haven't known well enough to be able to predict that they'd never do me any harm. And I'm not so crazy to think that I can beat a man. I'm gonna get me some outside help. Even a one-armed man I probably couldn't whup. You never hope to have a fire, and you may never have had a fire, but you get your fire drill instituted so that everybody knows what to do, how to get out.

COUSIN ROSA

FIELDNOTES: *Sugar's cousin Rosa, who has been diagnosed as bipolar, survives on government assistance and handouts. Too mentally ill to follow a pharmaceutical regimen, Rosa has good periods and bad. Sometimes she's homeless, sometimes she lives in a single-room occupancy hotel in downtown Springfield. Sugar sees Rosa only occasionally, and she would be a somewhat peripheral character in this book were she not the mother of Malcolm and Will, Sugar's teenage boys. In 1990, Sugar assumed their guardianship and they have lived with her ever since.*

Their story begins when, ever the caretaker in her extended family, Sugar sent for Rosa to come to Springfield.

It was 1986 when I first heard that they had come to take her away. So the stories were tricklin' back to Springfield: How Rosa and them were homeless. How Rosa was doin' some kind of weird rituals. There's no tellin' what else. How the boys would sneak to go to school. I've heard of kids sneakin' away from school, but these kids were sneakin' out the house to go to school. How they lived in squalor. Cats runnin' all through the house.

The family's remedy is "Oh, well, we're waitin' on the Lord to change somethin'." Duh! That's what *you're* for! For the Lord to work through *you*, but that's my family.

So I couldn't stand it anymore. By now the stories were that they were walkin' the streets in Milwaukee. That she had 'em walking at night. You know, crazy people like to walk at night. So they would be in the house during the day, not going to school, and walking at night, but nobody in my family would do anything. They'd just go, "Those are her kids and she's grown, what can we do?"

So what I did was I convinced her to come here, and I sent them bus tickets. And when they came, they stayed with my sister Kathleen. And Kathleen, being Kathleen, was expecting a form of sanity from Rosa that wasn't there. Rosa was always laying around in her pajamas while the dirty dishes piled up.

She got too psychotic for Kathleen, and her and Kathleen got into it because, of course, Kathleen was expecting normalcy from Rosa. Kathleen was all, "She won't clean up. She won't get up. She won't do these things." Why do people expect normalcy where there is none? It's just not gonna happen.

So, Rosa ended up on the streets. She emptied all her food outta the freezer, took the boys, and left. That night they ended up at the bus stop, with frozen food in a Safeway cart and the boys with their shoes neatly tucked up under the bench, prepared to lay down and sleep.

So me and Kathleen were driving around the city looking, and finally, we spot them. We screeched up, and then I kind of started a fight with her.

I shouted, "You gotta let me take these kids!"

But she didn't want me to take 'em.
I'm like, "Boys, get in the car!"
She's like, "Boys, sit down!"
"Boys, get in the car!"
"Boys, sit down!" So, after that, the police came, took 'em to the Crisis Center and then I had to go through the courts to get 'em out. I had to go against my cousin to save her kids.

I couldn't sit by and watch, specially in Springfield. This is my home. A lot of people know me. I couldn't have people sayin, "There's Sugar's kinfolks sleepin' on a bus bench." I couldn't do that, so I just had to do somethin'. People think I decided I wanted to take care of them. Caretakers don't decide they want to do shit. They are driven to do it.

Rosa can be very scary. She's very psychotic. You don't deal with that every day—someone sittin' in your house, laughin', talkin', lookin' upside your head. She gets frustrated being out on the streets. Somewhere in her mind she wants normalcy, but her illness won't let her have it. She wants to do the things that "normal" people do, and she can't. So she gets frustrated. She mills around life. It's kind of like you are a spectator in your own life. You can't even get in. So I imagine it's very scary for her. She maintains as best she can.

One day, she came over, and it was a good visit. And it was interesting too. When I have money for her, or when a span of time has passed when I haven't seen or heard from her, our paths will cross. So she showed up on the doorstep, and she never has done that, come without calling. It was interesting because she came in, and she was saying in jest, playfully but really seriously, "When are you gonna give my kids back? How long are you gonna keep my kids? I want my kids back. I think I'll just take 'em."

And I could see in my peripheral vision the boys had these stark looks of fear on their faces. The look that was saying, "Look, this is our mom, and we love her, but there ain't no way we wanna go with her."

FIELDNOTES: *When Sugar opted to raise her cousin's sons, there were few second thoughts. She was guided in her decision by her understanding of what families are about. This kind of "fosterage" is fairly common among poor African Americans. Circumstances vary, but many a ghetto childhood has lived at the home of an aunt or grandmother. Sometimes these arrangements are temporary practical adjustments to the demands of income production. For example, a mother may find a job out of town* and not be able to afford the expense of bringing a child along. In this period of welfare reform, grandmothers who thought they were past the age for child care have grandchildren thrust upon them when their daughters enter the workforce.

More often, however, some kind of personal family problem encourages relatives to offer their homes for a time. Sugar has cared for nieces and nephews when adolescent conflicts with their parents got to a breaking point. But long-term fosterage also occurs fairly regularly, as in Sugar's case when she intervened and wrested control of Malcolm and Will from her troubled cousin.

MALCOLM AND WILL

There's a basic foundation in Malcolm and Will that came from their mother, Rosa. There is nothin' special that I've done 'cept maybe nurturing what was put there by Rosa. I mean, I feed and shelter them, and I support 'em, but their fiber didn't come from me.

It's kind of puzzling. I mean, I can't look at them and say, "I gave them this. And she gave them that." I can't see clear-cut lines where I can claim anything special that I did for them. Except for maybe providing an environment where they could grow as opposed to bein' stifled. See, if they were in foster homes, that same spirit might not have been able to blossom. But I didn't put the spirit there.

Look at them. Malcolm's getting ready to go to New York with his class from high school. Goin' to the New York Stock Exchange. Will is looking up to his brother and kind of basking in the glow and lovin' it. And it's cool. They're really cool. They're fourteen and sixteen. When they don't work, they do their sports.

These teenagers are beginning to have busy, productive lives. Last summer, they participated in this summer school program. They did computer classes, they did tennis, and then they had some fun activities. They had karate, photography. They loved it. They were out of here every morning, goin' to summer school. And Malcolm always gets such glowing reports! He is jammin'!

They don't bring girls home or talk about 'em very much to me. Malcolm's let me know that he's not a virgin. We recently had another "condom-responsibility, please respect women, be responsible, don't be a whore, protect yourself and her" conversation.

He was sayin', "I'm not a whore." He says he doesn't even have a girlfriend. So then, I asked him about a certain girl I'd seen him with. But I really try not to pry.

A lot of times parents get intrusive like that: "What's her name, where's she live, how old is she, how many times did you do it?" That's not important to me; that's not my issue. I don't care if he never tells me her name. If she's nice, one day he'll want me to meet her, but I don't want to get so hung up that I alienate him by him thinking that I'm nosy and trying to just get in his life. If I give him something he can use, regardless, then that's all that matters. I don't have to know who the girl is to tell him to protect himself and be respectful.

What kind of husbands and fathers will my sons be? I don't know for sure. I think they'll be okay, but I don't know. I know my sons are hardworking boys, that they are empathetic, that they are responsible. And I hope that they will carry those things into their marriages. I don't know those to be qualities that necessarily Mr. Lester had. He started using heroin when he was sixteen. At sixteen, my son's goin' to New York with his class to see the New York Stock Exchange. At sixteen, my son has been singled out for award after award, and he's being praised. He was one of three students from his middle school who was chosen to meet Hillary Clinton when she came. He loves me, he loves his mother, he loves his aunties.

I've been honest with my sons. I've been open with my sons. I talk to my sons frankly. I have a sense of humor. I'm youthful, I touch them, I love them, I kiss them. I expect lots from them.

Once, I got drunk when they were around. So they've seen me lookin' like hell. And instead of tryin' to say I had the flu, I said, "A drunk ain't shit! Don't get drunk. This is not nice, it's not comfortable, it's ugly. You stink. It's nasty, it's disgusting. I wish I hadn't done it. I hope you guys don't do it. But here's a picture of somebody who went out and got drunk." That way they can make their own determinations, because they have a true picture. And they know that I'm human and honest.

FIELDNOTES: *Despite her best intentions, Sugar cannot expect her boys to grow up unaffected by the world outside her doors. She reminds them daily that they are kings and arms them with a strong moral code. She expects the best from them and for them, but high school and the larger urban culture may contradict her message. Like teenagers everywhere, Malcolm and Will sometimes behave like gangsters, act without thinking, and let their studies slide.*

One time Will brought home a D in Foods. Hello!? Now he needs to know that getting a D is definitely not okay. We gotta talk. As opposed to me yellin' at him—"What the hell is this? You must be a real *asshole* to get a D in Foods! You better not come in here with another D!"— we have a conversation: "Son, how the hell do you get a D in *Foods*? I'm expecting that you're gonna bring this grade up. You cannot bring in another D in Foods. Foods is so simple . . . " I don't tear them down, but I let them know that I expect them to do well.

I also give them the resources to do well. I try to provide for them. It's a struggle, yeah, but I don't say, no, you can't run track, baby, you better get a job if you want them new shoes!" I'm gonna try and get the shoes. He might not have four pairs of the shoes, but I'm gonna try to get him some of the things that he needs.

I know that I can find a way. I don't know if this means I've become middle class, because I had these same values when I was broke. Hence the hustler. But you can have middle-class values without being middle class.

WILL

I don't know what I'm gonna do about Will. I worry about those gangstas on the streets havin' too much of an influence on Will. Now he's dressin' like them! There's been several times I've had to say, "Son, pull up your pants!" Goin' outta here tryin' to sag! He's the one who's ditched school. He shot Tina in her face with a dart gun, one of those suction darts. What else has he done? Everything!

I try not to tell him, "Son, you sure are strange. Anything that is strange that goes on around here, you're the first suspect." But there's no sense in me lining up all fifteen kids on the block and sayin', "Did you do it? Did you? Did you?" First thing I do is go, "*Will!*"

The other day my kitchen shears disappeared. I know that boy did somethin' with my scissors. Sometime back he slashed up my couch. Now he's always doing these mischievous and destructive things. Finally, I sez, "If you tear up somethin' of mine, I'm gonna hurt you, okay? Your own toys, that's somethin' different, but leave my own stuff alone." What I gotta do now is not tell him *not* to destroy, but *what* not to destroy. I don't think I can tell him not to destroy, he's hell-bent.

I remember us when we were kids. We were scientific minded and we would dismantle things, but we wouldn't, like, take my mom's stereo and dismantle it. We'd take an old something that was in the trash, and we'd try to figure out what was going on. He's the kind that will take something that already works and mess it up. So that's my boy.

I'm gonna stay prayerful. I'm goin' to try to continue to encourage him to do activities. I signed him up for Odyssey of the Mind, that thinking contest school's do. They try to get kids to work together solving some problem.

I'm gonna try to keep a rein on him as good as I can, but I'm tellin' you, I've lost a lot of my energy for things like beatin'. I looked in his room today. The door almost pushed me back. How many times have I told him to clean his room? How many times have I punished him?

But, it's like, you gotta choose your fights. And it's somethin' that I teach my kids. So with Will, I don't care if he keeps the room filthy. I'm not gonna expend a lot of energy on it. But his destructive things bother me. The couch is a family thing. Now you're overstepping your boundaries. What I did yesterday was just told him he's off-limits from going in the back room. The Nintendo's back there.

Another thing I just quite haven't figured out about Will is that he still will not stop lying. He lies about any and every thing. You know how if you smash your hand in a car door? The scar that it leaves on your fingernail? You can see the blood up under and everything. He had that. I go, "Son, what you do to your finger?"

"Oh, I slammed it in a book."

Well then, soon as he does that, my radar shoots up and now we're on this quest.

"You slammed it in a book, huh? I've never seen a wound like that in a book slam. That must have been some slam."

"Well, a book fell on it."

"How did it fall? Did it fall from the top of the Empire State Building?"

"No, it fell out the locker."

"Son, you're lying."

One of the first clues I have that he's lying is that his voice gets higher and pretty soon he's doin' a soprano. And he could probably be an opera star 'cause he's *always* lyin'.

What really happened was he was roughhousing in the hallways of school and his hand got slammed in the door. I found out eventually. What I finally did, I got him to come to me, and I sez, "Son, you're lyin', and this is your final time to tell the truth. So as soon as you lie, I'm gonna slap the shit out of you. Okay, now, what did you do to your finger?" Then he fesses up 'cause he knows I'm gettin' ready to spin his head around. I think I let him off then. I told him to go off and play. Who cares? He's the one sufferin'. He got his hand slammed in the door.

But that's just one small victory. He just will not behave. The last report card his grades went to the bottom of the barrel, and I told him this time he should bring 'em up. If not, he'll be on kitchen duty again.

Last time I go, "Son, you're cleanin' up the kitchen pretty good, why don't we make this your lifetime job? What do you think about that?"

And he's goin', "No, I'd rather not."

I'm goin', "But you're so good at it!"

"No, I'll pass."

"Okay, well you better bring them grades up then."

I have to monitor his homework. I've stopped honoring that he says he doesn't need help. I make him show me his homework and make him let me help him. Normally, I'm pretty busy. So I used to go, "Does anyone need help with homework? Who needs homework help? Let me help you now. And, he'd be, "No, I'm okay." But what I found was that he wasn't doin' it. Or he wasn't doin' it right. So now, we sit here. We do the homework together. Will seems glad to have it, but I gotta kinda force it on him.

And over the holidays, I 'laxed. I let him play video games, watch TV. They went sledding. Pretty normal. Friends and stuff. But there was one little guy that Will was playin' with who he wanted to go over his house, and I wouldn't let him because the little boy had a marijuana-leaf necklace around his neck. I asked him about it:

"Son, you know what that is you have around your neck?"

"Yeah, I know what it is."

"You don't smoke, do you?"

"No, I don't."

I sez, "Well, maybe you should be careful about the things that you wear and do, because they say certain things about you and somebody might think that you smoke, and that's not a wise thing for you to do."

And he was just kinda lookin' off in the air, like, "Yeah, yeah, bitch, right, la-di-da."

And I'm, like, "Son, look at me when I talk to you."

And he kinda looks, but he wasn't childlike. And I looked at Will and I said, "No, son, you stay home. You ain't goin' around anybody that lets their child wear a marijuana leaf. You not playin' at his house."

FIELDNOTES: *As frustrated as Sugar gets with Will, she has had nothing but praise and admiration for his older brother, Malcolm. Both these young men are as handsome as the African princes from whom they are allegedly descended, but Malcolm seems to be moving into young adulthood on a flying carpet.*

MALCOLM

I remember when Malcolm had his first basketball game. And it's not that he plays basketball so good. But he's a team player. I hate to say the only team player, but almost. All the rest of these little boys, they think they're Michael Jordan. Soon as they get their hands on the ball, they're runnin', they try to go straight through and to the basket. Balls bouncin' here and there. But when Malcolm gets it, he's studyin', he's lookin', he passes the ball, he runs down court, he's guardin' his man. You can see him. He's playing basketball.

Malcolm was chosen to work for this community project called Youth Works. They have a youth business where they do weatherization. Right now they're in training, so they're learning about houses, about air seeping out of doors, that sort of thing. Then they'll be doin' caulkin' and stuff, and learning that. And on Saturdays they have recycling. They go around the neighborhood and get cans. And they also pass out flyers to people saying "Save your cans. We'll be back on Saturday." This job is ongoing; it's not just a summer thing. He can keep it till next year. So he got his check, $39. He gets maybe $4.25 an hour. And it's three days a week, Tuesday, Thursday, and then Saturdays.

The guy who runs Youth Works, he's like, "Oh, Malcolm, he is somethin'!" Like he's tryin' to tell Malcolm this: you don't have to be flashy to be cool. He's tellin' him to invest in CDs. The whole group took a field trip over to the credit union to get some how-tos of financial stuff. And I think Malcolm was like the only one that had an account there, knew the people and everything. So, he was like in there! He was doin' good.

FIELDNOTES: *On Sugar's fortieth birthday, I stopped at her school to wish her a Happy Birthday and give her a gift. She was photocopying some materials in the office. She wanted to talk in private, so we stepped outside and stood in the shade to chat. She had said to me on the phone, "Malcolm is emancipated." I didn't know what she meant until she told me this surprising story. It seems Malcolm and Will were fighting. She could hear them from the kitchen. She went upstairs to break it up, and Malcolm just totally lost it. He was furious. She told him to take a walk, go cool*

*down, and he responded in an "angry black dude" manner, all huffy and aggressive,
something untypical for him. At this, Sugar said she wasn't having that kind of
threatening attitude in her house. Perhaps he had been waiting for such an opportunity to leave. He got his stuff and moved out.*

*As Sugar was telling me the story of Malcolm's "emancipation," her narration was
so vivid, I felt as if I were standing in the room. She's an incredible mimic, has a real
talent for other black voices. In her narration, she managed to convey the need that
Malcolm had to show her he was a "man." At one point, he even asked her if she
thought he was going to hit her. Of course, her calm response was, "No, son. I know
you would never do something like that."*

I'm like, "Yo, raise up! You need to go cool off."

He's sayin', "I don't need to take a walk! You kickin' me out!" He's
talking in this hostile, aggressive way.

I sez, "No, son, I'm not kicking you out. You need to take a walk
around the block. Then, you need to come back so we can have this
conversation, okay?"

"No! I just want to get my stuff!"

He's actin' like this was his official notice of bein' kicked out. That
was bullshit!

So now, he's standin' there like he's gonna push past me and come
take his belongings. I'm sayin', "Now you about to get the police on
your ass. I suggest you go wherever it is you gonna go. And then we'll
discuss how you gonna get your things. You not gonna run me in my
home. You not gonna push past me, you not gonna tell me what you
gonna do in my house.

I would have called the police on his ass! He needs to learn that
there's a standard. You don't disrespect me and tell me what you're
gonna do in my home. No, nigger, I run this. I don't run very many
things on this earth, but this little corner of the world, I run this. If
you're not cool with me runnin' it, you have options. Exercise 'em!
Go live with your friends. You have choices.

If I say you're not gonna smoke weed in my house, you're not gonna
smoke weed in my house! He was smoking weed in the house several
times after I asked him, and he was lyin' to me. Hey, I ain't got time
for this, brother!

He was smoking weed on my front porch after we had the weed
conversation. I said he couldn't smoke weed in his room, so he sat on
my front porch, with all the doors open so I could smell it, and smoked
a joint.

He was testing me. But I'm not the one to be tested. I said, "Son, you smokin' weed? You're being defiant."

"You said I couldn't smoke in my room."

It was real steady, it wasn't some blowup that happened, and I said, "Get out!" I was constantly saying, "Son, these are the rules and these are your guidelines. You have options. You might consider where else you want to live if you want to continue these behaviors." What was I supposed to say, "How can I change for you, son? How can I be better? Shall I lay down on my back or my stomach so you can walk on me?" No.

I'm not gonna play that game. Life is too serious, it's too short. I love you too much to sit and let you jerk my damn chains. I'm not your toy now that you're goin' through this thing of teenagehood, which is cool, I understand. But there are some boundaries of respect, some protocol that you handle even with being a teenager and losing your mind. There are some things you just do and do not do.

FIELDNOTES: *I was shocked at this turn of events. Malcolm had always seemed so centered. Both Malcolm and Will had turned into extraordinarily thoughtful, polite young men. And, oddly enough, it was Will who had the bad-boy handle. Malcolm was the "good" brother.*

Malcolm played football, won awards at school, and wanted to go to a decent college. He never got into trouble. Just a few weeks before, I had been over there waiting for Sugar when Malcolm came and sat down with me on the couch. Did I want to see his wrestling medals? Was I interested in how he had had to go up (or was it down?) a weight class to stay on the team? He was going to be wrestling in Las Callas soon; did I want to come? He wanted to chat, and I liked talking to him. In fact, I thought so much of his potential that I had offered to split the cost of an SAT tutor with him. He hadn't as yet taken me up on it, but I couldn't help thinking, what could have happened to derail this young man?

She says he had been acting out for a few months. For example, he drank all the booze she got as gifts at Christmas and then lied about it. He flagrantly broke all kinds of rules, even though, to my mind, Sugar's behavioral guidelines are comparatively lax. He also had been telling Will that Sugar treated them differently from the other kids.

Sugar's analysis of this is that you can, to a certain extent, explain this by their ages. When you adopt kids, she says she has heard, it takes twice as many years as their ages for them to feel comfortable, to adjust. So, according to this logic, if they were seven and nine when she got them, then Will, now fifteen, has adjusted and Malcolm, only seventeen, still has not, and likely wouldn't until he was eighteen.

According to Sugar, the major "blessing" to come out of this is how Will has evolved since his big brother left home. He has become a pretty responsible young man for someone we not long ago thought of as an incipient gangster. Most of this surprising behavior is due to his being on his own to make decisions. It used to be that no matter how many times she asked the kids to call if they were going to be out late, they never did. This really made her mad. Now, since Malcolm is gone, whenever Will is out with his friends, he calls her, maybe two or three times a night, just to keep her apprised of his schedule. Sugar sees this as an example of how he is more of a person now that he isn't under the thumb of his big brother. Likely, Malcolm didn't want to call, and Will saw it as uncool to remind him that they should.

But without that influence, a considerate and attached-to-home side of Will is emerging. Sugar says he's thriving. He does his chores without being asked. It used to be that the boys would argue about who's turn it was to take out the trash. It would pile up because neither would give in. Now, every time he walks in the house, he takes out the garbage. He keeps the kitchen clean. He watches his own choice of TV shows; he got Malcolm's room. It's as if a load had been lifted from him. The brothers still hang out together, but it's a whole new world for this young man. So, says Sugar, there's a blessing in everything. And Will got the good end of Malcolm's teenage insanity.

Just a few weeks before this, while going over some material about the boys' mother, Rosa, Sugar had said she wanted to get the boys into counseling—that they had been through a traumatic childhood with their mentally ill mom and must be carrying around a lot of guilt.

Just as I didn't understand Sugar's apparent resignation to Malcolm's moving out of her home and into the home of one of his friends, I also didn't understand Sugar's eagerness to call the police in when Malcolm lost it that first night. Surely there was no need to make your private problems a police matter, I suggested. We're talking about who runs the house, not some kind of domestic violence or robbery. She was amazed that I didn't get it. Didn't I see that if he was "outta control," she was helpless? She was adamant that he had needed the lesson, and she wanted to get him into the "system," something else I didn't understand. Why would she want him to be on file with the police? Sugar explained that being in the "system" would be productive. It meant that as a juvenile, he would be directed to counseling, something she felt he needed.

> I just don't know. Right now, I'm allowing myself some inadequacies. Maybe this woman Malcolm's living with truly can parent him better than I can at this time in his life. Who am I to say that I'm the only person that can put some richness into this boy's life? I don't know a thing about this woman or her sons, those friends of his. But I don't think she's right bright!!!

I'm not worried about him, not at all. Will doesn't appear worried. Terrell's been over there, and he never comes back upset or anything. He will be all right. I hope he brings up his grades or he can't play football. How will that feel? All the guys are playing football while he's working at Target. How does it feel to have to pay bills? He's lost whatever chance he had to go to college on a football scholarship. He must feel bad about that. I was out there at nineteen with a four-month-old baby, and I ended up a queen! And he's a king, he just don't know it yet.

I still see him maybe once a week. He comes in, he's with Will or maybe his friends that he lives with. They're doin' teenage guy things. He speaks to me, asks me how was my day, what have I been doin', talks to Terrell. One day he came and read to Terrell.

I don't know how or when or if he would come back. Those are pieces that are outta my hands. I believe they're in God's hands. I don't have any type of control over it. I just take it day by day and let him know that I love him. There may not be a way for him to come back. That's part of life—sometimes you close doors. Sometimes you make a decision, and it impacts you seriously. Some are retractable, some aren't.

His coach called the other day. I kind of told him the situation. It takes a village, so I'm not ashamed to say "help me." He was sayin', "Well, it's a shame that he's messin' up his life. I guess he just don't want to go to college." And I said, "No, it appears he just doesn't want to go to college now. Everybody's gonna take a different course. I'm not gonna try to determine that college at eighteen is better than college at twenty or even thirty-four, when I went back." I tried to explain to him that he hasn't ruined his life. God don't put people here to ruin their lives.

I said, "Sir, I'm not writing my son off. I don't believe that a seventeen-year-old can mess up their life behind one thing or a few mistakes. He may be altering the course of his life right now, but I don't believe he's messin' up his whole life. I refuse to think like that."

And he said, "Too bad I wasn't there. Too bad a man wasn't there, 'cause I woulda beat him blind. I'd beat him till he couldn't see."

Hello?! Who is this fool, tellin' me something like that? But I just said, "Okay, and I thank you and I appreciate that." You go, boy!

So, in other words, he's not leading the life that the coach wants him to lead. So what? So he doesn't get a scholarship. Then maybe he

takes his ass down to the community college and he works a little
harder at it, and then he spends a couple extra years in college. And
then maybe he gets out and he raises a family and he becomes the
President of the United States. Or whatever! It's just a different course.

HOW TO BE A MOTHER, SUGAR-STYLE

But, What of the Babies . . . ?
(A single mother's poem) by Sugar Turner

"Let's go to the moon," he invited me,
with a smile spread across his face.
"We can trip among the stars,
bathe in the Milky Way,
come on, let's leave this place."

My heart pounded and raced within my chest.
I wondered which suit to pack?
Which lingerie?
Which dress?

My thoughts ran around
the circle of my mind,
and planned and schemed
on the joys I would find
on the moon, with this man
who was so, so fine.
They raced and screeched
and stopped on a dime!
"But what of the babies?"

"The babies? Your children?
Why of course they can't go.
My passion only extends
so far you know.
I like you well enough,
you're so sweet and so fine;
I love the soft feel
of your ample behind.

Your bedroom performance
is beyond and above;
but, frankly, those kids
are someone else's to love.
Can't you get a sitter,
a nanny, a nurse?
Hurry! Grab your suitcase,
your hat and your purse.
This offer is good only
for a limited time,
and our flight to the moon
leaves exactly at nine."

I looked and I cocked
my head to the side,
as if to get a better
look at this guy.
"Oh, now I see clearly,
since you've laid it on the line.
You want to love me,
but you don't want to love mine.
What of the babies? What indeed!
Those little children, I have to feed!
And clothe and teach
the ways of life;
protect and shelter
from stress and strife;
kiss small hurts and wipe warm tears.
I may not get to the moon
for a thousand years.
But what I DO get
cannot be measured.
No one can describe
the joy and pleasure
of receiving the love
only a child can express:
a wet kiss on my cheek,
a tight hug on my neck,
to be told 'I love you,'
and know that it's true.

My babies love me
no matter what I do.
It doesn't depend
on my sex or my dress.
It doesn't fluctuate
from more to less.
My children love me with an undying love;
that's all I need to know.
Since your heart can only
find room for one,
it's time for you to go.
I hope you enjoy your trip
to the moon, the stars, and the sky.
Now, I think I'll go watch cartoons,
just my sweet little babies
and I. Good-bye."

FIELDNOTES: *Before I met Sugar, I took it for granted that mothering meant sacrificing, putting your life on hold, often to the extent that you might have to live through your children and their achievements. Sugar has disabused me of the universality of that notion. She has her own life and can't be weighted down by mothering forever. She's guided her children, given them as much as she could. In other words, she's set them spinning, watched them grow. Now it's up to them. Yes, she wants them to find spouses and go to college, but mostly, she trusts that since she's done her job, they'll be fine.*

"MY KIDS, THEY DON'T WANT ME TO HAVE A LIFE"

My kids, they don't want me to have a life. My life is supposed to rise and set on them. And they will run away anything that sniffs at me, even if it's a dog. Any man, good or bad. And it's never, "Mom, we don't like him because he's not good for you." It's just, "Mom, we don't like him." And they don't have to have reasons. They'll find some: "His mouth is ugly. He wears those jeans with those patches on 'em. He wears white socks, Mom." Anything they can think of.

It's like I'm their fuckin' play toy that's put here to cater to them, play with them, and not have a life of my own. Within their minds, you are their possession. And you're supposed to be there until such time as they leave you rockin' in your rocker. Alone, no dates, and no man, because you didn't cultivate relationships while they were growin' up. And now you're this grizzled up old broad! And then they'll probably be goin', "Mom, why don't you date?" And if you don't make a conscious effort to have a life—fucking good or bad— if you don't choose to live your life, you will not have one.

I sat my darlings down and I sez, "I'm gonna have a life. I have not given up on love, which means I'm gonna keep trying. Which means I gotta keep datin', which means there's gonna be men in my life. And that means I'm gonna make some mistakes. And I'm human. All I need for you to do is love me and be on my side.

There's no man good enough for them. If I go into my room with a man and close the door, believe me, even if it has nothing to do with being sexual, maybe just a private moment, that door will start banging! Tina knocks like a Gestapo police. I fully expect her fist to come through the door. They don't want their mom to have sex.

One day back I says, "Dolly, I want you to take your brother. Me and Mr. Lester are gettin' ready to get in some water."

And she goes, "Together?"

And I go, "Yeah."

And she's making these fake retching noises over the banister, like you two old bats got the nerve to take a bath together and do whatever else comes after the bath!

But I got a right to go take a bath with my honey if I want to without being ashamed. Hey, I'm a woman! But your kids will never let you have that. You have to wrest it from them. I was sayin' to Terrell, "What's your name? My name is Sugar Turner."

And he sez, "No you're not, your name is Mommy."

And that's when it starts.

FIELDNOTES: *The inner-city black men Sugar's talked about are only part-time fathers at best. They have had children with various women (Mr. Lester had eight), but they are averse to committing to being either a husband to the mothers of their children, their "baby-mamas," or a full-time father to their offspring. As we have heard, one result of this pattern is an overemphasis on "Mom." I asked Sugar how this impacted her children.*

One time we were walkin' home from someplace with a bunch of other kids. I was walkin' behind the kids, and they were talkin' about their brothers and sisters. Tina was sayin' with such pride, I mean she was like chest-busting, "Me and my sister have the same dad." Where everybody else was sayin' my sister's dad and my little brother's father, and she was like one of the only ones in the group whose other sibling had the same parents. And I thought to myself, "Little does she know what's gonna happen." 'Cause I was pregnant right then with Terrell by Dusty.

Like I said, I'm always tryin' to be perfect mom. But if you hold yourself up on the pedestal that they put you on, you'll fuckin' crash. You can't do it.

When I told my kids that I was pregnant with Terrell, I literally have a picture of them goin' up the roof and spinnin' around in circles. They cried. They broke down. They told me, "No, Mommy, no! Don't have it!" They wanted me to have an abortion. I was so shocked. I get a baby, and they're like, "Shoot the bitch." They were like devastated!

This house is a Christian house. This house is, for the most part, a happy house. It's a free house. There's a lot of freedom here, yet there are rules. I don't know that it's so different from anybody else's mom who has dysfunctional boyfriends. We've talked many times about how Reggie or Mr. Lester was a picture of what not to do. Just yesterday I apologized to all my kids for even bringing those situations in here. I said, "I'm sorry. It was wrong to have them livin' here. I owe you an apology."

They said, "Hey, it's cool. You said your apology and everything is cool."

Yeah, they love me. And they know I mean to do right by them as best I can, and I bend over backward for them. So what are they gonna say, "Yeah, you evil bitch, you brought that man in here and he ruined our life!?"

I don't have to tell Terrell his dad's a stupid junkie. I'd rather arm my kids with something that can help them. He knows not to do drugs! Not heroin, crack, or even overuse alcohol. I think that's important: give your kids some far-reaching pieces that they can use.

FIELDNOTES: *Every time I drove from Las Callas into Sugar's life in the hood, I was confronted with the narrowness of my vision of the black family. I had carried myriad myths and stereotypes into this project, and I was embarrassed and somewhat horrified to recognize this tendency. Thankfully, the intimacy Sugar allowed helped me confront and then, in many cases, abandon these deep-seated assumptions. One of them was the old-fashioned feminist notion that the best place for women to be is working outside the home.*

As well, I had long eschewed the notion of the "welfare queen" as being little more than a bigoted generalization about black single mothers. What I found was that there are indeed welfare chiselers, drug addicts, and layabouts in the hood who avoid mainstream jobs and only want to hang around the house. They neither give a damn about their offspring nor would know how to manage them if they did. I heard about them, saw them on the street, and occasionally encountered them at Sugar's house. At the same time, however, I met honest, hardworking mothers—both on welfare or among the working poor—who seemed to be trying their best to support the family with dignity.

You just accept your mom. Even if you see your mom sittin' on the couch all day long watching talk shows and smoking cigarettes or crack, whatever! You don't really question—not to mom—your mom. You just love mom. And that's it.

When we were growing up, our little cousins' mom was like a total alcoholic, and their life was squalor. But they would not leave her. We tried to get them to come home with us, like trying to rescue a puppy. No way! My other cousin just recently had her mom's name tattooed on her hand. Your loyalty is to your mom who fed you. She can be the worst mom. If she prostitutes herself, she's still buyin' you tennis shoes with that ho money. It's all you got. And you're not lookin' to substitute mom with nothin'.

Your mom is your role model. Your grandmother is your role model. Your aunts might be your role models. If you are fortunate enough to have a good teacher, your teacher might be your role model. And that's it. There is a lack of other role models in the black community! Celebrities and their fame are pseudo–role models because you don't really believe that you will achieve that. So who you're really gonna be like is your mom.

Because of that, I try to build my kids up at every turn. And I've seen other mothers that don't. I wanna say that they don't know how because they don't practice at it, and because they might not have seen another way. You know that I have made a commitment to just being positive to the point of being Pollyanna sometimes. I guess I learned it from my mom. And from my faith.

I look at my friend Patty and her sons. I don't know that they smoke weed together, but I think they do. It's almost like they're bonding by getting high together! No way would I sit down with my child and smoke dope or have a drink. I ain't doin' it! That's not appropriate. But Patty was getting so desperate at not having some kind of a common ground with her kids. Partly, I think it was the lack of time. Patty's been in school for umpteen years. Sometimes she's too busy for her sons. Because you're just trying to exist, and you don't have the time, the inclination, or even the idea that there's more to do.

For instance, Gloria's working three jobs. I'm the one that's encouraging Felicia, her daughter, to go to college. I'm the one that's filling out Felicia's financial aid papers, her admission papers. Gloria goes to work, she goes home. She buys new furniture every year when she gets her income tax refund. She doesn't drive. She doesn't want to drive. She likes to go out, but she only wants to go to the Jam Spot. Her world is so small.

That's all she ever knew. I grew up and was exposed to some things, like art. We went to museums. My mom was on the fringes of the Panthers. We marched. We were teargassed. We read. We had books in our home. Gloria's mom is still in the same little apartment that she's been in all of her adult life. That's all they knew. Gloria and her sisters and brothers, they are some of the hardest-working people I have ever met in my life. They set goals and they reach 'em. Their goals are new furniture, a new TV. They save. They were taught to put things on lay-away (and they get 'em). But the goals they set seem small to me.

I chose to want more than that. It's not just that I made a decision to be a stay-at-home welfare mom when my babies were younger. I also chose to widen my world, and theirs. Some people don't make that choice. It's what I wanted, just a different way of seeing things, I guess.

FIELDNOTES: The following discussion about parenting was one of the very first tapes Sugar and I recorded. When compared to later conversations we have had about mothering, these events reflect a parenting style in transition. Yes, Sugar still believes in beatings, but she's largely abandoned them as useless. Instead, she's developed a sage philosophy about the importance of long-term lessons. Her approach is especially compelling when she compares it with the angrier, more "in your face" method used by her friends and neighbors. Although the children have grown and considerably changed since 1996, thus requiring a different kind of discipline and guidance, my sense is that Sugar is the one who has most evolved.

In the beginning, I was somewhat taken aback by Sugar's account of the common use of "whuppings" in her household and among other poor blacks. Mundane violence isn't part of my life. When, as a teenager, I cavalierly mouthed off to my mother, she slapped me across the face, and that moment is etched in my memory to this day. So I cringed when Sugar praised her young son for hitting my dog, and I flinched when she talked about being regularly beaten with an extension cord.

Don't look stunned now. Yesterday I went upstairs as normal. Everybody overslept, so I went upstairs to wake my kids up. I went up to wake the girls first, and I went to Dolly's room, saying, "Rise and shine, everybody up, rise and shine." Well, this time the door was locked. Doors are never locked in the house. It's a rule I have. And so I rattled the door, and I go, "Dolly, get up!" She opens the door and I keep going, "Rise and shine, rise and shine . . . what the fuck!?" My daughter has a man sleepin' in her bed! In my house. In her bed. With her. My sixteen-year-old daughter has her eighteen-year-old boyfriend . . . I was stunned.

The only term I can think of that really depicts what I'm feeling sometimes about my parenting is "castrated." And I don't know if this is a universal thing, that when your teenagers get to be teenagers you feel that you don't have control or somethin'. So I didn't quite know what to do. I've run out of punishments. I've run out of things to do for bad things that they do. I guess after sixteen years of parenting, you've whupped all the whuppings, you've made 'em write all the essays. I have tried every creative parenting thing that you can think of. I used to make them clean house, write book reports, sit and listen to me sing, *anything!*

I found out last year with Dolly that punishments don't work. And, I was thinking about this today too, that black society's this "matriarchal" society where we've ruled with fear—"Nigger, I brought you into this world and I'll take you out! I'll snatch you bald! I'll beat you till you bleed!" And, of course, it's done with love; but now, for fear of child-assault charges, social services comin' into your home, taking your kids away, you havin' to go to court, we no longer have that hold over our kids.

I don't feel like I got any clout anymore. With Dolly, I've tried *everything.* I've tried words. I've tried "Tough Love." Okay? And I go, well, why does she have no fear of me? What kind of an example am I setting? Is it because of all the loser men who've been with me?

When stuff like this happens, my first inclination is, I'm not even gonna tell all my friends 'cause the first thing they'd say is, "I would have whupped her ass!" That's the common thing: "I woulda went off." Well, I have seen how goin' off don't accomplish a thing after a certain age.

They respect me, but they don't *fear* me. Black kids always respect their moms, but when you lose what we call "Fear of the Lord," you got a problem.

When we were growing up, we feared whuppings. We got beat with extension cords. I mean, back in the day, if your mom told you to go get a switch, you was in such fear by the time you brought the switch back, she didn't hardly have to whup you. It's maybe a throwback to slavery. That's what we knew would work.

I stopped beating my kids a long time ago. Beating made me tired, strained, stressed. You end up as worn as the person you did this to. I knew I didn't want to keep suffering for something I didn't do. So I became a convert to what I call "creative parenting." I've made 'em sit here and watch me sing. That's not the most pleasant task in the world! They've written essays; I made 'em write out the Bible.

But then, you come to the point where now you're thinkin' about what exactly you're using as punishment. I don't want reading or the Bible to be equated with punishment. I don't want doin' chores to be a punishment. So I'm just like at a loss. They don't get regular allowance—if they have a need, then I fill it—so I can't be cuttin' off their allowance. And if they need shoes, you gotta shoe 'em. I can't say, "You can't have tennis shoes because last week you . . ."

And the killing part is that basically I got one of the better bunches of kids. I got a good bunch, okay? They ain't murderin', maimin', gang-bangin', druggin'.

Once I actually kicked Dolly out the house, and it backfired in my face. You don't sleep at night if you kick 'em out. You worry. All your friends are calling up going "Tsk, tsk, tsk." The same ones that were sayin', "Beat the shit out of 'em!" are now going, "Oh, I'd have never done that."

What'd she do *that* time? This had been when she'd been on that long, long deterioration: grades falling, ditching school, hanging around with the wrong people, everything. The final thing was that she had been on punishment for two months—lost her privileges. I had her write pros and cons—*why you did this, what you've learned from it.* And she was, oh, just the perfect angel. The day she got off punishment from this, she's out driving somebody's car without a license, and she hits a parked car. Of all the cars in the parking lot she could hit, she hits a cop's car. Not a police car, but the policeman's *own* car!

So, anyhow, she eventually got offa punishment for that. "Okay, I'm trying to give you a clean slate now. You've paid your debt to society. I'm not goin' to keep holdin' all this against you." First thing, she's, "Mom, can I go spend the night over Sheila's house?" I told her yes, and she packed a bag. I gave her cab fare. I thought she went over to Sheila's, but she went and spent the night with a boy! Fifteen years old! Never in my wildest dreams would I have thought of such a deliberate and calculated plot. Went and spent the night with a nig! Stunned again!

So I sent her over to her dad, Ernie T. I said, "Go live with your dad, okay? Let him handle you. You got two parents, and who's to say that the mom is the best to raise you. Maybe it'll be better for you to go over to your dad's. You shit on me, so let him do for you." He couldn't even give the girl bus fare. She would call me up saying, "Mom, I need some Kotex. Can you buy me some pads?" I mean the very basics this man cannot do. So it defeated my purpose. Not only was he giving her no discipline, but I was still supplying all her needs.

You know why she's so defiant? 'Cause I stopped whuppin' her. She don't have no fear. She knows I'm forgiving. She knows she's my child and I love her. She's knows that I've traditionally been a talker. You know—"let's talk this out. Baby, what's bothering you?" June Cleaver. All this white psychology stuff of figuring out what's the root problem instead of jumping your ass and whupping the hell out of you. okay? So I tried all of these nonviolent ways. They don't work, and now I'm completely out of ideas.

But one time, Terrell scared me. He told me such a big lie, I had to whup him! He was so convincing that if the lie hadn't been so outrageous, you would have had to *believe* that boy. I'm not sayin' Terrell's lying came from Mr. Lester, but I've seen it in a lot of black men. So it may be a child-lying thing. It may be a black-man thing or a man thing, I don't know. It's not a Mr. Lester thing. I can't blanket and say that every bad childhood thing my son does is related to Mr. Lester. Sin is sin.

Terrell got brand-new sunglasses. Three friends came over to play. He let one of them wear the gold pair, and Terrell wore the green pair. Later on that night Terrell couldn't find his glasses and came and told me that a gangster took his glasses. And I said we should check around and make sure we know they're not here before we accuse anybody of taking his glasses.

I sez, "This is what I remember. I called you guys in to watch the movie. You guys laid on the bed. We turned on *Morris the Moose*. I went and locked the front door and turned on the heat."

He sez, "The door was open."

I go, "No, son, I closed the door."

He sez, "It wasn't locked."

He sez a car drove up, stopped in front of the house, and a gangster got out.

Hello! It was so scary! He had a response to everything. He's finding the little details, just like Mr. Lester used to. And if you play those games with those men, as long as you give them an opening, they'll come back, and you'll be so confused by the end of the conversation, to where you don't know what to believe. Did a man really come?

I said, "Well, what did he look like? What color was the car?"

"Black. He came up and he took my glasses."

And I'm sayin', "Son, that just doesn't make sense." And you know why it scared me? Because I saw so much of our black men in that little exchange. When I told him, "Son, I doubt that story. I don't think you're tellin' the truth," he looked at me in my eyes and said, "You don't believe me." He didn't fold. He didn't go, "You're right, Momma. I made it up." He put it back on me. It was so strange. At one time I paused, and he indicated that the conversation was over and stomped up the stairs. And I'm like, "Hold up, mister! You come back here! I'm not done." To the point he said, "I saw it with my own eyes." Oh man, he was so convincing.

I'm a very reasonable parent, and I thought about it in contrast to my mom, who would just lift that extension cord and whale! But I did give him a whupping! As a parent you have to reinforce. I can't just talk to my boys about condoms once. I can't talk to Dolly about scamming just once. I need to let them know that I'm active in their lives and I care enough to come back to that subject, to revisit it if I need to.

So Terrell had his lesson in lying. And later on, he woke up in the night and said, "You're not mad at me, are you?"

And I said, "No, honey."

And he rubbed my nose, which is his love thing.

FIELDNOTES: *Sugar has a long list of little girls and young women that she has nurtured and supported. Several of her nieces have lived with her for months or years, and their mothers still send them to Springfield for what seem to be emotional tune-ups. Of all these girls, her niece Martha, who lived with her during the 1980s, is the one Sugar is most attached to.*

Sugar established a close parental relationship with Martha. Sugar's sister Ronnie has consistently failed to be the mother Sugar thinks she should be, a situation that obligates Sugar to step into Martha's life on a regular basis. The following moment took place when Martha was visiting for a few weeks. It shows how Sugar can cut to the heart of a problem and solve it faster than any shrink I know.

Martha was sittin' there with this big hickey on her neck sayin', "Sugar, are you mad at me? Am I on punishment?"

"No, baby, let me talk to you about bein' a queen. Let me tell you what somebody never told me: how special you are. That's the reason not to have a hickey." We role-played. And we did these scenarios, and I was the guy.

"Hey, baby come here."

"I don't want to."

"No," I told her, "the reason's not 'cause you don't want to, 'cause sometime you're gonna want to. The reason's because you're a queen, and your queenliness has to overshadow your wants. You may wanna be with this nigger, but you just can't go off every time your body wanna do something!"

We all want different things for people. I had let Martha go somewhere with one of her guy friends. So Aunt Cynthia comes over lookin' for her—she's Martha's guardian now.

"Does she have a chaperone?" She was mad.

I said, "Aunt Cynthia, you can't guard the pussy. You can't lock down the pussy. You gotta trust that somehow they're gonna make some choices. You also gotta allow in your mind that one of the choices may be givin' up the pussy. So, arm this girl as best as you can, and then trust her. Keep talkin' to her, but don't be sittin' around tryin' to be a hawk over the pussy!"

FIELDNOTES: *Before we met, Sugar had directed this desire to establish and coach positive personal growth by founding the Young People of Today motivational club for elementary-age kids. Members of the club learned that they were valuable by practicing to "be kings and queens." They modeled, they sang, they drew, they played with makeup, they put on shows. Basically, the club members expressed themselves and were broadly praised for their efforts by Miss Sugar. This club is currently on hold, but it figures in all of her plans for the future. At her fortieth birthday party, instead of accepting the traditional drink from well-wishers at the bar, Sugar passed a hat for donations to Young People of Today.*

This next piece demonstrates Sugar's need to save lost souls in a slightly more challenging arena. It relates what seemed to me a pretty startling turn of events. Some gangster girls were hassling Dolly and Tina, threatening to beat them up. A fight did take place, and Dolly got kicked in the face. I wanted to call the police, and, in fact, they were called by a neighbor who saw these teenagers tussling on her lawn. Throughout, although Sugar was upset about Dolly being hurt, mostly she focused on how she could extract these little hoodlums from their miserable lives by loving and nurturing them, thus showing them the way to a better life.

If I could, I would help those gangsta girls. The one girl who's smart enough to know she's too old now to be harassing Dolly, 'cause she's an adult and could do some real jail time, has enlisted her little monkeys like in the *Wizard of Oz*. So they fought Dolly and kicked my daughter in the face.

For all practical reasons, any normal person would be mad, but I'm not mad at those girls. I saw them at the bus stop, and I treated 'em like I treat any of my girls, these girls that call me Miss Sugar and love me. And I told 'em they should go to college. I wonder if anybody's ever told 'em that.

But I'm sad, because I can't do enough. I can't do what I want to do. I want to invite those girls to my house, into all my clutter and books. I want to tell them I'm not mad. Tell them they don't have to do all this fightin'. I want to ask them, "Is your existence only about finding somebody's ass to kick? Is that where you expend your energy?"

I hate it! We can't elevate ourselves, we can't go anywhere until somebody touches somebody else, touches a girl and helps 'em. And we're not doin' that. And so black people are wasting away. There's gotta be somebody to help these girls, but I'm not seein' it. I don't want to be so arrogant to think I'm the only one to give them a glimmer of hope in their life. Anytime these girls can walk up and down the streets day in and day out, meet my daughters at the bus stop, threaten them, then *somebody* ain't invested in 'em!

These girls are very narrow. Why would you want to fight? Why would you want to get your clothes dirty? Why would you want scars on your face? Is that your claim to fame, that if somebody calls you a bitch, you whup their ass?

You know, I believe all things work together for good to them who love the Lord. There's a great possibility that we have been sent into their lives. And they might just wonder, this crazy woman, what is it that she has that makes her *not* cuss us out every time she sees us when we kicked her daughter in the face? I know it's the Jesus in me, okay? If I didn't have Jesus in me, I'd be wantin' to kick their asses up and down the bus stop every time I seen 'em.

Maybe I can't save them, but I can show them there is salvation.

And I don't mean religious salvation, to be converted and be a Jesus freak. I mean to show them that they don't *have* to do this. That there are other options.

"THAT PURE FORM OF LOVE"

I think every young woman who had a child at the ages of thirteen through whatever teen years, and even in their early twenties, I think they should have another baby at thirty-four or thirty-five. Then their perspective is totally different, and they can raise that child better. It's like you get another chance. Because you have more to draw on. You're more knowledgeable, you're more patient, you're more loving. You want to know what's bothering the child. You're not as easily agitated by his crying. You are just a better mother. You have a wider experience level. You're a better parent just because you're older, and with age comes wisdom. So can you imagine if ninety-year-old women had babies? They would be the best mothers.

This recent slumber party that my kids had, one girl brought her baby, the other girl was gonna bring her baby. Two mothers. I remember sayin' that when we had slumber parties, we didn't bring our offspring. An invitation to a slumber party did not include your offspring. But now, slumber parties are two-generation things. There's babies in residence. But yet these young girls still want to come to slumber parties. Shanda's sixteen. Mimi's maybe seventeen. Sally has three. She's twenty. She had three by the time she was nineteen.

Why is this goin' on? Maybe you've grown up in households where you're not experiencin' the love that you think you crave. You know your mom loves you, but it's almost like that's a given. She has to do that. To have someone love you because they want and need you is a different kind of love. I guess it's a love I'm still searchin' for. I remember when Terrell was a baby, lookin' at him, holdin' him, and I was cooin'. I looked up and I said, "This is the love of a man that we searched for all our lives. Pure, innocent, no malice, nothing sexual." That's what we always wanted to get back to. That pure form of love. So we continue to go through man after man searchin' for this love thing.

Why they are sexually active so young—that's a mystery to me. My own daughter did it, and I still don't have a clue. Dolly has suggested things like "peer pressure," but I don't buy it. Peer pressure's a crock a shit. You gotta be stronger than that. You can't be a going off the edge of the cliff. Maybe it is a reality, but I don't remember being a follower or succumbing to a lot of peer pressure. I was pretty independent, as I've known Dolly to be.

When I was a girl, I was always a baby person. I was always a caretaker. When I was young, I would get anybody's baby. I baby-sat, I carried the baby, I held the baby, I just loved kids and babies. It's just a part of my makeup.

But it's not like you consciously try to get a baby. It's more like if you get one, you don't mind. I think that's maybe how a lot of teenage girls think. They've seen it be successful too many times. That if it happened, it's not a big deal. The level of success that they see is mostly to be successful with a child. That is success to them. You can't get 'em to see that you need more. They're not seein' successful role models in enough numbers to make it stick. But they love their mom. And their mom has a reasonably decent car, and she dresses okay. She is able to provide a decent Christmas, so what's not to want to emulate?

Yeah, their moms are sayin', "Don't get pregnant," just like I've tried to say to my kids, "Don't do what I have done. Don't repeat my mistakes." But they *do* do what you do. Your mouth can only do so much, and then your example does the bigger part of it.

And so these girls get pregnant really young; they repeat what they know. And what they know is that when they get pregnant, they usually don't see the baby's daddy for very long after that.

I've told Dolly that the boy that you choose now is not the man that you will be with. So don't get so hung up in this, 'cause he's gonna leave. But how could they have this dream of success when they haven't seen it happen? How can Dolly think she's gonna have a life mate when I still don't have a life mate? They're not out there. You can't find 'em.

And not only that, if you're growing, how do you find a life mate? I've outgrown all my men because I choose to widen my world and I choose to get bigger. So there's no life mates that are movin' with the same velocity that I'm movin', and so I can't help but lose 'em. They're casualties on my way to becoming the woman that I'm gonna be. And many times I've said that the man for Sugar today is not the man for the future Sugar. If I choose him now, I'm shortchanging her. When she gets there, she's gonna look at me and say, "What'd you bring that fuckin' bum for? Who is he? Throw him out!"

FIELDNOTES: *I am a natural-born matchmaker, but I confess to being utterly stymied on how to find a good black man for Sugar. When I have spotted someone attractive or interesting in a coffee shop or at a party, she invariably dismisses him. She says "he's too straight," or "he wouldn't like me," or "he's probably a tweeker, and you just can't tell." In other words, according to Sugar, I am totally in the dark as to what kind of man is appropriate for her. Sugar hasn't done all that well making her own choices, but clearly there is more to consider in making a match than I knew.*

"I CAN'T FIND A DECENT MAN"

Remember my list of men I've slept with? Most everyone on there has character. Just because of the fact that they slept with me or I slept with them doesn't say that they're not moral people. There was even an upstanding preacher on this list, upstanding, I suppose, 'cept for the time when he was trickin' with me!

Most of these guys never made me feel like I was in danger. Maybe three of 'em scared me. It's only the guys I loved who tried to hurt me. Mr. Lester hit me. Reggie fought me! Ernie T. tried to kick my ass. These other guys just wanted pussy. They didn't want to hurt me. The ones who hurt you are the ones you love, the ones you're tryin' to make lives with!

At least I knew what was goin' on with the tricks. They were the honest ones. They were the ones with character, actually. Why should I have been afraid of that? They never hurt me. But, you marry some bastard who tells you he's not on drugs, that he loves you and he wants to make a better life, and it's all a fucking lie, and you get hurt. That's weird. It should be the other way around.

Mr. Lester's name just recently went up on my list. He shouldn't have been on the list 'cause we were married and he didn't deserve to be on this list. He was special. He was gonna be the end of this list.

But it's funny, me and Mr. Lester weren't even havin' personal sex. He screwed me like I was a ho. And that's probably just what he was used to, and he couldn't separate himself from his other lives. Mr. Lester would jump up and wash himself off. That is a trick move. You washin' the ho offa you as soon as possible. You gotta get back to your wife. You gotta get back to your life. He makes you feel like you just got fucked and you didn't get paid. So even when I was married, I still didn't find the closeness that I've been lookin' for. And I've felt closer to other men that I've had sex with. Even some old tricks.

FIELDNOTES: *This analysis of how Mr. Lester's treated love-making was a painful confession for Sugar. Reviewing our materials, it was obvious that Sugar's voice had changed, and that she wasn't as eager to tell a tale as to create a history. This change in her was a natural development, given the redirecting of her life, but it also reflected the increased trust between us. I was included in her need to reach out to others, but she didn't want to help me; it was Sugar who needed a confessor. In that sense, we often mused that she should be paying me for our sessions, as they were so much like a psychiatric appointment.*

It's shitty. I can't find a decent man. I'm feeling it. It's fucked. We been fucked. And anybody that's makin' it out here's makin' it against so many odds and generations tellin' us that we're shit. But I don't give up hope.

I was down on Benton Street the other day, tryin' to talk to this handsome brother hangin' on the street corner. Oh my God, I'm like, "Brother, what's up with you? So what are you doin' today?"

"Oh, just drinkin' and thinkin'."

"Brother, if you drinkin', you ain't thinkin'."

"Well, baby, let me get with you . . ."

And I asked him, "Brother, why are you denying yourself your royalty? Look at you. You're handsome, you're tall, you're black, you're beautiful. You're shortchangin' yourself. What do you do? Go back to school. Do something with yourself."

"Oh, I'm gonna do somethin'. I'm gonna do somethin'."

It's just sad. It's sad. It really is. Our men are just defeated. And there just ain't very many available black men out there anyway.

Subtract the ones that are in jail, the ones that are gay, the drug addicts, the ones that want white women after they get to a certain level. I read somewhere it breaks down to like about 5 percent left that's able-bodied. And you know what that 5 percent really looks like? They are the men who got three or four women—or ten. Ten women for every eligible man! They don't have to value you. You are a throwaway bitch, 'cause they can get another. You better get with the program. And people wonder why a woman's not using a condom?

Shit! I'm desperate! I wanna feel love one time before I clock outta this motherfucker! It's shitty! And then you get married and you get an asshole too? One who's on heroin? Who can't change his life? Believe me, he doesn't have to. He doesn't have to value me because there's always another woman who will want him.

And what are our mothers telling us? "Honey you can grow up

and marry a rich man." Where the fuck at?! What are the bitches supposed to do, go in a ring and fight until the last one standing wins the man?

Or she'll say shit like, "Girl, don't you settle! Don't you settle for just anything." What the hell, you want me to be a old-ass maid? There ain't nothing out there! Unless I get some picked-over, down-trodden brother whose self-esteem is shit, who doesn't have anything. I talked to Jerry the other day—Jerry, who thinks he's my next husband. And he was saying, "Can we take our relationship to the next level?" Oh, Jerry, please no. NO! Jerry is about to be fifty, Jerry has nothing, is nothing, ain't gonna have nothin', can't get nothin'. I'm not going to say never, because God is great. But it looks pretty damn bleak for Jerry.

And so he's goin', "Why? Why?"

And I'm saying, "Jerry, I don't want to go there. I don't want to tear you down anymore."

But he keeps pressing me. I sez, "Okay, you have nothing. You going nowhere. You're not stable. You don't own anything. Everything you own could fit in three or four bags. I don't want another man like that. It's no judgment against you, Jerry, but I've had enough."

FIELDNOTES: *Until I met Sugar, I never really appreciated the extremely vulnerable position poor African American women were in vis-à-vis men. I was surprised to learn that women eagerly welcomed the absent fathers of their children when they came by once or twice a year to drop off $50 for the baby. I realize now that constantly worrying how you are going to get through the week or the month makes women behave in a way that middle-class people can't appreciate. Sugar has been so broke that no matter how she tried to get ahead and legitimate herself, she still ended up on the edge for weeks and months at a time.*

Women with fewer resources than Sugar are even more open to the "wrong" man than she. Like poor women everywhere, their options are severely limited, especially if they aren't smart, resourceful, or lucky. And what's fascinating is that although women complain about men, they are carefully inculcated into accepting what's out there.

I've always said I want to be with a black man. I love black men. I'm supposed to be with black men. They're my men. They're me. They can feel me. I like these people around me. There's a comfort level. They speak my language, they know my existence, they know my world. I want to let my hair down, and I want to just kick it. I like goin' to the Jam Spot. I like kickin' it with the brothers there. But those same brothers that I'm comfortable kickin' it with, the flip side of that is that they're depressed, they're unmotivated, they don't have anything.

And I've been to clubs and places where the guys wear suits and they hardly want you to touch their suits 'cause they paid so much for 'em. And they're so clean. And they're upwardly mobile, and they have these pristine apartments where they have art. Those guys are assholes! They don't speak my language. It's like two different worlds.

Those guys are not a solution to this problem. Love involves a whole dynamic. It includes the way I keep house, the way I dress, the way I smell, the way my kids behave. It includes my whole world. You can't love me and say you don't love my world. Or you gotta stop lovin' me.

My mom's like, "Oh, you just gotta widen your circles." I don't give a damn if I went to a doctors' convention, I still gotta bring him back to my little house in the hood, okay? I can't lift myself up, go into his world, and stay there. I got five kids. And by the time a man is makin' X amount of dollars, he probably wants a white woman anyway.

Let me explain that one. If you're makin' money, your circles change. I don't know why, but your circles just change. You wouldn't want to go to the Circle Club. You ain't slummin' in the ghetto. You ain't parkin' your Lexus in front of my house waitin' for some gang-bangers to come take it, okay? You go get your woman, you wanna drive into her garage in your Lexus. I got no garage. I'm not lamenting it. It's just the way it is. I don't wanna be with a rich man. I want a man like me.

It's a class thing. And there's nothin' wrong with it. I don't begrudge black men with white women. Some complain that they're takin' our men. But I say if he was your man, he wouldn't be with her! So the fact that he's with her means he's her man.

There was this article in Jet that was sayin' why interracial marriages are on the rise. That's one of them: white women symbolize the prize. And not only that, if a man has struggled, black women represent the struggle. And who the hell wants to be reminded of the struggle all the time? Of when you guys were on welfare, the time you ate commodity meat sandwiches, or when you only had one pair of tennis shoes and had patches on your pants; the women in those times are black women, okay? White women ain't in that picture. What represented what you were trying to get to was your car, your house, your this, your that. White women are in that picture. So when you get there, you don't want to be reminded of what you left behind.

But I'm telling you it's more than just that romantic notion that "you and me baby, we can make it." 'Cause if I have a good man, and we're really making it, five, ten women is gonna want him. And it's no reflection on me. They don't hate *me*. They don't want to see *me* hurt. They just fucking want something good for themselves too! So, we're stepping over each other out here to get even a glimmer of something decent. And our brothers know that.

The men want security. They *do* want a home. They want it, but they're not able to sustain it. They don't want it long enough. It's too easy for them to bail out. They don't have to want it. I want to have a nice home. I want my kids to grow up decent. And I *have* to want that. I don't have no fuckin' choice. I can't say, "I don't give a damn if all five of my kids go to hell in a hand basket." That is not an option. But for our brothers it is.

They know that if the clock's ticking, we gonna see which one of ya'll is going to get up and get this baby a sandwich, him or the mama. Now we're gonna sit here and we're just gonna wait a little longer. That woman's gonna get up. Brother, you can wait till that bell rings, 'cause your ass don't *have* to do nothing! We have to. And they know that we have to. And there's no gray area about it. Our love is tangible. It's what our kids eat and wear. Theirs is different. So you get a few men, if they do take care of their kids, they get praised, praised, praised. "That man sure takes care of his baby." What the fuck!? He does what? I don't get praised, and that's not what I'm looking for. But they get praised to take care of their kids. What the fuck!

Shit, I take care of mine in my sleep. I sleepwalk and take care of my kids. It's no choice. They get to get a pat on the back for the shit we do on the regular, day in, day out, normal, which devalues what we do. That's some backwards shit!

But I have hope. I have hope for my daughters. Sure I do. Why would I put my doom on them? Somethin's gotta give for my babies. I haven't given up. I love black men. I don't think our race is pitiful. But we've had a hard row to hoe, and we're suffering from it.

You have to accept it. Men are going to come in and out of your life. What are you going to do, sit and cry and about it? Be depressed all day, every day? The fact that we can't find a decent damn man? Are you going to turn into some man-hater? Are you going to start preaching to your sons that men are dogs? I don't see 'em as dogs.

They're strugglin'. They don't get it. They have it tough. Are they victims? They are victims of a lot, but they are not dogs. They are nice guys. They love their moms. They love their kids. But they might not love 'em enough to get up and get 'em that sandwich while that clock is ticking.

"WHAT ARE WOMEN LOOKING FOR?"

FIELDNOTES : *Sometimes when I try to explain human behavior, either in the field or with my students in the classroom, in my search for the big picture I ignore what's happening to the individual. Sugar had to remind me of this several times while I was trying to sort out the male-female interactions in her community. "It ain't just about money. It's gotta be about love too! It's about havin' a family, a partner, someone to hold."*

Sometimes it feels good just havin' a man in your life. It's a different good than saying I made a lot of money this week. Different than I'm a good mother and I'm raisin' my five kids good. Or I'm goin' to school good. Sometimes you just want that female good feeling. And it's not sex. You just want to feel special.

'Cause on one level, we don't *need* our men. Back to welfare. I make more money than Reggie, Dusty, Lester, any of them. So there's no sense to keep harping on "Honey, I want you to provide." I don't *need* you to do that. I want a time when I'm not Superwoman. I want a time when I'm not on stage. I want a time when I'm special, when I'm not Rosie the Riveter.

And I would like to have a man to interact with my son, but I don't want him to be a father. I've been able to provide a decent life. If you *never* spent a dime, my lights would never be out, my hot water would never be off, my cabinets would never be empty. But if I felt a little better because I felt a little special, we had a nice relaxing night, we watched a little TV together and did nothing, that would be cool. So what is that? I want a man for *me*! But I can't afford to be uppity. I can't afford to be picky. Beggars can't be choosers.

One of the things that I adopted is this "I don't care" attitude. If you love me, then I love you. If you don't love me, then I don't care. I can't make you stay. I don't control anything in this universe. I try to put some good karma out and hope some good will come back.

I don't want to keep goin' out there. I hate the dating ritual. I hate new relationships. I hate getting to know a new man. I hate that first intimate moment. I hate it. So I pray what I got works out. But it never does. I still end up back out there. I hate being the only single woman at a party. I hate walking in and seeing women grab onto their man. I enjoy goin' out with my girlfriends, but I hate having to.

And, I don't have a lot of confidence in my judgment as far as choosin' a man. I don't have a damn clue. I really don't. It's kind of scary. That's my blind area. And I can't really figure it out. I'm totally shaky in that area. My choices stink! And it's been that way *all* my life. I've never chosen right. Even in junior high school, I can trace it back way far. All of 'em came to a bad end, or they were a little thuggy, or they were like the boys at the halfway house I liked when I was in ninth grade. I've dated other types of men, but it goes nowhere. I hate them and they hate me. There's not that many guys around. Men like somebody my mom would pick for me wouldn't even spit on me if I was on fire.

I would like a man who is spiritual, honest, fair, loving, and generous, a man who was fair and nice and treated my kids well. I would like a man to be a provider. And I would like him to be loving toward me. I think that's what all women are looking for. Then, of course, we add all our superficial little things, like tall and dark, or green eyes and good hair, or light skin and gold teeth, or whatever else we want to embellish him with. But to me, I think I found the formula in what I would like in a man, but it doesn't mean I'm gonna get it.

What are women looking for? If they could sit around here and talk, what would they say? Of course, nobody wants a man to be beatin' on 'em. They just want to be treated like humans. They just want to be loved. They just want to be special. That's what I want.

I've never seen a man that is totally honest. I like to think of myself as one of the single most honest persons I know. When I tell people I don't lie, they look at me like that's the damn biggest lie they have ever heard. But I'm not a liar. I abhor lying. My kids have had some of their worst punishments simply for lying. I hate a man that lies. But I don't think there is a man out there that won't lie. They don't know how to be truthful, and to a degree women don't allow 'em to be truthful.

For instance, if a man has two women and he loves these two women, he won't tell either one of the women that he has this other woman. But to me, I say, be truthful and tell the woman and let her make her choice whether or not she wants to be with you. You may end up with two women. Or let her make her choice and say I don't care to be with you, I don't want to share you. But some women will choose to share you 'cause they want to keep you. But let it be her choice. Be honest with her. That's how I'd want a man to be with me.

Like with Andre; I didn't care if he had eighteen women, I wasn't goin' nowhere. That was my choice because he was honest, he was open. He didn't hide it. I wasn't tricked into it thinking I'm the only one, I'm special, I'm a princess. 'Cause you ain't. You're not. So, why do they lie? I don't know.

Is there a man with these qualities? Fairness? If they're lyin', they're not being fair. Generous? There's some men that *are* generous. Loving? There are some men that genuinely love their women. I think Reggie loved me, but he was lackin' in so many of those other qualities that it negated the love. It tarnished it, it took away from it and made it like it wasn't worth nothin'.

Meantime, men should be trying to elevate the woman, to make her feel special and to make her feel that he recognizes that we are the backbone of our race. That if it wasn't for us, black people would be extinct, 'cause these men have not done it. So they should do some special things. You would be surprised what a flower would do for a black woman. She will feed your ass for a month because that flower says she is special. It's just simple recognition.

We watch white women on TV getting romance. We want *that*. We take care of our men when they're rotten; how much more would we take care of 'em if they would add a human side to it? We know how to hustle. We know how to provide. We're not bitchin' all the time, though we might say you need to help us with the bills. It's not so much that the bills are pressing, 'cause we're used to struggling. But if you would help us with them, it shows a specialness, a willingness to give. It shows an emotional commitment that's far more important than the actual money. We just want to be loved.

I mean, black women are workhorses forever. We been in the workforce. We been the maid. We been the field hand. We nursed the master's kids. We haven't had a chance to be bubble-bathed. We don't pamper ourselves like that. Who has time? Do you feel worthy? Do you even think about it? Is it part of your life where you are even special enough to yourself so that comes into your thinking? We do our nails. That's outward. The bubble bath, nobody ever sees that. How come we don't do it? We do things that people will see. But inner things, forget it!

How come we don't think that motivational books are for us? Just 'cause we're so used to the day-in, day-out grind, and we don't make special time. That's what *Essence* magazine is about. That's what Susan Taylor Smith is always talkin' about. Get to the spirit within. Pamper yourself. Do things for yourself. Feel good about yourself. Love yourself and all that. Why does she have to drum that into our heads? 'Cause we haven't been there.

But the women that are listening to her are the women that are inclined to do it anyway. The *Essence* women are upwardly mobile. They work. They wear business suits. They're in corporate America. They're middle-class black women. So these kinds of articles don't trickle down to the lower-class black women. They don't get to her. So the middle-class woman gets to raise even higher because now she's feeling better about herself. And this woman that's down here still don't get it.

Like the women in *Waiting to Exhale*. I didn't like them. They weren't me. I had been so hyped up for that movie. Everybody said I would love this book. They told me this woman would be me and all my friends. And I didn't see that. These women, their whole purpose in life was to get dicked. Who spends their life worrying about sex? That seems to be what they were worried about. They were stupid. They sat around and they called each other "bitch." My friends don't do that. And they'd cuss each other out. You don't do that. I guess Terry McMillan and her friends think that's how it goes. But I didn't recognize those women.

You don't call your girlfriend "bitch!" You might let somebody slip one or two "bitches." You can call yourself a bitch—I do. But then it gets too much . . . I did not like those girls. The fat one, I remember wonderin' why she was so down on herself. In our society, the voluptuous woman is queen! I've had men who would not look at me twice 'cause I didn't have no meat on my bones. So I am not prime property. In this book, the fat woman, she was manless. She talked about how no man looked at her. What world is she livin' in? Terry McMillan's not payin' attention to what's happenin' in black society. A fat woman can get a man before I can. If she was a depiction of fat black women, she wasn't true to my life. Maybe in the middle class, the men want thinner women.

Okay, then there was another girl, the girl with the big fake boobs. Ain't no black women goin' to get no big, huge, grapefruit-size fake tits! We don't need 'em. We ain't into that. And if we did, they would be orange size. So that totally threw me off. Then there was another couple of girls that talked about their girlfriend horribly when she was not around. They talked about her and called her tramp. And they're supposed to be such a close-knit group. And we're supposed to think they love each other. (I'm thinkin', "These are some two-faced ho's.") The other one who drugged herself because her man was goin' with this white girl? I don't know. And then her kids talked to her like shit. No way. So those women in *Waiting to Exhale*, I didn't recognize them. Maybe it's all a middle-class thing. I'm not middle class, I'm a poor black woman from the hood. So what do I know about what those girls do up there? They weren't really talkin' to me.

FIELDNOTES: *Sugar also feels this way about most black talk-show hosts, whom she considers sellouts. They're just too middle class, too concerned with "teaching how to paint grapevines around your archways to make your breakfast nook cheery, or how to make your face look thinner, or what to wear on a cruise." Sugar would like to have her own talk show that would explore a balance of lighthearted and serious topics relevant to African American viewers. She's already got a show planned where black women talk about why they don't use condoms. Another show would be about the often-ignored issue of the difficulties black children have being adopted. Or how single mothers live for their kids, often without that love being returned. Lately, she's been thinking of designing the show around herself as the black Dr. Ruth. Whatever the central theme, Sugar certainly has a lot of useful advice to dole out.*

"YOU CAN'T UNRING A BELL"

If we're gonna change things, we gotta start with our sons. I don't hold out a lot of hope for me findin' this decent man. We gotta build a new man. Yes, we have to offer him jobs, but the boy has to go to college. The mothers have to raise up the boys, 'cause we still gonna be raisin' 'em up ourselves. There's no redeeming these men that's out here now. You can't unring a bell. You can't go back and raise these men. People are always sayin' the white man's got us down. Okay, so we've already established that. Now what are you gonna do about it? How many black men do you see goin' back to college? They give up. We gotta widen our boys' world. We gotta make 'em better.

One of the reasons that black men are so rotten, especially now, is because they've grown up without men. It's not somethin' that happened overnight; it's the process. Men my age have grown up without fathers, and they have grown up with moms who didn't have men, so they were kind of pampered. They were almost kind of elevated. You know how women are about their sons. I think black women might have transferred a lot of their love to their sons. These sons have grown up to be selfish.

But it started a long time ago when the men started getting pushed out of the home. When we got out of slavery, and we started trying to bring ourselves up, we couldn't help it that we were poor. But then welfare came along and said we'll help black women, but we won't help black men. In fact, we'll help you as long as you don't have a man. It started a long time ago.

I gotta stay hopeful, stay prayerful, teach my boys what I know and hope that things begin to change in some way, that maybe fate will bring them the one woman they will love and cherish. Maybe they'll meet her at college. Maybe Tina will meet the one guy, maybe I'll be wrong. I don't know, somebody's doin' it! There has to be somebody out there who has a husband they've been married to for thirty years.

But, is there anyone that's really faithful? Sure, there are some. I have to believe so. Have they been faithful their whole thirty years? Quite possibly not. Probably not. Does it matter to their marriage if they don't have all of their husband? Or is that somethin' that we're resigned to?

What are we really telling ourselves? Do you know he sleeps with other women? Did you tell yourself that he doesn't? How many women have you heard say, "I took him back. He was unfaithful to me, and I took him back. And I took him back. and I took him back." Why? So that you can say I'm Mrs. So-and-So, that we raised our family together? What I want to know is, did your sons grow up watchin' him tip out on you?

But you got to keep trying, or you never have male companionship. You're bitter. You're old. You're dried out. And you're shriveled up. Is one better than the other?

I don't know that men are the only ones that fuck it up. There's just so much pressure on them. Like with Mr. Lester, he was always competing, and he could not not compete. And he shouldn't have had to have to compete with me.

Every moment of the day, Mr. Lester was bustin' his ass at his job. It was physical work. Lotta drivin'. He was makin' $6 an hour. You can't do shit with $6 an hour! Nothing! It fucks up everything. Here I am making thirteen, and yet I'm sayin', "Honey, I want you to pay your share of the bills; I want you to carry your weight." He can't do shit with that little bit of money!

"Well," he sez, "if I put mine in the pot, if I come and meet you where you're meetin' me on bills, I'm totally fuckin' broke." So, basically, this means I have to give him an allowance! Which causes friction because to be a man, he needs to have his own money. It's fucked!

So when I come to him and say, "Honey, you gotta pay your half of the gas and light bill," there's a fight.

"Bitch, why did you even have to bring that up to me? You know good and well the position I'm in."

So then I think, "Well, he's just barely makin' it. I'll take care of it myself." And I start resentin' him. It's scary. And it's sad.

However, as a single male with $6 an hour and a hustle, you could look somewhat successful among the people who value $6 an hour and a hustle. But as a husband, $6 an hour and a hustle ain't shit! As a single man, you can maneuver out there a lot better without bein' encumbered by a family or kids.

And once you're gone, then you can pop in on your baby-mama every once in a while and give her fifty dollars and kind of be able to hold your head up. You can *pop* in with fifty dollars, but you can't live here with fifty dollars. So you come in every few months, and it's not much, but it's something, because it's not like the woman can't use it, and it's all that that nigger's got. So I think it's easier on the men's mentality and their self-esteem in a lot of ways to be away.

5 FEELING BLESSED

TBE   So, you tell me, Miss Bible Expert, what's the meaning of Scripture for me, for my life?

ST   You don't *get* it? The more you understand on your own, the more you will know that everything has an application to your life. Rarely does something not have some application. Even if it just makes you go, "Lord, I just want to reassess. Am I cool?" Like Job's friends, after he had all the boils on his body and his family done died, and he's sitting in sackcloth and ashes, and he's lost his property, his friends come down and ask, "Job, you know you done *somethin'* wrong. We're your boon coons but we gettin' ready to just tell you how wrong you are, and how God would not have came down on you like this for no reason. So fess up. *What'd* you do?"

TBE   The ebonic approach to Job! So what finally happened?

ST   He finally got vindicated. He came back. He was better. He still had his testimony. But it also showed that it's okay to question God. It's okay to say, "Lord, *why* am I goin' through this? I know you got somethin' better planned, but right now I don't see it. What is goin' on?" People think you just gotta be so "Okay, it's cool. God gave it. He said it. I accept it." You know, it's like, "What is up with *this*?"

TBE   What about Abraham, who did what God told him and was ready to sacrifice his son, Isaac?

ST	Whew! So scary! What a cliffhanger!
TBE	And then God says, "Only kidding!"
ST	Girl, you got a warped sense of humor.

FIELDNOTES: *Sugar's spirituality is the governing force in her life. Her day-to-day existence starts and ends with God. She is centered by prayer and contemplation. Rarely does she make a decision without waiting to see if "the Lord speaks to me on it." Sugar is the first person I've ever known with this degree of certainty about God. Her approach is deeply embedded in the kind of personal Christianity commonly found among African Americans, but it is colored by the idiosyncratic way she has of removing herself from institutions that offend her. Churches offend her, pastors offend her, worshipers who are only good Christians on Sundays offend her. Although she goes to church, and regularly consults the Bible for guidance and inspiration, Sugar's spirituality is best expressed in the way she lives her life.*

"MY FAITH GIVES ME HOPE"

I know that I'm armed with some things that a lot of people aren't. And I know that some of the things I am armed with even rich people don't have: the peace that I have, the faith that I have. Hey, we're here for a reason. God didn't put us here for nothing. God didn't put us here just to be. So everybody has a spirit and whether or not they're nurturing their spirit or basically doin' anything with it than propelling their body around, it's still there. There's nobody walking on this earth that doesn't have a spirit.

I see blessings in everything. When people say, "Well, how you doin'?" I say, "I'm doing great" even if I'm having a bad day. I'm blessed if the sky is blue. If the sky is gray, I'm blessed that there's a sky. If the bus comes on time, I'm blessed that it's on time. It could have been twenty minutes late. So I just try to see the glass half full. Real full, as a matter of fact.

My faith gives me hope. I say "my faith" because say if at the end of all this there was nothing, my faith would still have sustained me. It helps keep me grounded and focused. It keeps me optimistic. It gives me joy. It drives me. I believe in something much larger and more powerful and omnipresent than myself. I know it's God that keeps me going.

The Good in the Bad (1985)

I thank the Lord for struggles, for problems and for pain,
Because I know each backward step is toward my ultimate gain.
I try to look at each wrong event and focus on the right;
A positive outlook and a sincere prayer always help me see the light.
There was a time when trouble came,
I weeped and sobbed and cried,
Until I stopped and remembered every cloud is silver-lined.
There is a lesson to be learned and wisdom I can get,
But I can never acquire these gifts if I just sit and fret
Or mope and brood or curse the Lord or roll my tear-filled eyes.
No, the way I spell adversity is blessing in disguise.

I'm very comfortable with issues that other people worry about. Like how late my daughters are out at night. I know I've trained them well. They have a decent foundation that I have been able to instill in them. And they're God's children. They're not mine. And there's nothing I can do about anything they're doing when they're away from home. Yeah, Dolly was in a car wreck, and I broke down cryin'. But she came out with only a scratch on her finger and a bruise on her head. I know I cannot stop a car wreck. I cannot stop a bout with alcohol. I have to have peace. I have to believe that they're gonna be all right. And I have to be prepared for it if they are not. So I put more energy into that type of thing than into worryin'.

I believe that God is going to take care of them, keep them safe. And if He doesn't, then there's going to be a reason why they're not safe, and I'm going to be able to endure it, whatever it is. And whatever it is, is going to be a part of my growth as well as their growth.

Am I worried about how I'm going to pay my rent? Not at all. It's going to be fine. I know that it's going to be part of my continued testimony to women who are tryin' to become self-sufficient. I know God did not bring me this far to fail. I know that, worst-case scenario, if I had to move out of that house—God forbid—I still would be able to make it. I just know that it's going to be fine.

I guess I've always been optimistic. It comes from my spirit. That came with me down the chute. It just is. But most of my optimism is associated with my faith.

"WE ARE REALLY SPIRIT WALKING AROUND IN THESE BODIES"

I don't think faith has a lot to do with religion. I don't particularly care a lot for religion. I believe religion is man-made. I believe that faith is a spiritual thing. I believe that we are spiritual beings in earthen vessels. We are really spirit walking around in these bodies. That's what's used to carry our spirit around while we're on earth. So religion is kinda what man uses, and makes laws and dogma and rules and crap, to keep people under control and divided and docile.

I don't think it's the same thing as being spiritual, because I don't attend church every Sunday, but I rely on my spirit. A lot of people call it gut instinct. They call it women's intuition. They call it common sense and mother wit. Different words for what I know to be spirit.

God is speaking to me through the Holy Spirit. Because I'm a Christian I believe in that. But I believe that if I had no knowledge of the Bible, I could still be spiritual. Because we are spiritual beings. I think there's a spirit that's just inherent in us that will lead us—if we listen to it—to do right, to do good. I think everybody has the spirit inside of them. I think they have the choice, though it may be unconscious, to nurture it or use it or lose it. My kids have it. Because I've worked to instill it, make them aware of it inside them. Is it this big spiritual talk we have? Not necessarily. I talk to my sons about making good choices, about respectin' people, respectin' women, guarding what they put in their minds.

They were up at one of their friend's house, where this boy had a locker full of pornography—hard core. So the conversation I had with my boys was that you have to guard what you put in your mind, that pornography can be very addictive, that it can be very dangerous, that it can cause you to have unnatural expectations of women. You gonna be hard-pressed to find a freak like that, and so your expectations are gonna be wrong. I told them that I didn't want them to have those kinds of images of white women, didn't want them to set their ideal of a woman on some unreal freaky white broad, but they have black women in there too. And then they will look for that. I want them to have healthy images of some black woman that I hope they would marry one day.

And did I expect that as young men they would never see pornography? No, but I thought that the difference is that, say your friend has a book, you leaf through it, you look at it, you gawk at it, maybe, okay, you pass it on, you go on out, you do somethin'. But to lock yourself up behind a closed door for hours, to just saturate your mind with that? That's dangerous. So I let them know yes, I know that this is somethin' that young boys are going through, but yes, I also think you need to govern what you put in your brain.

To me, that's a way I'm giving them spirituality because that's something deeper. Governing yourself, that's a deep concept. Your mind is a deep concept. And it's more than just, "Boy, you better not let me catch you lookin' at no nasty books!" Because that doesn't go anywhere, it doesn't draw anything from them. It doesn't connect with anything in them. That's just my voice tryin' to tell them what to do. And I can't tell them what to do.

"I HAVE A PROBLEM WITH ORGANIZED RELIGION"

I was raised in the Baptist church, lotta ritual, noisy, vocal. "Say amen!" I grew up in the church. I directed the choir. I led "Red Circle," where the girls teach younger girls Bible study lessons and do little girly things. I found it to be a source of comfort, a source of guidance. It helped keep me grounded.

But I have a problem with organized religion. I have a problem with charlatans telling me what to do, what to wear, and that they are my link to God. I know they are not my link to God, because God said they ain't. God said I can go to Him. And I do. And I don't need no self-righteous nig that on the flip side is tryin' to get in my drawers.

I attended a church. The first day I went to the church, the pastor tried to jam me, invited me for dinner or something. Was asking me did I have a husband, and held my hand and looked me in my eye—all this crap. That Reverend is known for messin' with people. Dirty little man, dirty little church.

There was one little girl, four years old. She sat next to me. I would try and quiet her down. Her mom was glaring at me from the choir stand 'cause I was saying, "No, baby, you gotta sit down. When we talk, let's whisper." Trying to keep her in control so she wouldn't ruin it for everybody else. While she sat there, she drew a picture of a penis in three stages of erection from soft to hard. It was a penis with the head and hair at the base. I never seen nothin' like it in my life! Three of 'em she drew!

And I go, "Oh, that's interesting. Oh, baby, what's that?"

But she didn't have no words to tell me. I said, "Who showed you that?" She garbled something I didn't understand. I'm new at this church. I didn't know how to go to her mom and say, "Hey, look! This four-year-old girl drew a penis! In church."

And I'm seein' the pastor tell me that the reason this child is acting out in church is because she's a drug baby. Later on I saw the mom in the store, and she told me she had to send the girl back to foster care. In other words, she gave up this little girl to keep her away from some drug-crazed man who was probably sexually abusin' this girl. I couldn't stay there at that church.

The church that I went to before that, I didn't really feel welcome over there either. It's a small black church up the street from my house. They weren't warm, though they tried to give the illusion of being warm. Churches tend to be cliquey and suspicious. It's kinda like you gotta go through some kind of rites of passage. Jesus didn't act that way.

Now I go to a Christian church. There are people in every stage of humanity. There were homeless people there. There were people in suits. There were people dressed like I was. It was good. It seems like the congregation is mostly white now! But it didn't start out like that. It's a nice church. The preacher, he preaches from the Word, not off the top of his head.

THE PASTORS "GO TOO FAR"

We weren't put here on this earth for ourselves; we were put here for other people—to serve and sustain and help—so it is important that you have a community of other believers. But they don't have to be Baptists or they don't have to be Catholics to be a part of the spiritual community. It's the community of spirit that people have to tap into. A church should have scholarship programs. It should have mentorship programs. It should be feeding the poor. It should have a food bank, a clothes bank, day care. The role of the church is to lead the people that needs leading, to give them some inspiration and some guidance.

But what I've seen is that they're goin' too far. The preachers try to manipulate and influence too much what's comin' from the Lord. They make you feel that you must go through them to talk to the Lord.

In the Baptist church, you hear a lot of embellishment and what *they* think. A lot of "bragimony"—not testimony. They get up and they may talk about how "Jesus wept." Very simple, Jesus wept. There's a whole lot around "Jesus wept." Why he was weeping, how he felt when he was weeping, what it meant. But you get a Baptist preacher that might go, "Jesus wept! And grandmother wept! And momma wept! And see, you gonna weep! And there's gonna be days when you gonna weep!"

Ah, shut up! Take me back to the Word!

I think a lot of times they have a kind of an agenda of what they want to preach that particular day. They take a verse out of context and build a sermon around it, as opposed to taking a sermon out of the Bible and *illuminating* it for the flock. So they take "Jesus wept" and with those two words they can make a whole thing about how "black people wept and how we been weepin' and we gonna weep. And momma lays up and cries rivers on her pillow every night while her son is in jail and out doin' drugs . . . !" Ah, but there's a whole piece around Jesus wept, and if you take that, you can craft somethin' a little more akin to what was the intent and not just what you are trying to tell me. So I don't like to see the Word used like that.

When Jesus wept, as I recall, it was in the Garden of Gethsemane. I believe this is when Jesus was going to the cross, this was the last week of his life. He takes his three cronies, you know, his ace boon coons. He tells them, "Wait here, I'm gonna go a way's off and pray." And he goes and prays. And they fall asleep. And he comes back and asks them, "Couldn't you guys wait for me? Couldn't you basically be there for me?" And they couldn't. And he wept.

Now there's a whole piece there about how your friends let you down at this pivotal moment of your life. How agonized he was, knowin' that he was gettin' ready to die. On and on and on. There's so much there. The Bible is so abundant. You don't have to go into takin' these two words and doin' what you will with them.

For me, I'm not there for the "Say Amen, Preacher Man!" thing. Obviously, people enjoy it. But I suspect that people get caught up in that and don't come away as full of knowledge as they could. Sure, they're getting something out of it, maybe a sense of community and a unity and a feel of spirituality. They're getting filled up on Sunday and they're gonna go back and live their lives for the next week. They're feeling like they're participating. And maybe they are. I can't speak for them. But I don't recall feeling like I was comin' away with somethin' that I could really use from that.

But testifying is good! I love to hear people testifying. If I testify, I might normally start out by sayin', "Givin' honor to God, I just want to say that it is my privilege and my pleasure, my honor and my obligation to get up and speak and tell how good the Lord has been to me." And I might tell of maybe some incident durin' the week. Try to be as general as possible. It's not their business the specifics. To me it's just an opportunity to speak for God, to tell that God has been good to me. Which I think we should. It's our witness. And if we don't, if we all fell silent, the rocks would cry out. There's a part in the Bible where the crowds were praising Jesus and speaking for Jesus and things. And the authorities wanted him to shut them up. And Jesus said, "If I were to do that, the rocks would cry out." You're not going to suppress the glory of God. No way, you can't do it. The trees are cryin' out! Spring is cryin' out. You can't do it. And before I let a rock speak for me, I'm gonna tell how good the Lord has been to me, because He's good to me every day.

FIELDNOTES: *I knew that I was comfortable with Sugar's spiritual side when I asked her to pray for my friend Stuart. He had lymphoma and there was a scary bone marrow transplant taking place. I decided to call upon her because, among my friends, she seemed to be the only one in constant communication with God, and maybe her prayers would get some serious attention. Sugar was glad to do it, but she could never remember Stuart's name. So she just called him Seymour Weinberg. She didn't mean anything by this "Hymie-town" idiom, she said. She loves everybody. And she prayed for Stuart/Seymour. She prayed and he recovered.*

"I OPEN UP MY BIBLE AND BOOM!"

So I always read the Bible. Probably since I was eighteen or nineteen. That's how I educate myself. I read all over. I read lots of Bible commentaries. I use my concordance. Mine is the *Strong's Exhaustive Concordance*—tells you the root and the meaning of every word in the Bible. So I can trace back and find out what a word really means. It takes it back to the Hebrew or the Greek. So I use that. And I read *My Daily Bread*. Just now I'm reading a book called *The Real Jesus: Who He Was and What He Taught*. So I read different books.

The Bible says, "Study to show thyself approved" and that you should "hide the word in your heart." A lot of times I read it just for guidance. It speaks directly to me. I just say, "Lord, open up Your word to me and help me get some understanding about this situation." And I open up my Bible and boom! Right there! I open it to a random page. And other times, I'll choose passages to read that's not just random. My whole family, we all have Bibles, we read 'em. We used to have regular family Bible night, but it kinda got so busy. We pray together. We are spiritual as much as possible.

My Bible study time is usually in the morning. And my Bible study place is my bathroom where it's warm. So I've got my books right there. I've used my art history book from the course I took at college to help really illuminate some things for me. That course was so helpful to me, because it made me able to *see* what I was readin' about in my Bible study. So when they talked about how a man who can't control his own spirit or his own temper is like a city without walls, I could see how in those days the walled city was their protection, and if you can't control yourself, your wall is down. And so I can visualize those types of things.

I can open up the Bible anywhere, and it will speak to me. I like Proverbs a lot because Proverbs are easy and they're very wise. This is Proverbs 24, verse 13. "My son, eat thou honey for it is good. And the honeycomb is sweet to thy taste. So know thou wisdom to be unto thy soul. If thou hast found it, then shall there be a future and thy hope shall not be cut off." So to me that's sayin' that wisdom and learning and knowledge is very sweet. It's like honey to your soul. So it's more than just knowledge in your head. When you get wisdom, it should go into your soul, so that it drives you and it guides you, it leads you and it steers you.

Then I'd try to do some kind of historical thinking. I'd think: Back then, it's not like they could just go to the store and get a candy bar. They didn't have a whole heckuva lot of choices, so honey was like this treat. So now when I'm tellin' my son to eat honey and that it's good and it's sweet, I'm seein' how really sweet they're sayin' that it is. More than us just goin' and getting' honey off the shelf at the store. What they had to go through to get it. So that kind of illuminates the sweetness of it. And I look at it: so wisdom was *that* sweet. To my soul. So that touches me and tells me something.

Then I can go to Proverbs 17, which basically says, "Better is a dry morsel in quietness than a house full of feasting with strife." For me, as a person who loves peace in my house and whatnot, that speaks to me. I can say, "Amen." I agree. I'd rather have my little bitty food.

Matter of fact, the other day, Jerry was over. Jerry believes he's gonna be my next husband. So he's over and he's gettin' somethin' out the refrigerator. And he's like, critical: "How come you don't have any food?" To not have Jerry there shadowing my ass every moment, I'd rather have that empty-lookin' refrigerator. So, it's better a dry morsel and quietness therewith than a house full of feasting with strife.

Anywhere I turn in the Bible, it's just full of practical wisdom that we can use every day, but you have to have a heart to learn, a heart to understand, and a heart not to try to manipulate. Like where the verse is—many churches still use it—about where women shouldn't braid their hair. What it says is, "Women, don't concern yourself with the adorning of your body, the gold, the fine colors, the braiding of your hair, the rouge, blah, blah, blah, if you're empty inside." So that's how people take things out of context. It's not sayin', "Don't braid your hair." What it's actually saying is, if that's all you're thinking about, if you don't have nothin' in your spirit, nothin' within, you might as well not braid your hair. 'Cause you're nothing. But they just say: "See, right here, it says 'women should not plat their hair.'"

Hey, don't be tryin' to intimidate me with that kind of shit, 'cause I'm gonna read. And that's another thing the Lord wants us to do, He wants us to know for ourselves so that we can be discerning. And when we are maybe sittin' in the church where the preacher is givin' us the whole crock of himself, we don't have to jump up and say, "Preacher, you givin' us a crock of yourself!" Instead, we can say, "Well now, that doesn't sound right. Let me go back and let me study that. Let me understand for myself." Everybody's gotta be accountable by themselves. I'm not going to go to heaven and say, "Well, Reverend said . . ."

There's also books on abortion and marriage. Should you stay in your marriage and get beat up? It will guide you, but it's not political. Politics is kind of like religion: it's man-made. God just values life. However, God's not gonna send you to hell if you get an abortion. And there may be other consequences that you're gonna go through, as with anything in your life. Every choice that you make, every fork in the road is going to lead to something. And if abortion is one of 'em, so be it.

There's any number of people would say that there's no way that I should be divorced. Well, I had to come to that decision within my-self, my own spirit. That's why you have to have a personal relation-ship with God. So that when all else is going on and every preacher is sayin', "Don't divorce him, don't divorce him," you're able to make a decision. Right or wrong, I know that I thought this out, I prayed on it, and I know that my Lord is going to forgive me.

"I CAN HAVE A RELIGIOUS EXPERIENCE ANYWHERE"

I like church, but I can have a religious experience anywhere. I can walk outside my door, I can sit in my house. I love my living room. I just marvel at, like, *everything*. The fact that water runs hot outta my faucet to me is a miracle. And that I can go to the grocery store. I can praise God for small round rocks. I just see God everywhere.

Like in my biology class we saw those cells goin' around inside of a leaf, and they looked like little cars in a traffic jam, moving, driving around. That's just too, too awesome. God made 'em, but how intricate! I mean, you see a big mountain, you like, "Whoa, God!" But when you come all the way down to like the cell level of a plant and you realize that in every leaf out there, little cars are goin' around, that's too cool!

The Holy Spirit will speak to you if you will listen. He will speak to you in any number of ways, but you have to prepare yourself and be in tune. And often it's in a still, small, quiet voice. Sometimes we have so much goin' on, we will not hear. So the waiting is the preparation for when you will hear. You have to know the way God operates.

Some of it is waitin' to align yourself with the way God thinks. The way that He behaves. And I also believe that the Holy Spirit that is in me is the same Holy Spirit that guided the writing of the Bible. It's not a separate spirit. So I trust that spirit to lead me the way it led them.

"GET YOUR WHITE ROBE AND YOUR WINGS!"

I see a life after death. In my limited human perception, we're like these glowing creatures in white robes up in heaven. But I think that's because that's about as lofty as we can get with our minds. We can't really visualize spirits floating, or however they move around. We don't even know whether they are like a Casper-the-Ghost shape or smoke or glowing white-robed creatures. And I see hell with fire. I don't necessarily see devils with pitchforks, because I believe the same spirit type of beings will be there, they just won't get the white gear! They get some psychedelic tie-dyed thing they'll have to wear forever!

So I do see life after we die, but I know my vision is very limited. I wouldn't put a lot of stock in it. I wouldn't be tryin' to preach to somebody about it: "Make sure that you get right so that you get your white robe and your wings!" Those are just human terms that we use to make it comfortable for ourselves and make it understandable because we can't even imagine the glory of it all.

There's angels here on earth, and some of them look like us. Oh, yeah, like in that movie It's A Wonderful Life, I believe there are "angels unawares." That's like that old lady with one leg that sits downtown with those pencils. Say I could pass her because I knew my change was short or my hands are so full of bags I can't get to it. And by the time I get to her, I may begin thinking how abundant my life really is, that my hands were full of bags. She may be an angel, not there to test us, but to encourage us, to bring the greatness out of us, to provide opportunities for us to do what we're here to do, which is to minister to each other. It's not as if I pass her by I'm going to get struck down by a lightning bolt. I may feel guilty and think that I should have. It's something to just keep us going back to our focus, which is God.

My Word tells me that the poor is always going to be with me. And I believe that. Ain't never been a time when there wasn't poor people. How do I change it? Eradicate poverty? You're not gonna do it. We're not going to change the order of things. So I do what I can, because we're here to minister to people. I give $20 to that poor couple begging for fifty cents. I brighten my little corner of the world.

And then it depends on who you consider the poor. Are you talking about the poor in spirit? Are you talking about the poor physically? The rich man who's bound to pornography, he's very poor. So if you want to eradicate poverty, which one? Choose one. It's not going to go away. So you do what you can. You figure out what your mission is, and you do as much as you can on your mission.

We're not saved for ourselves. We're not just here for ourselves. I have a little analogy that I like: Say the world is reduced to ten people. And those ten people all had an itchy back, and everybody tried to scratch their own back. Bullshit! But if all ten of you guys stand in a circle and start to scratch, everybody's satisfied. Everybody's back is scratched. Higher, lower, in the middle. We're here to minister to each other. And not so that we can become more saved or get a bigger mansion in heaven or whatever. Our works don't save us. We're saved already, and the spirit in us should move us to want to do good work. The question we need to ask ourselves is, I have this blessing that God gave me, so how do I spread it and share it and touch others and just do good things?

FIELDNOTES: *For several years Sugar and I have lived with a quiet mutual respect for each other's religious sides. In fact, I've kind of warmed to the personal thing she has going on with God. The pragmatist in me doesn't allow for that kind of faith, even though I can see how her personal connection to God has guided Sugar through some very tough times. Mine is a more studied, respectful distance from a powerful deity. I haven't had the private, soulful conversations Sugar has had with God. And sometimes, when she's waxing eloquent about the spirituality that warms her soul, I feel a little lonely.*

This year, Sugar said she was interested in attending my synagogue on Yom Kippur to see what was happening there. But then, in the confusion non-Jews often have about the different Jewish holidays, she asked if there was going to be a big dinner. "No," I said, "that's Passover. Actually, we fast on this day." "Well, then," she said, "never mind."

POLLYANNA AND COUSIN ROSA

FIELDNOTES: *One summer afternoon, Sugar wanted to talk about a recent visit from her cousin Rosa. As she began, I was expecting Sugar's usual spin on her cousin— that she wasn't taking her pills or had said some crazy things, that kind of thing. As it happens, the session ended up far more serious than anything we had done before. Confronted with Rosa's pitiable condition, and her own inability to save her cousin, Sugar emotionally took stock of her own life.*

Right now I'm feeling depressed! Can you imagine every day thinkin' like this? Feelin' like this? You can't! There's too much to be happy about! My gas and lights is on! My little hoopdy is workin'! I can go where I want to. I got a credit card, my health. Hello! I have kids that love me. I have people who love me. I have people who rely on me.

And at the same time, Rosa needed to come off the streets last night because she's seein' corpses. You think I got it bad? My cousin's seeing corpses—everywhere! I just took her over to the hospital. I don't know that she has meds. I just tell her that she needs to get in touch with her caseworker. I can't really offer her a place to stay. I got problems? This woman is talkin' to herself. Usually her mental state seems like it's pleasant: she's laughing to herself and talking to herself and having these conversations that don't look like they're causing her any great harm. So the fact that she's seein' corpses now is scary. She sounded frightened. She wanted to get off the street last night.

And I'm layin' in my nice warm bed. That's why I can't stay depressed. I got a girlfriend who's been working sixteen days straight just to make her rent. Working at a nursing home, turning people over, lifting people. Compared to that, I'm on *vacation* at my job. I'm rushin' to get to a meetin' so I can teach people how to model. My daughter's drivin' a new car. I got handsome sons. My little son wants me to go to "Beauty Shop Day" at his school. You can't stay down! And I'm not down! You can't. It's not an option. It's not an option for me to be depressed.

I don't know where Rosa's been sleeping. She just came back from Milwaukee. She arrived in all that snow. She was sayin' last night, and I could just hear the desperation, "I can hang if I really have to. I have places where I can go. I can sit up in coffeehouses. There's people that I can talk to." But what she was really sayin' was, "I need to come in. It's scary out here."

Rosa's sons didn't see her. It was about midnight when she caught a cab in. They had gone to bed. They left for school about 6:30 in the morning, and she was sleepin'. So, basically, they didn't know she was here. What am I gonna do, "Hey, guys, your mom's comin'! She's seein' corpses!" Pretty scary. That's no occasion for a family get-together. Sleep, honey, sleep. And she slept so hard. And I could tell she hadn't slept. And I just went over there and I just prayed over her. She's scared.

What do I have to be sad about, unless it's for her? My cousin is seein' dead people. She's frightened. She's homeless. So maybe it seems like I take some things lightly, but in the whole scheme of things, if I died of AIDS tomorrow, I would not have suffered the way that she has suffered. If I clocked out of here tomorrow, I would be able to say I had a life!

It's pretty tough. I've pretty much made up my mind that if she calls and needs to sleep again tonight, I'll let her. But I can only sustain that so long before everybody starts being mental. It makes you crazy. One time, a year or more back, Rosa was here for several days. She didn't have any clean clothes. So I wanted to take her to the Goodwill. And she was so unkempt. She wasn't filthy, but she had had her clothes on for several days, so she was dirty. And I felt guilty about bathing and cleaning myself up because I didn't want to make her uncomfortable or look like I was better. For a split second I thought I shouldn't do the shit that I do normally. It makes you crazy. You really get twisted. To inflict that on kids! I don't know when I'm gonna get them in counseling. I just don't know how to approach it or when's a good time. I don't know. But they're gonna have to talk to somebody. I know they want a mother they can be proud of. And I know they feel guilt that they can't be proud of her. It's not her fault they can't be proud of her, and it's not theirs.

I can just remember one time—how old was I? Fifteen or sixteen. I was in a car with some people, we were smoking weed, kickin' it, right? We were drivin' down the street, and one of the girls in the car is beginning to talk about this woman on the street who was Rosa. And she was sayin', "Look at them big ole titties, and look at her!" And I never said a word. I was embarrassed, and I couldn't say, "Bitch, that's my cousin! You better shut the fuck up!" I can just imagine the boys bein' on the bus and it passing by and she's sitting talking to herself. And somebody sayin', "Look at that crazy lady."

Is it any wonder that I'm like this Pollyanna, bubbly, optimistic nut! Consider the alternative—I could be a mean, ugly bitch! "Fuck you, I don't have a man! Damn you, my cousin's crazy! Fuck off, I'm tryin' to raise five kids! I just had to pay $856 dollars for some rent in a house I'll never own!" And I could go on and on and on and on! There's no choice. I have to just buoy myself daily and know that even if someone were to look at my life, they would say that's pretty dismal. But look at these people in the Balkans! Just look at them and just cry! How dare someone walk around here and talk about how miserable they are. I think it's a disgrace, it's totally ungrateful and gross. There's people that are just truly, truly sufferin', and me not havin' a man just pales.

FIELDNOTES: *How much of Sugar's Pollyanna attitude is due to being "blessed" I can't say. No matter how much Sugar insists it is true that God keeps her safe, I fret over the near misses she's had and worry that bad things are going to happen to her.*

One major area of concern is that she doesn't use condoms. She's gotten tired of my nagging her about the fact that sleeping with a needle-using junkie made her extremely vulnerable to AIDS. In spite of careful lectures to her children as to the importance of safe sex, this woman is not a fan of rubbers. When confronted, she admits that she wonders what's going on as well. She knows she should be having safe sex but doesn't.

What are we thinkin'? Even us black women wonder why we don't have protected sex. What is it we're tryin' to find? Why do we keep doin' it even after a scare? Maybe it's somethin' about the smell of the latex bringin' you down. Or it's inconvenient. Maybe you think it's gonna be just this time or whatever. Truth is, nobody wants to use protection. I mean it's such a personal act. We're being intimate here. We're havin' sex. With a condom, it's so impersonal, it's like you're not really having sex.

There's times when I have unprotected sex, and there's times when I don't. A condom says to a woman "You're not special," even though it's really the other way around. With condoms, that's fuckin'. Let's say you were screwin' two men. You wouldn't want to use a condom with the one that you like. Because you wanna think this is real love. If your man says he ain't usin' no condom, you go, "Well, oh, I'm special. He doesn't want to use a condom with me. That means he loves me." Stupid! What a ditz! Is trading off that moment of feeling special worth it?

I've been tryin' to examine if I am scared to be alone with myself. As much as I love myself and as much as I love my solitude, am I scared to be lonely? And I think maybe I am. Am I scared not to be necessary in somebody's life? In so many people I feel that I'm necessary in their lives. But in relatin' to a man, I believe God put man here for woman, and woman for man. And so there's a whole part of what I'm supposed to do here on earth that I don't get to fulfill. So it's like there's a chunk of my spirituality that's also not complete because I don't get to play that role. I don't get to have that part of my life.

And to think I don't have a man and may never—that is like a blip. It's a blip on the screen of my life. It's sad. But it's not as sad as it can get. Me not havin' a man is no comparison to my cousin not havin' a mind. Me not havin' a man is no comparison to Rosa bein' so crazy she can't raise her sons. So I have parts of the life, I have parts of the dream, but I don't have the whole dream. So what, you gonna go kickin' and screamin' into the night because you didn't get the whole piece of pie? You got some pie. Your ass betta be glad. So, I'm glad. I just am. I just have to be.

EPILOGUE

FIELDNOTES: Today, when Sugar looks back on the life she had flaunted and described to me in lurid detail, in many ways she is ashamed. She knows she's made a lot of bad choices. But what to make of the mistakes and the poor judgment now? Clearly, there is an important lesson to be learned from examining Sugar's past. Though she is dismayed when she reviews her life, she is also somewhat aglow when she reflects upon its new, more positive direction.

To begin with, she took advantage of an entrepreneurial training program—part of the state's attempt to "end welfare as we know it"—which is where we met. Those months of business training convinced her that only through education could she reach her goals of being an independent working woman with a credit card, a bank account, and, maybe one day, a house of her own. So Sugar applied her hustling moves to going to college.

SUGAR GOES TO COLLEGE

I love college! Because I'm good at it. And it's fun. And you have proof that you're doing good—by your grades. Nobody can take this away from me. I modeled for years, and one time Gates took it all away from me by sayin', "Yeah, but you still bob your head." I reflected back on all the fashion shows I ever did and just started trippin', like, "Why didn't you tell me? I'm not a good model?" Mr. Lester tried to take it away from me when he said I was nothing. But I know that if I apply myself, it's easy for me to be good at stuff. You just own it then. I own the knowledge that I got in college. If I never get a degree, I own what I saw under that microscope in biology class. Nobody can ever take that away from me.

FIELDNOTES: *Sugar's college years were, as she says, an experience just as positive as the rest of her life. She went in purposeful and came out more so. She actively engaged in her studies and participated in student life, becoming vice president and then president of the Human Service Students Association. Her grades were so good that she was asked to become a key-carrying member of Phi Theta Kappa, the honorary society of two-year schools. She found the classes fulfilled her in ways that would, I am sure, stymie most college students and infuriate or, perhaps, delight their professors.*

I found it all fascinating when she talked about her courses, which professors she loved or hated, and how she was fitting in with the other students. During that first year, Sugar asked me to read drafts of her English papers. I was surprised—and very pleased—to see how insightful and articulate she was.

One English class essay Sugar remembers fondly was called "Perfect Hatred," and it was about how people misuse the word "hate," how they should save the word "hate" for child abuse and stop talking about "I hate Mondays." I liked that essay, but the one I've included here is more compelling. It seemed such a clear expression of the lesson she was quickly learning about argument and analysis—just what I want my own students to appreciate. When I asked her what it meant, she said, "When you start writing research papers, you have to defend your stand. And it has to be on a higher level than "I wrote it. And that's good enough!" She really loves the first line.

Three Sides to Every Coin

There are three sides to every coin, and America's pockets are full of change. This change is jingling all over the country as people express their views on subjects ranging from pornography to race and education. The assigned reading has basically instilled in me a new-found respect for the research paper as well as an underlying fear. I feel that the authors of the variety of readings that I just digested offered well-thought-out and -documented arguments. With each successive reading, I found points with which I agreed wholeheartedly. Other points caused me to scowl with disagreement. I found this true of each piece, and that is when the fear set in—the fear of the daunting task of forming an opinion so strong that I would want to share it with the world. And also the fear that once I formed this viewpoint, then I would be committed to offering a position much stronger than the elementary "Did not!" "Did too!" "Poo-poo head!" "I know you are, but what am I?" Oh, how I wish that everything I needed to know I had learned in kindergarten.

FIELDNOTES: *Sugar has stacks of essays that are honest and idiosyncratic. She gave me several to read, and all were similarly compelling.*

ST   Let me read you somethin' else—from my English class when we were learning to form our "point of view." The question is "Are fourteen-year-old boys old enough to assume the burden of fatherhood? Should they be held responsible for their actions?" So I took the stand of writing from the boy's, the girl's, and the mother's point of view.

The Boy's Point of View: Well, I want to take care of my baby. I *do* want to be a part of his life. I mean, I *wanna* be responsible, but I can't really. I mean, I don't know how this happened! I mean, I know how this happened, but I wasn't even ready for this! Man, how in the heck am I gonna take care of a baby? I can't take care of no baby, man. It does feel kinda cool though. I'm gonna be a daddy! But it's scary too. Me and my girl, I mean my ex-girl, we ain't getting along so well now. I guess it's her hormones or somethin' like that. I don't know, man. She's all cranky, and I can't do nothin' right around her. So I just leave her alone. I'd like to get a job, but I'm too young. Ain't nobody givin' a young brother a job. But when I do, I'm gonna get my son all the fly gear. I'm gonna get him some Nike gear from head to toe. And I'm gonna let him run with me and my boys.
     Is this fourteen-year-old ready to be a daddy?

TBE   You wrote this? You made this up? How am I gonna get the voice on the printed page? It's not as good without the voice. I have to also get the head movements you're doing.

The Girl's Point of View: First of all, I don't know what he talkin' about "son." This baby's goin' to be a girl. I just know it. I can feel it. And besides, my grandmother says I'm carryin' her high. Just look at this belly. Well, me and the daddy ain't talkin' right now. I'm just tired of him. He just don't wanna be serious 'bout nothin'. Play,

play, play. I don't know why I got mixed up with no *freshman*, anyway. I shoulda got me a senior. He ain't serious. He don't go to school half the time neither. Now, how he gonna take care of a baby? Yeah, I shoulda thought about that before we . . . well, you know. Birth control? Yeah, I tried it, but it made me sick. And besides, I couldn't be bothered with rememberin' no little pill every day. And listen to him talkin' 'bout "Nike gear!" That's all he wanna do with his little money is buy Nike gear. He didn't save no money from his summer job, and he didn't buy the baby nothin'. Not nothin'! Not a diaper. He don't know what responsibility is. I'm the one that's gonna be takin' care of Chiniqua. I already got her name picked out: Chiniqua Chiffon Monique Michel Jones. I named her after all my best girlfriends. [*She giggles*]

The Mother's Point of View: There she goes with that Chiniqua stuff. Why she can't name the baby a normal name I'll never know. But then, in reality, the one who'll be raisin' the baby goin' to be me. Yup, grandma always gets stuck. I raised her by myself, and now I'm gonna be a granny. She's a good girl. Gets good grades, too. She just slipped up. Lord knows I talked to her about sex and birth control. Even took her down to the clinic. But she says the pills made her sick. What am I supposed to do? Force 'em down her throat? And that boy! He's an okay boy, but he don't have the sense God gave smoke. I told her that. I sure wasn't ready to start takin' care of no baby. But I guess I better *get* ready. I raised her all by myself. I can handle it. Of course, she'll be doin' her part, but I know the big work is gonna fall on my shoulders. [*Sighs*] I don't know. Sometimes it's so hard out here. I just get so tired.

The girl's father and the boy's parents were not available for comment.

For a while I've felt I was at the top of my game. Absolutely. But then it becomes a different game. Eventually, you see that you need somethin' different. I was thirty-five years old when I decided to go back to college. I was on a path of enlightenment and self-improvement. It was my awakening. My start on the upward learning curve. And, of course, Tracy encouraged me.

I began to go on this trek for formal education being that I was already such a good student in the "school of hard knocks." Of course, I love to read. I always loved school, and I love learning. So I guess it was just time. I went to Springfield Community College basically because it was cheap. It's right downtown. I couldn't see myself in a dorm room somewhere. So it was a logical choice.

I wanted to better my business skills. Right on back to the hustle. "Entrepreneur" is just another word for "hustler." I wanted to be a better hustler. So I went to college because I wanted to legitimize my entrepreneurial endeavors. What with the hairdressing, the fashion shows, all the things that I did, I wanted to be able to make my businesses work better. So I felt I needed to get some education. That's when I started with the Coretta King Center, taking entrepreneurial business classes to try and tie it together. And when I went to the center, I saw that I needed more.

I know you might think it's funny that I didn't take any business courses at college, but by now you gotta know that I ain't talkin' about business per se. I went to college to improve my hustle, yes, but a big focus of that was to explore further community service. I've always been a servant and a community activist and a person who's real involved in the community. Community is my business. So I took up Human Services to help me explore more how I can serve people. Next I'm going into High-Risk Youth and Non-Profit Management. That's my focus: helping youth, helping people, working in my community, just bein' a community resource.

I was thinkin' about getting a teacher's certificate, but teachin' is too small. The High-Risk Youth and Non-Profit Management makes me broader. It makes my business and what I do broader. Because with those skills I can teach—which is what I been doin' from the days I taught those girls how to be a whore. I call myself an "educator" because that's what I do.

TBE   Or you could call yourself a guru!

ST   Yeah, that!

Tracy makes a difference through her work. She's a college professor. My work is my servitude. My work is helpin' people and loving and embracing, uplifting and building esteem. And so mine is less tangible. She writes a book, does a paper. I move somebody's furniture, adopt a child. But it's the same work. I didn't go to college to be rich. I hope to get rich somewhere down the line, but first I want to enhance my servitude. Because if I could become a better servant, I could be closer to getting rich.

There's no money in it directly, but the karma's good and the karma's gonna bring the money. The universe is gonna bring the money. It just has too! There's the biblical principle of castin' your bread out on the waters and it will return to you. It's kinda like puttin' somethin' out there and it's gonna come back. So you just *do* what's right. And right will come to you. And it's gonna come to me in the form of money. Because I desire to be a philanthropist, which I can't do if I don't have money. It makes sense to me. Servants gotta eat!

TBE   So, you went to college to become a community entrepreneur and servant. (There's a new major!) You were on welfare, you were on Section 8, you were not working. You had the hairdressing business. You had been to the Coretta King Center for entrepreneurial training, which is where we met. And I inspired you, as if a voice from heaven . . .

ST   She said modestly.

I went to college when welfare reform was coming in, and by then they were telling people that you had two years to get off and all that noise. So the timing was pretty good. Damn good. But I had started at the Coretta King Center before then, and welfare supported me a little, with things like child care and my bus pass. But when I went to college, education wasn't really on the welfare agenda. They were givin' you two years of school, but they weren't payin' for no college. If you want something a little deeper than, say, your dental certificate, welfare didn't condone that. They didn't want you to do that, and still don't. They won't support that. You figure it out. I opted for Springfield Community College 'cause I could get in there. I didn't give a damn about what welfare would pay for. I was like any college student. I got scholarships and loans. I paid for it myself.

The welfare people were bothersome, but I didn't really consider it a "hassle." It was their option. And it was my option to do whatever I had to do. They paid for child care for maybe my first semester, or it might have been my first year. I only had a year left. I had went to the Coretta King Center, and they were basically tellin' me I couldn't do the program I had chosen 'cause I only had two years. "Sez who, honky?!" If you put your faith in them, then you are stuck and under pressure. My faith is in somethin' higher than the welfare system telling me I can only go a year, that I have to be on the fast track, I can only be a dental assistant 'cause I've already used up one of my years. "Sez who?" You don't become a hustler listenin' to shit like that.

SCC's a commuter college. It's filled with people who come from the hood. People trying to make a living. Women wanna get that two years of schoolin' before they have to come offa welfare. And gosh, I remember the pressure they were under. They were like *insane!* Tryin' to make sure they passed every class, knowin' they only had these two years. Feelin' the pressure of knowin' that after their two years their schoolin' would not be paid for. Deadlines! I didn't have that pressure. I spent three years in there on a two-year program.

So it wasn't surprising to see these welfare queens goin' through all these gyrations and pulling their hair out, wringing their hands, sweatin' blood. They had to get *out!* But they didn't have no hustle. They were smart, but there are areas where they weren't usin' their smarts as much 'cause they were under so much pressure.

It was a chore, because I had two unsupportive bastards during my college career who would not help me, support me, believe in me, turn off that damn TV, stop smoking crack, or anything else. So it was hard. But mostly, I would study early in the mornings or late at night. I like to get up at five and do what I gotta do. I got good grades.

I loved college. College was basically more of the same in my life. I just was Sugar. I'm pretty consistent with that. I didn't become some college girl. I am who I always was: Sugar Goes to College.

FIELDNOTES: *Sugar and I were going through her stuff from college. I had once written that her house was "cluttered," a word that offended her. Now I was duly impressed at her organization. She had separated out all her classes and had the papers, comments, readings, and notes in distinct folders by year and semester. She even had little plastic sleeves for the anonymous comments that other students had made about her speeches: "Girl, I hung on every word." "It is always rewarding to listen to you." "I know I'm going to get something good out of what you are going to say." "God is working with you. Keep moving." "No signs of nervousness."*

Her materials from Biology recalled the pleasures of looking through a microscope, but her discussion of that class also revealed how unmovable she was in her religious convictions.

I always think of that Biology class when I wash dishes. How water cleans, how it removes dirt. It clings to the dirt molecules and then, like, moves it away. And then if you add soap, it further. . . . Cool stuff.

What do you call them in the leaves? Cells? The things that travel around like little traffic, bumper-to-bumper traffic on the highway. They move around like little green cars. That was Biology. I loved it 'cause it was so awesome to see something like that. It just reminded me of the awesomeness of the world. God's got little itty bitty cells traveling around like little traffic. It just let's you know *you're not runnin'* this.

I know that God created the world. No doubt. No question. Never changed. No fish walked up outta no mud puddle. It's too intricate. No way! I just know God made man, He made all the animals. He hung the moon and the sun in the sky. This could not be some accident or some survival of the fittest. And because I live in Africa or because the air is thin, my nostrils became bigger? I can't buy that. It just doesn't make sense. You got Lucy, this ape woman? Nah! Now, you mighta had them, they mighta been there too. But God made 'em.

Just like the Big Bang. I believe the Big Bang. God did it. Biology just reinforced that for me.

I dropped Hatha Yoga I 'cause they started getting spiritual, and I couldn't hang with that. I didn't go there for religion. I got out of that what I went in there for. That's my approach to college. I wanted some breathing techniques, and when she got into that Hatha Yoga piece, the "mantra" stuff, I don't need that. My spirituality's intact. It was cool. And I wasn't mad at her, but I was gone.

ST   I dropped Elementary Algebra 'cause I have a math phobia.

TBE   You're gonna have to do this class unless you can figure out a way to get past the math requirement. You could get a tutor.

ST   Yeah, I'm thinking about a tutor or else claiming maybe math deficiency or handicap.

TBE   Come on!

ST   Hey! Who you talkin' to?

TBE   (The lightbulb goes on.) Whatever you have to do! [*Both laugh*]

My teachers responded to me the way I'm accustomed to people responding to me: favorably. Then again, I'm no dummy. I tried to do my reading, asked intelligent questions. So I anticipated they would respond to me the way they would to any active, interested, prepared student—which I was. Plus, I'm attractive, and kinda easy to get along with. I'm fairly articulate. Hey, attractive people are responded to better, they get quicker service in restaurants, the whole *blah di blah*.

I never got a bad grade. Starting way in the beginning: Keyboarding, where the woman now uses my story as an example of the woman who cut her fingernails and is so enthused. The story is that I went in there with these Dragon Lady fingernails, and I was tryin' to type. And the teacher stood over me after a couple of days, and she said, "You know, you type wrong the fastest that I have ever seen. I suggest you cut your nails and learn right." And the next day I came with my nails cut. Ready to learn right. And I learned, and I passed the class. No big deal. I got an A.

TBE   Did you ever get a critical remark on your papers?

ST   Yeah, somebody said I was "opinionated to the point of being obstinate."

TBE   And your response to that?

ST   What the hell is "obstinate"? [*Both laugh*] Then I figured out what obstinate is: it's unchanging and stuck where you are. And you can't see another person's point of view. I thought that that was an unfair assessment of me. But I believe in what I believe in, and I stick by it. I guess that sounds like obstinate, don't it?

I just had fun in my classes. Whew! Sometimes they came in handy! There was that time when I had come to hang out with some of Tracy's friends. It was one of my first social things with people of the "Caucasian persuasion" up in Las Callas. Tracy invited me to dinner, and I went. Nice house, nice little kids, just kickin' it. It was fun, and I mingled.

Then after dinner we sat and everybody was talkin' about this upcoming presidential election and the debates that went on. And I conveniently just happened to have watched the debates, so I was able to interject strategically placed intelligent comments! If I hadn't had a class assignment to watch the debates on TV, I wouldn't have been able to be a part of the group. And they would have been lookin' like, "Oh, this stupid black girl! You don't know anything about this."

But some of my classes I will *never* use! Well, let's look at Philosophy. It was tough. They were talkin' about brains in jars. You know, "I think, therefore I am." Stuff like that. It was hard for me because there wasn't really a *black* philosophy. And these old, white, drug-addict junkies made all these rules. And it was hard because some of it makes a lot of sense and we still hold to 'em today. But today we look down on a tweeker, but we revere this old tweeker Freud? I don't know. It was hard because there really wasn't a big right and wrong. So you never knew quite how to answer.

I did like it, and I was able to get by. But there were a lot of places where you could get into an argument about religion. You know, this doesn't make sense. But I had enough brains to say to myself, "Your goal is to pass this class, not to argue and all that. So what you need to do is basically digest this and answer the way you know that it needs to be answered, whether or not you believe it." I can't write all my answers: *God created the earth. God created the earth!* I disagree with the professor! You gonna fail the class, butthole. You're not here to change philosophy. Them old guys is dead. Their stuff is etched in stone.

FIELDNOTES: *Sugar still has a few courses to complete before she gets her Associate Degree. Then she has to consider where to enroll in order to get her B.A. Even though she's not in school right now, like all college students I know, she is constantly changing her major. It is an accepted fact between us that she will go back to school one day. But for now, she thinks she has done a good job achieving her first set of college goals.*

My goal was not to get a degree. My goal was to enhance myself and my business. So every day I went in there, I achieved my goal. Every day that I made intelligent comments in the classroom, I achieved my goal, and every day that I got an A on a paper. College was just a good, cool, fun experience, as is my life. It's just a continuation of my life.

FIELDNOTES: *And Sugar's life does go on. The children are in school or in college. A wonderful new job with a non-profit organization keeps Sugar very busy. She's a professional-level director of a women's health program. She has a staff, a budget, and the respect of the community. Hairdressing is only an occasional activity now. She confesses that being legitimate feels great. In fact, she's finally achieved another of her important goals: just recently she wrote out a check for $1,500 for her daughter's living expenses at Spellman College.*

She continues looking for love, but with the decided motive of finding a suitably reliable and adoring mate who will allow her the white-picket-fence fantasy she had learned about growing up. There's a new man who's looking like a pretty good potential husband to her, but we agreed to leave that be without comment.

About three months ago, we stopped taping. It was an odd sensation to find ourselves in the middle of a conversation without the tape recorder whirring. But we had decided that no matter what was going on in Sugar's life, by the new millennium, we had come to the end of the project. We were both tired of Sugar's life. And, in some ways, we figured that the process had self-destructed. We had gone too far, become too intimate, lost our distance. In fact, she made me take out a few very private sections where she insisted she had been talking to her "girlfriend," not to the anthropologist interviewing her.

Sugar went through a lot of emotional changes reading the draft of the whole book. I had never seen her quite as weepy before. She was sick and tired of being a specimen, she said. She wanted out from under the microscope! I acknowledged that, but I knew that what really saddened her was reading this clear, uncensored account of who she was, facing the hundreds of pages we were calling her life.

I confess that Sugar's emotional response to her story threw me. I had witnessed her tears, but they had never implicated me before. Now I felt as if I had been added to the list of those who had betrayed her. I got over feeling bad, but the experience made me reflect carefully on this whole endeavor. What exactly had I done here? I had gone into this work with the same social-scientific purposefulness I used in all my other ethnographic projects. I had a scholarly goal—to work collaboratively with Sugar to write a testimonio—and I had met that goal. A book would be produced, perhaps a play or a movie would emerge. I had made a friend, and together we had lived through five years during which she had changed enormously. She had blossomed. But what of me? Was the production of a book all that I could point to?

When I first thought about this, I considered that, on some levels, I was pretty much the same person I had always been. I was an anthropologist home from the field. I had another publication for my CV, and maybe it would get me a full professorship or even a little money. I had inserted this urban-poverty piece into my career and in the process had recharged my scholarly energies. A lot of my colleagues were getting bored writing about the same people, the same village, even the same continent as when their careers began. I had been lucky to get into this other reality in a fieldwork site so close to home. Now that it was done, I could simply reshelve my books on urban poverty and move on to the next project.

Except that Sugar was in my life. And having her in my life meant something. I couldn't get on a plane home from Guatemala and remove myself from the intimacy of that relationship now that the work was done. Instead, I have become some kind of hybrid researcher with the head of a social scientist and the heart of a friend. I tried to peer at Sugar through my ethnographic lens, but she had insisted that I come out from behind the tape recorder, and indeed that had happened. For the first time in my career, I have been involved with my informant and have been a real part of her life, with no attempt at scientific objectivity. If I was going to be in her life, I had to really be there.

We weren't ethnographer and informant, that oddly predictable but uncomfort-